A Dictionary for the

MOORISH HOLY KORAN

"The Wise Man cultivates his mind with knowledge." (MHK 26:9)

Compiled & Prepared by:

Brother Abdul Raafi Saadi Bey

&

Edited in part by:

Brother Carlos Arzola Lopez-El

authorHOUSE

AuthorHouse™
1663 Liberty Drive
Bloomington, IN 47403
www.authorhouse.com
Phone: 833-262-8899

Published by AuthorHouse 12/06/2021

ISBN: 978-1-6655-4055-1 (sc)
ISBN: 978-1-6655-4114-5 (e)

Print information available on the last page.

Any people depicted in stock imagery provided by Getty Images are models, and such images are being used for illustrative purposes only. Certain stock imagery © Getty Images.

This book is printed on acid-free paper.

CONTENTS

PRAISE AND HONORS

First and foremost, we must give all praise to the Father of the Universe. None other than Him is worthy of all thanksgiving, adoration, and praise. He is known by various names and titles. We of the Moorish Islamic community call Him ALLAH, for there is none higher than Him.

We extend the highest honors that can be bestowed upon any human to our beloved leader, redeemer, and guide, Prophet Noble Drew Ali. We are forever thankful to our Creator for sending us a Prophet, Messenger, and Angel in our likeness to lead us back to the Oneness of ALLAH.

We extend our honors to all those who have come before us to prepare the way for our entering into this civilization. Theirs was a mighty task. They carried the sword and slew the beast so that we may be able to enter.

We further extend our honors and gratitude to those Moors, Moorish-Americans, Moslems, and all who continue to fight the good fight and stand firm on behalf of the righteous who may be weak and are not able to stand alone. This work is dedicated to those mentioned above, because without them, there would be no us.

INTRODUCTION

The First Edition is intended to be a springboard for research. The authors, with an inquiring mind, have conducted their personal research and have shared their findings in the enclosed material. For the most part, the definitions that are given can be found in a standard Webster's New Universal Unabridged Dictionary. The authors intended to give the best definition that correlated with the instruction in which the word is found. The numbers found in parentheses at the end of every given definition indicates the instruction in which that word is found. For example, "Recompense = reward. (3)" means that in Chapter 21, the word recompense can be found in instruction #3. Not only is this done to make it easier for the reader to find the word if he/she is using only this dictionary, but it is also done to make it easier for the reader to locate the word in The Holy Koran of The Moorish Science Temple of America. It also serves to distinguish one definition from another if the same word appears in that same chapter but may have a different definition than the previous or latter one given throughout. In an additional effort to make this work reader-friendly, we have placed the words in alphabetical order. After each chapter, we have used the leftover space to allow the reader to add his or her own notes.

The authors of this work do not intend to use this material to convince anyone of their personal perspectives and/or opinions. We have shared numerous works be members of the Moorish Science Temple of America, as well as works from various writers of the Moorish diaspora. We understand that we each have our portion of understanding, but this portion should be intended to guide us into the Universal Understanding. It is our hope that this work will inspire individuals to pick up the mantle of responsibility and begin to dig deeper into the teachings of Prophet Noble Drew Ali. For far too long, we have allowed ourselves to become complacent in our current conditions, which have been dictated by those who have no true and sincere interest in the betterment of humanity. These individuals are obscurants who wish to "feed their sheep" while they sheer them as they eat. This was not what our Prophet brought.

Use this work for good acts, as this is what this work is intended for. In the future, it is our objective to produce a second edition with an "advanced" understanding of the teachings of our Prophet Noble Drew Ali.

The Holy Koran
OF THE

Moorish Science Temple

Of America

Divinely Prepared by The Noble Prophet

DREW ALI

By the guiding of his father, God, ALLAH; the great God of the Universe.
To redeem man from his sinful and fallen stage of humanity back
To the highest plane of life with his father God, ALLAH

Africa = a continent located below Egypt and between the Atlantic and Indian oceans, consisting of about 53 countries. It is the second largest continent in the world with about 11,700,000 sq. miles in size.

Appointed = predetermined; arranged; set.

Authority = a power or right delegated or given.

Delivered = given into another's possession or keeping; set free or liberated; made known.

Egypt = a country in N.E. Africa with a civilization dating as far back as 4000 B.C. It was known in ancient times as Kemet. (See definition of *"Egyptians"* in Chapter 45.)

Europe = a continent in the Western part of the landmass laying between the Atlantic and Pacific oceans, separate from Asia by the Aural Mountains on the East and the Caucasus Mountains and the Black and Caspian seas on South East.

Events = occurrences, especially ones of some importance.

→ An event is usually an important happening. The 18 missing years of life works, and teachings of Jesus are of great importance to the followers of the Prophet Noble Drew Ali because it demonstrates the stages of unfoldment of Brother Justice and gives a pattern and starting point, so that we too can begin the unfoldment of the God-Man that is within each and every one of us.

Expenses = costs or charge.

Falsely = not properly, accurately, or honestly; with malicious or ill intent.

Genealogy = a record or account of the ancestry and descent of a person, family, or group; descent from an original form or progenitor; ancestry.

Good = morally excellent; virtuous, righteous.

Happiness = the quality or state of being delighted, pleased, or glad, as over a particular thing.

House = a building in which people live; residence for human beings.

Humanity = the human race

India = a republic in South Asia: a union compromising 25 states and 7 union territories. Prophet Buddha is said to have been born in India circa 566 B.C.

→ In addition to the aforementioned information, I will further quote from Brother J.V. Pimienta-Bey's work, "Othello's Children in the New World," in which, in quoting J.A. Rogers' work "Nature Knows No Color Line," he informs us that "Indi" was an ancient Latin word for 'Black People' in general. The antiquity of the name 'Indian' is a Eurocentric reference for a very dark-complexioned peoples, is thereby illustrated."

Keys = something that affords a means of access; a book, pamphlet, or other text containing the solutions or translations of material given elsewhere.

Know = to be cognizant or aware of; to be cognizant, or aware, as of some fact, circumstance, or occurrence.

Learn = to acquire knowledge of or skill in by study; instruction, or experience; to gain (a habit, mannerism, etc.) by experience, exposure to example, or the like.

Life Works = tasks of a lifetime.

Little Ones = one's children; our offspring.

Loosened = slacken or relax; to let loose or set free from bonds, restraints, or constraints.

Palestine = known in ancient times as the land of Canaan. An ancient country in Southwest Asia, on the East coast of the Mediterranean.

Pamphlet = a complete publication of generally less than 80 pages stitched or stapled together and usually having a paper cover.

Peace = cessation of or freedom from any strife or dissension; a state of mutual harmony between people or groups, especially in personal relations.

Secret Lessons = "Secret" indicates that something is being kept from the public at large.

→ At the time of the Prophet, what had been kept from the public was the lessons that are now found in The Holy Koran of The Moorish Science Temple of America. ALLAH, knowing the time of the season, appointed the Prophet Noble Drew Ali to bring, or reveal, these secret teachings. Now we have the necessary tools to begin climbing the 3-step ladder along with the 12-step ladder until we reach the pinnacle of that which life is spent to build the Temple of Perfected Man.

Servant = a person employed to perform domestic duties in a household or for a person.

Set = to put into some condition; to cause to pass into a given state or condition.

Teachings = acts of imparting knowledge of or skill in; the giving of instruction in.

Thy = thou; you.

Thyself = thee; yourself.

Worthy = having great or adequate merit, character, or value; of commendable excellence or merit.

PAGE 3 (Lower Part)

Algiers = a seaport in and the capital of Algeria in the Northern part, and one of the former Barbary States in North Africa: now modern Algeria.

Canaanites = members of a Hamatic people that inhabited parts of ancient Palestine and were conquered by the Israelites and largely absorbed by them.

Etc. = et cetera; and others; and so forth; and so on (used to indicate that more of the same sort or class might have been mentioned, but for brevity have been omitted).

Hamathites = descents of Canaan, who was a descendent of Ham.

Industrious = working energetically and devotedly; hard working; diligent; skillful.

Joshua = the successor of Moses as leader of the Israelites. (See Bible Deut. 31:14-23; 34:9).

Kingdoms = states or governments having a king or queen as its head.

Land of Canaan = the ancient region lying between the Jordan, the Dead Sea, and the Mediterranean; also, biblical name of Palestine.

→ Brother J.V. Pimienta-Bey states in his work "Othello's children in the New World," that "upon reviewing the history of the near-Asian lands, one finds that such places as Canaan and Moab were once extensions of what we now call the African Continent." He further fortifies this point by stating that "in fact, many historical, theological, and linguistic studies show ethnic connections between 'Moor' and the ancient people of Canaan, Moab, Kush, Judea, and Kemet." (pg. 17).

Moabites = inhabitants or natives of Moab, which was an ancient kingdom East of the Dead Sea, in what is now part of Jordan.

Morocco = a kingdom in Northwest Africa.

Moslem = one who has submitted his will to the will of ALLAH, and knows the truth of the Oneness of ALLAH and Man

Tripoli = one of the former Barbary States of North Africa: later a province of Turkey, now part of Libya.

Tunisia = one of the former Barbary States in North Africa, once notorious for its pirates: constitutes modern Tunisia.

→ For a clear and deeper understanding of page 3 of The Holy Koran of The Moorish Science Temple of America, it is suggested that the reader pick up a copy of Brother Nathaniel Chambers-El's book, "Moorish Holy Koran Commentaries: The Illuminated Pages." Brother N. Chambers-El is truly a servant worthy of his hire for this and other books he has blessed us with.

NOTES:

·····CHAPTER I (1)·····
THE CREATION AND FALL OF MAN

Apace = rapidly; with great speed.

Attain = to achieve; to arrive.

Attribute = distinctive features or objects associated with someone or something.

Beacon Light = a source of guidance.

Birthright = any right or privilege to which a person is entitled by birth. This birthright is being the Lord of all the plane of manifest, which we lost but will regain.

Blessedness = divinely or supremely favored; blissfully happy or contended.

Boundary = something that indicated bounds or limits.

Bud = an undeveloped or rudimentary (beginning) step or branch of a plant.

Carnal = flesh. In this instance, a "garb" of flesh.

Cease = to be no more.

Cherubim = "a celestial being and member of the second order of angels. Known as 'Karybiyum' in Islam, the Cherubim continuously praise ALLAH by repeating tarbih (Glory to ALLAH) and dwell in peace in an area of the Heavens that is inaccessible to attacks from Iblis, or the devil; a high order of Angels that are celestial attendants of ALLAH." (M.D. / Sis. Rashida-El)

Circumscribe = to encircle; limited.

→ Man is made in the image of ALLAH, but he is not ALLAH. Therefore, since man was created by ALLAH, he cannot limit or try to encircle that Supreme Intelligence which is ALLAH. We must bear in mind that man is a spirit and <u>A PART OF ALLAH</u>, but he is not ALLAH. Man must elevate his thoughts to infinite wisdom in order to glimpse at his possibilities and unfold those attributes of ALLAH which he has within.

Creation = invention; the bringing into existence by the Supreme Creator and Author.

Creative Fate = "Creative" means having the quality or power of creating. "Fate" means the supposed force or power that determines events. In this case, we understand that power is but an illusion and that force is the Will of ALLAH and his Omnipotent; that power is that WILL in manifest. Therefore, Creative Fate is ALLAH.

Essence = the intrinsic or indispensable properties that identify something.

Estate = property or possession.

Ether = the upper regions of space; the sky or heaven.

→ In this instance, I lean more in agreement with Sis. Rashida-El in her description of ether as being a "gaseous substance when vibrating very fast cannot be seen by eyes of men in flesh. The slower the vibration, the more dense the gas becomes, allowing men to see the materialization of life and thus see ALLAH'S will in action." (M.D.)

Fall = to move to a lower position.

→ The fall of man is not necessarily a negative occurrence. The Prophet states in the Moorish Holy Koran, "and so this carnal nature soon became a foe that man must fight, that he might be the strength of ALLAH made manifest." (Ch. 1).

Finite = measurable; capable of being subject to limitations and conditions.

→ Finite-mind is the mind of the physical man, measured by time and has a limit. However, in its own way, "the manifests of *life* on every plane unfolds into **perfection** of their kind." The Prophet teaches us in our Moorish Literature ("What is Islam," pg. 10), the object of man's life, according to Islam, is its complete unfoldment. Islam teaches that man is born with unlimited capacities for progress. The mind of the physical-man is limited by the experience of the physical world, but the mind of the Spirit-man, which is within, is unlimited as is the mind of ALLAH.

Function = to operate; the purpose for which something is designed to exist.

Garb = wearing apparel; attire.

Hark = listen attentively; to pay close attention to.

Heritage = something that comes or belongs to one by reason of birth.

Holy Breath = ALLAH, who animates all that is in creation.

Husbandman = ALLAH; a farmer.

Infinite = having no boundaries or limits; illimitable or eternal.

Manifest = visible; conspicuous; to become evidence; able of being seen with mortal eyes.

Manifold = having many features; of many kinds; numerous and varied.

Might = may; used to express possibility.

Mineral = any of the inorganic elements, as calcium, iron, magnesium, potassium, or sodium, that are essential to the functioning of the human body and are obtained from foods; any of a class of substances occurring in nature, usually comprising inorganic substances, as quartz or feldspar, of definite chemical composition and usually of definite crystal structure, but sometimes also including rocks formed by these substances as well as certain natural products of organic origin, as asphalt or coal.

Ordained = conferred with Holy order; decreed, bestowed.

Perfectness = exactly fitting the need in a certain situation or for a certain purpose; thorough or complete; pure or unmixed.

→ The suffix *ness* denotes quality and state. Within man is the ability for perfectness.

Plane = a stage; level.

Potency = strength; capacity to be, become, or develop.

Protoplast = the very word "proto-" is a prefix and means "first," or "original." "Plast" means "living substance." Taken together this leads me to believe that it is a reference to the first *living* substance or matter. Every physical object seen with mortal eyes consists of matter.

Seed = a fertilized ripened plant ovule (a minute structure from which a plant develops after fertilization), having an embryo (an organism in its early development stage, especially before birth or germination), capable of germinating to produce a new plant.

→ Here the seed being spoken of is symbolically man.

Seraphim = the highest order of Angels; Seraphim ("burning ones") continue to praise ALLAH, as they fly over HIS presence.

Soil = any place or condition providing the opportunity for growth or development.

Source = any thing or place from which something comes, arises, or is obtained; supplier.

THE CREATION AND FALL OF MAN

Spirit-man = That part of ALLAH that is within man, never susceptible to death for as long as ALLAH lives, Spirit-man lives, and ALLAH is not bound to death as finite things are.

Tarry = to remain or stay, as in a place.

Thought = an idea or notion.

Time = a system of measurement.

→ Since ancient *times*, systems have been developed for measurements. Every living thing is measured by a system. Depending on your beginning stages of research, you can find similarities within the systems used in the Mayan, Aztec, Julian, and Gregorian calendars, extending to the Ancient Egyptians. All of these consisted of the observation of the moon, stars, planet alignment, sun, etc. A system for measuring men is by observing his physical evolvement from his infancy to his second infancy, etc. Time is also measured by milestones, or events marked in history. Since the physical aspect of men is measured by time, a point will arrive when he will cease to exist as well as every other living thing.

Unfold = to reveal or display; open.

Unto = to.

Untrammeled = unrestrained or free from obstacles.

Ye = you.

Yea = yes; indeed.

Wisdom = One of the attributes of ALLAH as spoken in Ch. 10:14; ALLAH; the quality of being wise.

NOTES:

Archelaus = son of Herod.

→ "The son of Herod the Great by his Samaritan wife, Malthace. He was given the most important district of his father's real estate, Judea, Samaria, and Idumea. He was more cruel than his father and was disposed by Rome. He ruled from 4 B.C. to A.D. 6. In an attempt to protect his throne, he ordered the death of all infants of Jerusalem, not knowing that John and Jesus came to lead the people to the path of ALLAH and not to claim his throne although Jesus was of the line of King David. (1)

Book of ALLAH'S Remembrance = a record of all that there is, was, and evermore to be.

→ According to Bro. R. Thomas-Bey and Bro. M. Jeffreys-Bey, "The 'Akashic Records' are known to Moorish American Moslems as 'The Dial Plate of Heaven,' 'ALLAH'S Own Record Book' and 'The Book of ALLAH'S Remembrance.' It is non-perishable, non-physical, non-material, permanent registry of every thought, word, deed, and occurrence from time immemorial to the present. The Akashic Records can also be described as 'The Universal Mind of ALLAH.'"

They further state that "when the mind and soul of an individual man or woman, is purified with Wisdom, Will and Love, he/she becomes wholly in tune with ALLAH, thus giving him/her full access to the 'Book of ALLAH'S Remembrance,' that he/she may copy the massages from its sacred, non-tangible, non-perishable non-physical pages…" (Catechism on The Holy Koran of The Moorish Science Temple of America). (25)

Carnal Men = the physical aspect of man with its lower nature and desires; those whose main focus, objective, or goal in the physical manifestation is limited to those things dealing with the mundane. (15)

Claimant = a person who makes a claim. (2)

Comprehend = to understand. (15, 20, 23, 25)

Council = an assembly of persons summoned or convened for consultation, deliberation, or advice; a body of persons specially designated or selected to act in an advisory, administrative, or legislative capacity. (2)

Cycle Age = a round of years or a reoccurring period of time, especially one in which certain events or phenomena repeat themselves in the same order and at the same intervals, *i.e.*, seasons, the alignment of planets, the rotation of planet earth, etc. (12)

Dark = evil; wicked, destitute of knowledge or culture; lacking spiritual understanding. (15)

Debased = reduced in quality or value; lowered in rank, dignity, or significance. (18)

Deeds = acts or gestures, especially as illustrative of intentions, one's character, or the like. (18)

Deem = to hold an opinion; think. (12)

Deliverance = an act or instance of delivering; salvation, liberation. (6)

Egypt = a country in north-east Africa.

→ "The great civilization of north-eastern Africa, which, when united, included both the upper (southern) and lower (northern) kingdoms. It is identified as Mizraim in Hebrew, the duel ending "ayim" perhaps indication the upper and lower kingdoms of ancient Egypt. By the time Abraham arrived in Egypt during the First Intermediate Period, the great pyramids of the Old Kingdom Period (2700-2200 B.C.) had already been standing for some 500 years. The subsequent

EDUCATION OF MARY AND ELIZABETH IN ZOAN, EGYPT

rise of the Middle Kingdom Period (2040-1786 B.C.) parallels the arrival of Jacob and Joseph. Extensive archeological excavations at various sites throughout Egypt reveal an advanced culture expressed in architecture, agriculture, music, military prowess, and religion. The Pharaoh was considered to be a god incarnate whose word was law." (King James Study Bible). (4)

Elihu = a master teacher who taught Elizabeth and Mary and prepared them to set the lives of John and Jesus in motion in fulfillment with their missions to the sons of man. (5, 7, etc.)

Elizabeth = mother of John and cousin of Mary. (5, 6, etc.)

Gospel = a doctrine regarded as of prime importance; glad tiding, especially concerning salvation and the kingdom of God [ALLAH]; something regarded as true and implicitly believed. (14)

Grove = a small wooded or forested area. In this case it would appear to be a place where meditation, teaching, and other religious activities took place. (9)

Happenings = any events considered worthwhile, unusual, or interesting; episode. (7)

Harmony = agreement; accord; harmonious relations; a consistent, orderly, or pleasing arrangement of parts. (19)

Herod = ruler of Palestine.

→ "Known as Herod the Great. Given authority over Palestine (37-4 B.C.). To win the favor of both Romans and Jews, he carried out lavish building projects, including the cities of Caesarea and Samaria, and the new temple at Jerusalem. Herod had 10 wives and the deserved reputation of being a cruel and unscrupulous

despot. Because of hatred and ambitions for power among families, and because of Herod's consuming suspicion that someone might try to usurp his throne, he executed one of his wives, Marianne, and his three oldest sons: Archelaus, Antipas "the Tetrarch" and Phillip. Herod also embellished such foreign cities as Beirut, Damascus, Antioch, and Rhodes." (King James Study Bible). (1)

Holy = spiritual; dedicated or devoted to the service of God [ALLAH]; "...*holy zeal*...." could be taken to mean spiritual fervor or spiritual eagerness, desire, or endeavor. In the case of Jesus and John, they were to be educated and have their spiritual qualities awakened. (17)

Infant = a child during the earliest period of its life, especially before he or she can walk; baby. (2)

Jerusalem = capital of Israel, in the Judaea Heights between the Mediterranean and the Dead Sea.

→ "A sacred city and well-known capital of Palestine. The earliest known name for the city was Urushalem. Salem was a natural abbreviation for Jerusalem. David united the kingdom after Saul's reign and quickly made Jerusalem the political and religious capital of the kingdom. Jerusalem was chosen as the place for the capital because it was centrally located between the northern and southern tribes and because the topography of the city made it easy to defend. David gave the city the name 'Jerusalem' and it is also referred to as the 'City of David.'" (1)

John = forerunner of Jesus; son of Zacharias and Elizabeth. (3, etc.)

Joseph = husband of Mary, father of Jesus, and legal heir of king David. (4)

EDUCATION OF MARY AND ELIZABETH IN ZOAN, EGYPT

Judean Hills = the hills in the country of the southern portion of Palestine. (M.C./Sis. Rashida-El). (4)

Light = spiritual enlightenment; spiritual illumination or awareness. (15)

Lo = look; see; also used to catch the attention of an individual to a statement or phrase. (26)

Lofty = extending high in the air; of impossible heights. (22)

Manifest = to make visible.

→ By His words, actions and deeds Jesus made *visible* true love. (22)

Marveling = wondering; the feeling of wonder. (6)

Mary = wife of Joseph, mother of Jesus, and cousin of John's mother, Elizabeth. Mary was also a teacher to Jesus. (Ch. 2:17 Moorish Holy Koran). (4, 6, etc.)

Measure = the extent, dimensions, quantity, etc., of something ascertained especially comparison with a standard; the act or process of ascertaining the extent, dimensions, quantity, etc., of something. (12)

Messenger = a person who carries a message or goes on an errand for another. (26)

Milestone = a significant event or stage in life, process, development, or the like of a person, nation, etc. (12)

Missions = assigned or self-imposed duties or tasks; calling. The missions of John and Jesus were issued by man, but rather it was from a Higher calling directed towards humanity. (17)

Native = a place or environment in which something or someone came into being. (27)

Native Land = being the place in which a person was born, or a thing came into being. (27)

Naught = nothingness. "*...that nothing can make them one but love...*" (20, 22)

Ordained = destined; selected for or appointed to. (8)

Pave = prepare or facilitate. (24)

Preparation = a proceeding, measure, or provision by which one prepares for something. (13)

Purity = freedom from anything that debases, contaminates, pollutes, etc. (24)

Registry = a record or list of acts, events, etc. (25)

Reigned = ruled; governed. (1)

Remembrance = a retained mental impression; memory. (25)

Rend = to separate into parts with force; to tear apart, split, or divide. (22)

Restoring = bringing back to an original place or position. (19)

Revealers = one's who make known, disclose, or divulge something. (16)

Sacred = of or relating to religious objects and practices. (9)

Salome = a master teacher of Mary and Elizabeth. (5, 9, etc.)

Sure Foundation = a strong foundation.

→ The Prophet Noble Drew Ali instructs us that understanding is the rock on which man builds himself. We must therefore be sure that we gain the proper spiritual understanding so that we may unfold the potencies of ALLAH that are within. We must also be able to distinguish the difference between gnosis and mundane knowledge. A sure foundation signifies a strong base. (11)

Teach = to impart knowledge of or skill to.

→ Teach can refer to any practice that causes others to develop skill or knowledge, in this instance it is referring specifically to gnosis, or spiritual knowledge. (18)

Thoughts = products of mental activities; the capacity or faculty of thinking, reasoning, imagining, etc. (18)

Thrice = 3 times; in this case many times. (10)

Throne = the office or dignity of a sovereign. (2)

Wont = accustomed or used to. (9)

Words = speech; talk. (18)

Words of Life = speech that brings about spiritual awakening.

→ Words are energy and thus can create, save, or destroy, and so we must be careful of the words we use and should use positive words to bring about positive results for humanity and keep in mind that we are instructed to use kind words by the Prophet Noble Drew Ali. (27)

Zeal = a fervor for a cause, person, or object; eager desire or endeavor; enthusiastic devotion to a cause, ideal, or goal. (17)

Zoan = Tanis; an ancient city in the Egyptian Delta and seat of the 21st Dynasty. An important port for over a millennium. (4)

NOTES:

Bitterness = harsh, disagreeable acrid taste, like that of aspirin, quinine, wormwood, or aloes; acrid of biting. (13)

Blessedness = blissfully happy or contended; bringing happiness and thankfulness. (12)

Body of Desires = those mundane or worldly desires arousing from the lower-nature of the flesh. (7)

Bound = tied; connected. (2)

Breeds = produces or brings about; to cause or be the source of. (11)

Carnal Self = of, pertaining to the flesh.

→ The word "carnal" derives from the Latin "carnalis," or flesh. The carnal self is the flesh, or this vehicle we possess, and it's used by the Soul so that it may travel in this world of things made manifest and gain its lessons. (7)

Clothed = dressed; covered with or as with clothing. (6)

Cores = the central parts of fleshy fruits, containing the seeds. (13)

Dark = evil, iniquitous; destitute of knowledge or culture; having very little or no light. Dark implies a more or less complete absence of light, or spiritual consciousness. (23)

Deems = held as an opinion; regarded. (17)

Demand = to ask for with proper authority; claim as a right.

→ "*...not demand love in return...*" means that love will be given because it is the right spiritual thing to do and not because we feel it must be done if we are to receive something in return. The Law of Reciprocity will take care of that, whether what we give out is good or evil. As we sow, so shall we reap. (3)

Desires = longing or craving, as for things that bring satisfaction or enjoyment, in this instance of mundane or carnal nature. (7)

Dethroned = removed from a throne; overthrown. (22)

Disguise = that which disguises; something that serves or is intended for concealment of identity, character, or quality; a deceptive covering, condition, manner, etc. (17)

Distorted = misrepresented. (7)

Embodiment = given a bodily form to; to personify. (9)

Ether = the skies; atmosphere; a realm of a specific type. (7)

Exalted = elevated; raised in rank or character. (22)

Falsehood = something false; deception. (9)

Form = the structure, pattern, organizational, or essential nature of anything; idea; a particular condition, character, or mode in which something appears. (6)

Gall = bitter; unpleasant. (13)

Goliath = the giant warrior of the Philistines whom David killed with a strong from a sling. (I Sam. 17:48-51); a very large, powerful, or influential person or thing. (23)

Grove = a small wooded or forested area, usually with no undergrowth; a small orchard or stand of fruit-bearing trees. (1)

Harmonies of Life = the unification of one's life with all of creation; Peace in life.

→ When one's will is in tune with the Will of ALLAH, there is harmony amongst all. The Will of ALLAH is not of chaos. It is the will of man that causes the chaos/cares that we experience. As it is man's will that creates chaos, it is this very same will that creates harmony between man and creation. Thus, it is that we are Moslems. (11)

Harms = to cause physical injuries or mental damages; moral injuries; evil deeds; damages. (11)

Hate = to dislike intensely or passionately; feel extreme aversion for or extreme hostility toward.

→ Hate, the simple and general word, suggests passionate dislike and a feeling of enmity. We as students and followers of Prophet Noble Drew Ali must learn to love instead of hate, and one of the first steps in accomplishing this objective is to be able to identify the difference between hate and love. (17)

Hatred = intense dislike or extreme aversion or hostility. (11)

Illusion = an illusion is a sensory impression or perception that is false or incorrect. "Incorrect" here means that what we see (or hear, feel, or the like) does not correspond with the objective situation as it can be determined by measurements. (8)

Jealousy = jealous resentment against a rival, a person enjoying success or advantage, etc., or against another's success or advantage itself. (17)

Justice = the state or quality of being just; righteousness, equitableness, or moral rightness. (10)

Lewdness = lustfulness; vulgar, lascivious. (11)

Light = something that makes things visible or affords illumination; an illuminating agent or source, as the sun, a lamp, or a beacon. In this instance, purity. With purity of heart, we can see the true essence of humanity and creation. (23)

Love = a profoundly tender, passionate affection; deep and enduring emotional regard. (See Ch. 48). (10)

Lust = intense sexual desire or appetite; uncontrollable or illicit sexual desire or appetite; to have intense sexual desires. (17)

Made = produced by making, preparing, etc., in a particular way. (6)

Manifest = made clear or evident to the eye or the understanding; made capable of being perceived by the senses; material. (9)

Mercy = an act of kindness, compassion, favor, pity, tenderness, etc. (10)

Misery = distress or suffering caused by need, privation, or poverty; great mental or emotional distress; extreme unhappiness. (12)

Murder = the killing of another person. (11)

Murky = obscure or thick with mist, haze, etc., as the air; vague, unclear, (7)

Myth = a fictitious story, person, or thing. (20)

Nether World = lying or believed to lie beneath the earth's surface; internal; lower or under. (17)

Pass Away = to come to an end; to cease to exist. (8)

Peace = freedom of the mind from annoyance, distraction, anxiety, an obsession, etc.; silence; stillness. (12)

Perils = dangers. (16)

Pleasant = pleasing, agreeable, or enjoyable to the senses. (13)

Promises = things that have effect of an expressed assurance; declarations that something will or will not be done, given, etc., by one. (12)

Pupils = students. (1)

Pure = without guilt or blemish; innocent; sincere. (3)

Ransomed = freed or liberated. (16)

Redeemed = rescued; freed; liberated; brought back to its original or intended state. (21)

Reflection = a representation, counterpart; an illusion; something that appears to be but is not the essence of the subject.

→ A reflection is *not* the original object. (7)

Reply = answer; respond. (14)

Right = fair, good, or proper. (10)

Saviour = a person who saves, rescues, or delivers. (22)

Slander = to defame; a malicious, false, and defamatory statement; to malign. (11)

Study = application of the mind to the acquisition of knowledge, as be reading, investigating, or reflection; deep thought, reverie, or a state of abstraction; to think deeply, reflect, or consider. Study implies an attempt to obtain a grasp of something by methodical or exhaustive thought. (14)

Sympathize = to feel or express compassion; commiserate. (19)

Theft = the act of stealing; the wrongful and carrying away of the personal goods or property of another. (11)

Thrice = three times, as in succession; on three occasions or in three ways; very; extremely; in threefold quantity or degrees. (16)

Throne of Power = the chair, or seat, occupied by a ruler.

→ In this instance the ruler, whether as aught (righteousness), or naught (foolishness), will be demonstrated in out words, actions, and deeds. (22)

Truth Reversed = falsehood. (9)

Unity = united; to come into one, in agreement, cause, course, etc. (Heading)

NOTES:

····CHAPTER IV (4)····
DEATH AND BURIAL OF ELIZABETH
-MATHENO'S LESSONS-
THE MINISTRY OF DEATH

Assure = guaranteed; sure; certain. (16)

Binds = connects. (3)

Block = a solid mass of wood with one or more flat or approximately flat faces. "...*a block of wood can do the same*" basically means that anything can serve as a pointer. (15)

Canaan = the ancient name of the land of Israel. According to the Bible, Canaan was the grandson of Noah and the son of Ham. In the Amarna Letters, the Phoenician coast is described as the land of Canaan. (26)

Ceremonies = the formal activities conducted on some solemn or important public or state occasion; a formal religious or sacred observance. Ceremony applies to more or less formal dignified acts on religious or public occasions. (17)

Comprise = to be made up of. (20)

Conception = the ability to form or understand mental concepts; a concept, plan, or thought. (8)

Conquered = to be victorious over.

→ Brother John was *victorious* over self, that is, he conquered self. At this time, he was 30 years old. (See Ch. 14:5). (31)

Cord = a string or thin rope made of several strands braided, twisted, or woven together; any influence that binds or restrains. (3)

Crisis = a dramatic emotional or circumstantial upheaval in a person's life; turning point. (8)

Departed = passed away, as from life or existence. (6)

Elijah = a prophet of ALLAH.

→ "Elijah was a prophet of God [ALLAH] during the reigns of Ahab and Ahaziah in the Northern kingdom of Israel (c. 873-852 B.C.). Elijah shaped the history of his times and dominated Hebrew thinking for centuries afterward. His prophecies emphasized the unconditional loyalty to God [ALLAH] required of the nation of Israel. His strange dress and appearance, his fleetness of foot, and his cave-dwelling habits all suggest a robust, outdoor-type personality." (King James Study Bible). (9)

Engedi = a small community in Israel.

→ "Engedi bears the name of a perennial spring that gushes from a small promontory about six hundred feet above the Dead Sea. The remarkable water supply in the midst of such a desolate region led to the creation of a small community at the site. Engedi was on the barren western shore of the Dead Sea about 35 miles southeast of Jerusalem, 18 miles southeast of Hebron, and part of the allotment of Judah. Because Engedi lay on the eastern edge of the rugged wilderness of Judah, David hid himself in this area when he was fleeing from King Saul. It was watered by a hot spring that came forth about three or four hundred feet about the base of a large cliff and yielded an abundance of fresh water that created an oasis rich in semitropical vegetation and vineyards. Engedi is a modern-day tourist attraction." (King James Study Bible). (29)

Fiery Drinks = liquors or condiments that cause a burning sensation; highly intoxicating drinks. (13)

Ford = a place where a river or other body of water is shallow enough to be crossed by walking. (26)

Forms = sets of words, as for use in religious ritual or in a legal document; a formality or ceremony, often with implication of absence of real meaning; any assemblage of things of a similar kind constituting a component of a group. (17)

Grieved = in great sorrow; grief. (2)

Harbinger = a person who goes ahead and makes known the approach of another. (9)

Hebron = "One of the 'central' cities in the southern hill country of Judea some 20 miles south-southwestern of Jerusalem on the road to Beer-Sheba. It is situated at one of the highest points (c. 3,040 feet above sea level) on the central mountainous ridge and is one of the oldest continually inhabited cities in Palestine. Originally, Hebron was called Kirjath-arba. Hebron was built seven years before Zoan (Tanis) in Egypt." (King James Study Bible). (1)

Hence = meaning "away from here." (4)

Hierophant = an interpreter of sacred mysteries or esoteric principles. (30)

Infancy = the state or period of being an infant. (13)

Inner Life = Spiritual life, or intellectual life. (17)

Inspiration = stimulation of the mind to a high level of feeling or activity. (7)

Jericho = A town in the Jordan Valley, on the Israeli-occupied West Bank.

→ One of the oldest inhabited cities in the world. It is situated in the wide plain of the Jordan Valley at the foot of the ascent to the Judean mountains. Jericho is about 8 miles northwest of the site where the Jordan River flows into the Dead Sea. The city is about 800 feet below sea level and has a tropical climate that is at times very hot. Even though only a few inches of rainfall are recorded each year, the city is a wonderful oasis. Known as the 'City of Trees,' Jericho has many date palms, banana trees, balsams, and henna." (26)

Jordan River = a river in Southwest Asia, flowing from South Lebanon through the Sea of Galilee, then south between Israel and Jordan through West Jordan into the Dead Sea. It is approximately 200 miles.

Kindred = collectively, a person's relatives; family members. (1)

Matheno = an Egyptian priest. (26, 27, 29)

Messiah = "The Anointed One of God;" "the Redeemer." (10)

Mission = the business with which one is charged. (10)

Nazarite = "to be set apart."

→ "Nazarite" means "to be set apart" and is explained as a separation unto [ALLAH]. The vow was taken by men and women who desired to consecrate themselves in an outstanding or unusual manner. It was a total consecration to the service of God, usually for a specific period of time. At the completion of his vow, the Nazarite had to offer the same range of sacrifices as Aaron did in his ordination. The Nazarite's long hair and the high priest's diadem and anointing oil are all called 'nezer,' for in both cases these were outward symbols of holiness expected of them. The same root 'nezer' translates as 'consecration' or 'head of his consecration,' denoting the characteristic mark of the Nazarite, his uncut hair, which had to be returned to God in sacrificial fire when the vow was completed. (King James Study Bible). (13, 30)

Nile = the longest river in the world, flowing north from Lake Victoria to the Mediterranean. It is over 4,000 miles long and served as the bloodline for the ancient people of Kemet. (29)

Noble = majestic or grand; having high moral character. (7)

Outward = pertaining to or being what is seen or apparent, as distinguished from the underlying nature, facts, etc.

→ "...*does not come with outward show...*" could be taken to mean that the cleansing of the soul, with its ceremonies, forms, and/or rites, are mere formalities with a deeper purpose. Once the individual begins the inner rite of cleansing the soul, it will come forth and show itself to all. "As a man thinketh in his heart, so is he." "As above, so below; as below, so above." (22)

Pattern = an original or model considered for or deserving of imitation; an example, instance, sample, or specimen. (14)

Pointer = a person or thing that points or shows a direction. (15)

Preparation = a proceeding, measure, or provision by which one prepares for something; any proceeding, experience, or the like considered as a mode of preparing for the suture. (20)

Purity = freedom from guilt or evil; freedom from anything that debases, contaminates, pollutes, etc. (11)

Readiness = a developmental stage at which a child as the capacity to receive instruction at a given level of difficulty or to engage in a particular activity; the condition of being ready.

→ Jesus taught that "unless you are converted and become as little children, you will, by no means, enter the Kingdom of Heaven." The benefit of the mind of a child is that the child's mind is pliant and receptive. Therefore, it is more open to receiving knowledge. As adults, we have been trained to believe otherwise. Our wills have been removed from our possession and in the hands of those who have no interest in our benefit. As Brother Marcus M. Garvey once stated, "You've been educated, now you must be re-educated." (11)

Reform = to improve by correcting efforts or removing defects. (21)

Rite = the prescribed form for conducting a religious or other solemn ceremony. (18, 20, 22)

Sages = profoundly wise persons; persons venerated for their possession of wisdom, judgement, and experience. (9)

Sakara = Saqqara: Temple of the Brotherhood in Egypt, located in the Valley of the Nile.

→ "Ancient Kemet is a land of many firsts, and chief among them is the distinction of being the home of the world's first skyscraper. The first stone building ever constructed still stands majestically within the vast complex of temples at Saqqara. It is called the Step Pyramid. There is a total of 15 royal pyramids at Saqqara. Most are in varying stages of disrepair, but they were all developed from the same prototype." (Anthony T. Browder's "Nile Valley Contributions to Civilization," pg. 100), (29)

Selfishness = devotedness to or caring only for oneself; concerned primarily with one's interest, benefits, welfare, etc., regardless of others. (6)

Span = the distance between two points or extremities. (16)

Strive = to make strenuous efforts toward any goal; to contend in opposition, battle, or any conflict; to struggle vigorously, as in opposition or resistance. (19)

Symbolic = serving as a symbol of something. (18, 22, 24).

Tarried = remained, or stayed, as in a place. (26)

Tasks = duties, especially ones assigned directly to an individual. Task usually refers to a clearly defined piece of work, sometimes of short or limited duration, assigned to or expected of a person. (4)

Tis = a contraction of "it is." (26)

Treads = forms by the action of walking or trembling. (16)

Tried and True = reliable, trustworthy. (4)

Valley = an elongated depression between uplands, hills, or mountains, especially one following the course of the stream, in this instance the Nile River. (29)

Worth = usefulness or importance, as to the world, to a person, or for a purpose; value. (4)

Zacharias = the father of John. (1)

NOTES:

AFTER THE FEAST * THE HOMEWARD JOURNEY * THE MISSING JESUS * THE SEARCH FOR HIM * HIS PARENTS FIND HIM IN THE TEMPLE * * HE GOES WITH THEM TO NAZAREHT * SYMBOLIC MEANING OF CARPENTER'S TOOLS

→ In this chapter, we are given the proper tools with their symbolic meanings to begin building the Temple of Perfected Man. We are all responsible for the building of our personal temples and so to build the temple properly, we must place ourselves in the mindset of a carpenter. A good perspective of what a carpenter is, was used by the great Japanese samurai warrior, Miyamoto Musashi. In his book, "The Book of Five Rings," he states: "If Heiho [the path to enlightenment] is to be compared to carpentry, the general is the master carpenter who knows everything about the nature of the carpenter's square and who is knowledgeable about the ways of the region and the particular ways of that household for which the carpenter is building the house." From the beginning, before we start our construction of a dwelling, the carpenter "learns the measurements of the temples and the plans of the palaces and constructs the house which people use." Brother Jesus mentions the tools necessary for the proper construction of the Temple of Perfected Man, and as Miyamoto Musashi states, "a necessary accomplishment of the carpenter is to have sharp tools…" "The necessary accomplishments of the carpenter are that his work not be warped and that joints are aligned."

Ascend = to move, climb, or go upward; to rise to a higher point, rank, or degree; proceed from inferior to a superior degree or level. (21)

Ax = a chopping tool with a bladed head mounted on a handle. (16)

Block = a solid mass of wood, stone, etc., usually with one or more flat or approximately flat faces; a short length of plank serving as a bridging, as between joists. (18)

Bounds = limits or boundaries. (15)

Carpenter = a person who builds or repairs wooden structures, as houses, scaffolds, or shelving. (11)

Character = the moral qualities, standards, principles, and the like of an individual. (13)

Chisel = a wedge-like tool with a cutting edge at the end of the blade, often made of steel, used for cutting or shaping wood, stone, etc. (19)

Compass = an instrument for drawing or describing circles, measuring distances, etc., consisting generally of two movable, rigid legs hinged to each other at one end. (15)

Conduct = personal behavior; way of acting. (14)

Desires = wishes or longing for; craving; wants. (15)

Disputing = engaged in an argument or dispute; arguing or debating. (6)

Doctors of the Law = (See Ch. 14 for definition). (6)

Dome = a vault, having a circular plan and usually in the form of a portion of a sphere, so constructed as to exert an equal thrust in all directions; a domical roof or ceiling. (20)

Drive = to send, expel, or otherwise cause to move by force or compulsion. (17)

Faith = confidence or trust in a person or thing. According to the teachings, what man knows is truth. (20)

Feast of Pasch = The Feast of the Passover.

AFTER THE FEAST * THE HOMEWARD JOURNEY * THE MISSING JESUS * THE SEARCH FOR HIM * HIS PARENTS FIND HIM IN THE TEMPLE * * HE GOES WITH THEM TO NAZAREHT * SYMBOLIC MEANING OF CARPENTER'S TOOLS

→ The annual Feast of the Passover commemorating the birth of the nation of Israel and her deliverance from Egypt. Typologically, it pointed forward to the greater deliverance from the bondage of sin to be provided by the "Messiah." Passover takes its name from the Hebrew term related to the death angel passing over those who had applied the blood (of the unblemished lamb) to their homes. Passover time was a great high day among the Jews and thousands of pilgrims flocked to Jerusalem each year to observe it. (King James Study Bible); "Pasch" or "Pesach" in Hebrew means "passing over." (1)

Galilee = (See Ch. 6 for definition). (3)

Hammer = a tool consisting of a solid head, usually of metal, set crosswise on a handle, used for beating metals, driving nails, etc. (17)

Hope = the *feeling* that what is wanted can be had or that events will turn out for the best; to look forward to with desire and reasonable confidence. (20)

Joint = to true (position as to make it balanced, leveled, or squared) the bottom of (wooden plane body) to allow even movement along the surface of the work; a connection between two pieces of wood, metal, or the like, often reinforced with nail, screws, or glue. (18)

Kindred = a person's relatives collectively. (3)

Knotty = the hard, cross-gained mass of wood at the place where a branch joins the trunk of the tree; an involved, intricate, or difficult matter; complicated problem. (16)

Ladder = a structure of wood, metal, or rope, commonly consisting of two sidepieces between which a series of bars are set at suitable distances, forming a means of climbing up or down. (20)

Line = a cord, wire, or the like, used for measuring or as a guide; a string with a weight on one end, used to check the straightness of a wall. It is believed that this same tool was used by the ancient "Egyptians" during the construction of the pyramids. (19)

Love = the benevolent affection of ALLAH for his creatures, or the reverent affection due *from them to ALLAH.* (20)

Nazarenes = Nazarenes are descendants or inhabitants of Nazareth, Jesus' hometown. Later, Jews would refer to the followers of Jesus as "the sect of the Nazarenes." (1)

Overtaken = happened to or befallen someone suddenly or unexpectedly.

→ In the instance the parents of the child Jesus thought that harm had overtaken him. We must bear in mind the experience His parents went through when Jesus was first born and so it is justified for His parents to have reacted the way that they initially did. But it was Jesus who put their worries to rest when He informed them that He must be about His Father's work. (8)

Passions = powerful or compelling emotions or feelings, as love or hate; strong amorous feelings or desires; strong or extravagant fondness, enthusiasm, or desire for anything. (15)

Pinnacle = the highest point. (21)

AFTER THE FEAST * THE HOMEWARD JOURNEY * THE MISSING JESUS
* THE SEARCH FOR HIM * HIS PARENTS FIND HIM IN THE TEMPLE *
* HE GOES WITH THEM TO NAZAREHT *
SYMBOLIC MEANING OF CARPENTER'S TOOLS

Plummet = also called plumb bob; a piece of lead or some other weight attached to a line used for determining perpendicularity, for sounding, etc. (19)

Righteousness = the quality or state of being just or rightful. (15)

Samaria = ancient capital of Israel.

→ "Samaria was built about 880 B.C. By Omri, the sixth king of Israel. Samaria occupied a three-hundred-foot-high hill about 42 miles north of Jerusalem and 25 miles east of the Mediterranean Sea. This hill was situated on the major north-south road through Palestine. It also commanded the east-west route to the plain of Sharon and the Mediterranean Sea. It could easily be defended because it was on the hill; however, its great weakness was that the nearest spring was a mile distant. Samaria fell to the Assyrians in C. 722 B.C. and its inhabitants were carried into captivity." (King James Study Bible). (2)

Saw = a tool or device for cutting, typically a thin blade of metal with a series of sharp teeth. (19)

Sought = seek; to search for. (3, 4)

Square = There are several types of square tools. I would think that the reference made here is to the Try-Square, which is a device for testing the squareness of carpentry work or the like, or for laying out tight angles, consisting of a pair of straight edges fixed at right angles to one another. Clearly this tool could fit the symbolic meaning given by Jesus. (14)

Symmetrical = well-proportioned. (16)

Trinity = a group of three; three. (20)

Temple = an edifice or place dedicated to the service or worship of a deity or deities; any place or object in which God [ALLAH] "dwells." (6, 21)

Ungainly = not graceful; awkward, clumsy; in an awkward manner. (16)

Useless = worthless. (16)

Workshop = a room, group of rooms, or building in which work, especially mechanical work, is carried on.

→ In this case, the workshop is the mind. (13)

Zebedee = father of James and John, who were two apostles of Jesus. (4)

NOTES:

LIFE WORKS OF JESUS IN INDIA AMONG THE MOSLEMS

Band = a company of persons, joined, acting, or functioning together, in this instance a band of Hindu Priests. (2)

Chief Hillel = chief rabbi and teacher.

→ "Hillel lived in the late 1st century B.C., and early first century A.D. He was born in Babylonia, and at the age of 40 went to Jerusalem to study. He founded the bet Hillel, or House of Hillel. Hillel was famous for his saintliness and scholarship, and rabbinic literature describes his patience, self-control, and loving care for his people. His seven rules for interpretation of the scriptures formed the basis of rabbinic hermeneutics. Among his ethical maxims, which were collected in 'Pirke Avot' (Ethics of the Fathers), are many upon which the humanitarian precepts of modern Judaism and Christianity are based. These include: 'The more property, the more anxiety; the more schooling, the more wisdom; the more counsel, the more understanding; the more righteousness, the more peace.' His description of the teachings of Judaism contains the golden rule stated in the negative: 'What is hateful to you do not do unto your fellow man. This is the whole law; the rest is commentary.'" (King James Study Bible). (4, 6)

Conceptions = the act or power of forming notions, or concepts; understanding. "...*clear conceptions*..." demonstrates the clarity in the understanding of spiritual matters Brother Jesus had at this age in his life. (20)

Day Star = the sun.

→ The day star is the sun and brings light and life to us. Jesus came with light and life and paved the road with brilliant acts towards humanity and left a blueprint for the sons of men. (5)

Entranced = filled with delight or wonder; put into a trance. (8)

Favored = one who has found favor in the sight of ALLAH (God) or another. (12)

Galilee = "The regional name for the northern part of Palestine, extending from the Esdraelon plain some 50 miles north and from the Sea of Galilee about 30 miles to the west. Its primary feature is the 13-mile-long Sea of Galilee. It lies 695 feet below sea level with the Jordan River flowing through it. Some towns of Galilee that were situated on the seashore were Capernaum, Bethsaida, Tiberias, and Magdala. Of these, only Tiberias exists today. Other significant Galilean towns include Nazareth and Chorazin." (King James Study Bible). (9)

Gave consent = gave approval. (16)

Gorgeous = splendid or sumptuous in appearance, coloring, etc. "...*gorgeous train*..." is a splendid procession of person, vehicles, animals, etc.

→ In the past, this method of travel was used by kings, queens, etc. In this case, it was a caravan. A caravan is a group of travelers, as merchants and pilgrims, journeying together for safety in passing through the deserts, hostile territories, etc. (9)

India = a republic in S. Asia; a union comprising of 25 states and 7 union territories; formerly a British Colony, gained independence on August 15, 1947. India has one of the oldest civilizations in the world. In the Indus Valley civilization can be traced back 5,000 years. Brother Jesus taught in Orissa, India. (1)

Joseph = Jesus' father. (14)

LIFE WORKS OF JESUS IN INDIA AMONG THE MOSLEMS

Longed = having an earnest or strong desire or craving; to yearn.

→ "*longed to go…*" means Jesus was eager to go with Ravanna, driven by the desire to gain knowledge. (16)

Magian Priests = wise men, who were originally the priestly caste among the Persians and Babylonians. They were experts in the study of stars.

→ According to the Oxford Concise Encyclopedia, "The sages who came from the East, follow a star [in search of] the infant [Jesus] in Bethlehem." (6)

Object = target. "*…object of his search…*" means the target he (Ravanna) was looking for. (10)

Orissa = (See Ch. 8 for definition). (17)

Patron = protector. (15)

Prince = a non-reigning male member of a royal family. (1)

Prince Ravanna = a wealthy prince of India. (1)

Province = the parts of a country outside of the capital or the largest cities. (17)

Rising Sun = the east. The sun rises on the east and sets on the west. "*…take him to the east [India]…*" (Chapter 6:15). (17)

Royal = of or pertaining to a king, queen, or other sovereign; descended from or related to a king or line of kings. (1)

Sought = to seek or search for. (14)

Temple of Jaguanath = Jagannath: Hindu Temple. (19)

Vedas = the entire body of Hindu sacred writing, chief among which are four (4) books: The Rig-Veda, the Sama-Veda, the Atharva-Veda, and the Yajur-Veda. (19)

Whence = where; "*from what place?*" (4)

Wrath = strong; stern, or fierce anger; deeply resentful indignation. (7)

NOTES:

Abides = dwells; remains. (13)

Appearing = coming into sight; becoming visible; coming into being. (9)

Belief = an opinion or conviction.

→ According to the Moorish Holy Koran, belief is the first step in salvation, the ladder reaching from the heart of man to the heart of ALLAH. It is what man thinks *perhaps* is truth. It is the beginning of the journey toward salvation. (28, 31)

Certainty = the *state* of being certain; without doubt. (26)

Conditions = existing circumstances; circumstances indispensable to come results. (9)

Conjoined = joined together; linked. (13)

Consciousness = special awareness of, or sensitivity to a particular issue or situation. (23)

Deific = made divine; deifying. "…*deific life*…" as Moslems, is when the will of man and the WILL of ALLAH are one. (26, 31)

Ethers = "substance that differed from all other matter. It could not be seen, felt, or weighed and was present in vacuums, outer space, and all matter." (9)

Evermore = always; forever. (10)

Faith = confidence or trust.

→ Faith is the second step in the ladder of salvation. It is what man *knows* is truth. (25, 29, 31)

Falsehood= lack of conformity to truth or face; deception; that which *seems* to be; an illusion or a lie. (4, 6)

Flesh = the body, especially as distinguished from the spirit or soul; the physical or animal nature of humankind as distinguished from its moral or spiritual nature. (13)

Force = mental or moral strength; an *influence* on a body or system, producing or tending to produce a change in movement, shape, or other effects. (15)

Fruition = attainment of anything desired; realization; accomplishment.

→ Fruition leaves no room for doubt. This is man himself, the truth. It is the complete salvation of man when he and ALLAH are one. (30, 31)

Gnosis = knowledge of *spiritual* matters; mystical knowledge. (20)

Holy Breath = ALLAH; that which animates all. (10)

Illusion = an illusion is a sensory impression or perception that is false or incorrect. "Incorrect" here means that which we see (or hear, feel, or the like), does not correspond with the objective situation as it can be determined by measurement. (15)

Jaguanath = Jagannath: in Hinduism, name of Krishna or Vishnu. (1)

Knows = that which men perceives or understands as fact or truth; apprehending with clarity and certainty. To know is to be aware of something as a fact or truth. (29)

Ladder = a structure of wood, metal, or rope, commonly consisting of two sidepieces between which a series of bars or rungs are set at suitable distances, forming a means of climbing up or down.

→ The ladder spoken of above is a spiritual ladder, which is a means for us to rise and set our will in tune with the WILL of ALLAH by following the three steps of Belief, Faith, and Fruition. (27)

Lamaas Bramas = a priest of India. (1)

Lightning = a brilliant spark discharge in the atmosphere, occurring within a thundercloud, between clouds, or between a cloud and the ground. (17)

Manifest = readily perceived by the eye or the understanding; evident; to make clear or evident to the eye or the understanding. (6)

Naught = be without result or fruition; nothing; zero. (6, 8)

Omnipotence = the quality of being omnipotent. (26)

Omnipotence = almighty or infinite in power, as God [ALLAH]; having very great or unlimited authority or power. (16)

Perhaps = maybe; possibly. (28)

Power = ability to do or act; capability of doing or accomplishing something; characteristic of those having authority or influence. (14)

Pray = beg; beseech or implore. (25)

Priests = persons having authority to perform and administer religious rites. (1)

Reflexes = the reflection or image of something, an object, etc.; noting or pertaining to an involuntary response to a stimulus, the nerve impulse from a receptor being transmitted inward to a nerve center that in turn transmits it outward to an effector; occurring in reaction; responsive. (9)

Rock = a firm foundation or support. (20)

Salvation = deliverance from the power or penalty of sin; redemption.

→ The suffix -ion in salva*tion* denotes action or condition. This demonstrates that salvation comes only by action, not inaction. This informs us that we must put work in to achieve salvation. (27)

Saved = rescued; redeemed. (31)

Sensing = a mental discernment, realization, or recognition; to grasp the meaning of; understand; to become aware of. (21)

So and So = in such a manner. (9)

Strangely = in a strange manner.

→ The suffix -ly means "-like," and so "strangely" then must mean in a strange-like manner, which is important to point out because it informs us that we are mixed in a strange-like manner, or an unusual, extraordinary way, but only because we haven't taken the time to study self and figure things out. Once we take this time to study self, as instructed by our ancient forefathers and the Prophet, then things would not be "strange," but familiar and we can begin our task of climbing the 3-step ladder in our quest for deific life. (12)

Strive = to contend in opposition, battle, or any conflict; to struggle vigorously, as in opposition or resistance. (13)

Surely = without doubt; the state or quality of being sure. (26)

Truth = ideal or fundamental reality apart from and transcending perceived experience; the reality lying at the basis of an appearance, the manifested, veritable essence of a matter. (2, 3, 4, 5)

Understanding = superior power of discernment; prompted by, based on, or demonstrating comprehension, intelligence, discernment, empathy, or the like. (19)

Waves = disturbances on the surface of a liquid body as a sea or lake, in the worm of a moving ridge or swell. (17)

Winds = air in natural motion, as that moving horizontally at any velocity along the earth's surface. Wind applies to any such air in motion, blowing with whatever degree of gentleness or violence. (17)

Wisdom = knowledge of what is true or right coupled with just judgement as to action. (22)

NOTES:

JESUS REVEALS TO THE PEOPLE OF THEIR SINFUL WAYS

Assist = to give support or aid to; help. (14)

Bear in Mind = to give considerable thought to; to keep in mind. (12)

Behold = to observe; look at. (3)

Blessedness = divinely or supremely favored; fortunate; blissfully happy or contended. (20)

Car of Jaguanath = Juggernaut: an idol of Krishna, at Puri in Orissa, India, annually drawn on an enormous cart under whose wheel devotees are said to have thrown themselves to be crushed as a sacrifice. (2)

Countenance = appearance, especially the look of expression of the face. (15)

Covet = to desire wrongfully, inordinately, or without due regard for the rights of others. (14)

Deed = something that is done, performed, or accomplished. (12)

Dove = any bird of the family Columbidea, especially the smaller species with pointed tails; a pure white member of this species, used as a symbol of innocence, gentleness, tenderness, and peace. (17)

Entranced = filled with delight; placed in a trance. (23)

Foe = enemy; a person who feels enmity, hatred, or malice toward another. (13)

Frenzied = wildly excited or enthusiastic. (2)

Hauled = pulled or drawn with force; moved by drawing; to drag. (2)

Holy One = Supreme Creator; ALLAH. (15, 24)

Idol = an image that is worshiped; an image or other material object representing a deity to which religious worship is addressed. (6)

Image = a mental representation; idea; conception. (10)

Incense = an aromatic gum or other substance producing a sweet odor when burned, used in religious ceremonies, to enhance a mood, etc.

→ In this case, it is symbolic for righteous deeds done. The Prophet advises us to let our good deeds outnumber our bad deeds, and when we pass away, we won't have anything to worry about. (20)

Jaguanath = Jagannath: in Hinduism, a name for Krishna or Vishnu. The word "Jaguanath" means "Lord of the World." (2)

Katak = a city of Orissa. (M.D. / Sis. Rashida-El). (1)

Kin = a group of persons descended from a common ancestor or constituting a family, clan, tribe, or race. (13)

Krishna = in Hinduism, an avatar of Vishnu (*infra*) and one of the most popular Indian (from India) deities, who appears in the Bhagavad-Gita as the teacher of Arunja. (4)

Lamb = a young sheep. (17)

Mortal = subject to death. "*...mortal eyes...*" would refer to finite men. (9)

Needless = unnecessary. "*...needless waste...*" means unnecessary waste or useless expenditure, as in animal or food, as sacrifice to ALLAH.

→ When we see ALLAH in all, we treat everything with reverence and our minds are exalted and serve as the alter of worship for our Supreme Creator and it is demonstrated in our lives. (17)

Noise = sound, especially a loud, harsh, or confused kind; a non-harmonious or discordant group of sounds. "...*noise of tongues*..." could be taken to mean outward show, or simple words; ALLAH lives through the words, actions, and deeds we display. (6)

No Kin = those who are not members of your family, clan, etc. (13)

Orissa = "a state in E. India, known as 'Kalinga' in ancient times."

→ Orissa was once a Buddhist state and later a Jain region before being converted to Hinduism. Through the centuries, dozens of kingdoms, local and foreign, have ruled Orissa, and many have left their mark in huge temples and other structures.

"Bhubaneswas once had 7,000 stone temples; many were destroyed by past invaders, but 500 remain. Especially well-preserved is the Great Lingaraj Temple, of about 650 A.D. At Konarak on the Bay of Bengal is the celebrated Black Pagoda, an elaborate temple to the sun of God, built in the 13th century. Nearby is Puri, a city of great antiquity and importance in Hinduism, with its mammoth 12th century Temple of Jagannath. Hundreds of thousands of pilgrims attend Puri's "Rath Yatra," or Car Festival, each June." (1)

Poor = having little or no money, goods, or other means of support.

→ Moslems are to be charitable and aid those who are less fortunate. If we lack in this department, all we have to do is execute the teachings of Prophet Noble Drew Ali, as he instructed in Ch. 32 of our Moorish Holy Koran. (14)

Sacrifice = the offering of an animal, plant, human life, or some material possession to God, a deity, etc., as in propitiation or homage.

→ ALLAH no longer demands such sacrifices. The sacrifice of self for the betterment of humanity is the best sacrifice. (16)

Sacrificial Altars = specific surfaces or areas designated or set apart for the sole purpose of making sacrifices. (21)

Scores = a great many; large amounts. (2)

Serve = to act as a servant; to render assistance; to be of use, help, etc. (13)

Shrine = "...*idol shrine*..." any structure or place consecrated or devoted to some saint, holy person, or deity, as an altar. (6)

Still Small Voice = "the spirituality of you, which is your definite part, or degree of the Omnipresent Spirit of God [ALLAH], is your true self." (The Theological Science Society, Vol. 1, pg. 5). (7)

Stranger = a person with whom one has no personal acquaintance; a newcomer in a place or locality. (13)

The Holy Breath = ALLAH; that which gives LIFE to all. (9)

Thought = the product of mental activity; idea or notion; the act or process of thinking. (12)

Vishnu = a deity believed to have descended from heaven to earth in several incarnations, or avatars, varying in number from nine to twenty-two, but always including animals. His most important incarnation is the Krishna of the Bhagavad-Gita; "the Preserver," the second member of the Trimurti, along with Brahma the Creator and Shiva the Destroyer.

Waste = to be consumed, spent, or employed uselessly or without giving full value or being fully utilized or appreciated. (17)

Weak = not strong; lacking in bodily strength or health as from age or sickness. (14)

Wine = something that invigorates, cheers, or intoxicates like wine.

→ "*...wine of carnal things...*" are those things of the material world, of the finite world, that become our obsessions and are placed above the Supreme Creator – ALLAH. (5)

Within = in or into the interior or inner part; inside. (10)

Word = speech or talk. (12)

Worship = to render religious reverence and homage to; to place on the level of ALLAH or higher.

→ There is but ONE ALLAH and all else comes from our Supreme Creator. (24)

→ There is a difference between ALLAH speaking with your tongue and ALLAH living in the noise of tongues, as mentioned in instruction 6 and 15. In order for ALLAH to speak with our tongues, we must allow our will to become in tune with the WILL of ALLAH so that our words, actions, and deeds be in tune with the message being brought. Noise of tongues indicates discord and confusion, something that ALLAH is not.

NOTES:

JESUS ATTENDS A FEAST IN BEHAR AND HERE HE TAUGHT HUMAN EQUALITY

Accuse = to charge with a fault, offense, or crime. (22)

Accuser = person who accuses. (20)

Ach = a wealthy man of Behar. (3)

Aggrieved = wronged, offended, or injured. (4)

Asp = any of several venomous snakes, especially the Egyptian cobra or the horned viper. (6)

Baubles = showy, unusually cheap, ornaments; minor art objects. (8)

Behar = Bihar: the tenth largest Indian state, and the second largest in population of the leading states in the Indian union. Although typically Indian, it has many important Buddhist and Jain shrines. Behar is in the lower Ganges valley. (M.D. / Sis. Rashida-El) (2)

Blades = leaves of plants, especially of grass or cereal; the broad part of a leaf, as distinguished from the stalk or petiole. (26)

Burs = rough, prickly cases around the seeds of certain plants, as the chestnut or burdock. (24)

Charming = pleasing; delightful; using charm.

→ "...*charming forms*..." could be referring to the physical appearance of the opposite sex that are appealing from a lower nature perspective. (17)

Choicest = worthy of being chosen; things that are preferred or preferable to others; carefully selected supply. (24)

Consort = to keep company; associate. (6)

Courtesans = prostitutes or paramours, especially ones associating with noblemen or men of wealth. (4, 15)

Covet = to desire enviously. (17)

Darnal = Darnel: any of several grasses of the genus Lolium, having simple stems, flat leaves, and terminal spikes. (24)

Deceit = to mislead or trick; trickery. (18)

Desire = to wish or long for; crave; want. Desire is a strong feeling, worthy or unworthy, that impels one to attain something that is seemingly within reach. (16)

Drunkards = persons who are habitually or frequently drunk. (15)

Extortioners = persons who engage in extortion; oppressive or illegal extraction, as of excessive price or interest; to wrest or wring (money, information, etc.) from a person by violence, intimidation, or abuse of authority. (4)

Fame = spread reputation, especially of a favorable character. (1)

Harvest = the gathering of crops (*infra*). (29)

Harvesters = a person who harvests (*supra*). (29)

Held Their Peace = were humbled to the point of silence. (20)

Holy Smoke = expressing a "holier than thou" façade while deep down inside they deceive. (22)

Indices = index: indications; things used or serving to point out; signs, tokens, or indications. (9)

Kernel = the body of a seed within its husk or integument (natural covering, as a skin, shell, etc.) (28)

Life Sums = the substance or gist of a matter [in this instance, life] comprehensively or broadly expressed; life works. (12)

JESUS ATTENDS A FEAST IN BEHAR AND HERE HE TAUGHT HUMAN EQUALITY

Loathing = strong dislike or disgust; disgusting. (23)

Loud Professor = pretended wise; the one who is always pointing out the faults in others and enjoying this act while professing to be "holier than thou," and deep inside his mission is only to deceive. (23)

Merit = claim to respect and praise; something that deserves or justifies a reward or commendation. (9)

Mockery = ridicule, contempt, or derision; a derisive, imitative action or speech. (23)

Polished Coat = a façade; something used to hide one's true self and/or intentions. (14)

Pure in Heart and Life = free of or without guilt; living life in Islamism, where one's words, actions, and deeds are not used to cause suffering, and where one rests in the House of Peace. (15)

Reputation = the estimation in which a person or thing is held, especially by the community or the public generally. Reputation is a word which refers to the position one occupies or the standing that one has in the opinion of others, in respect to attainments, integrity, and the like. (7)

Revel = to take great pleasure or delight in. (23)

Robboni = rabbi.

→ Since in this instruction of word "Robboni" is followed by the statement "Master of the Wise," I would think that "Robboni" derives from "Rabbi." The word rabbi translates to "My Master," in Hebrew. A rabbi can also be a title of respect for a Jewish scholar or teacher. Jesus was indeed a teacher. The title of this chapter (Ch. 9) itself states, "and here He *TAUGHT* human equality." (5)

Sacred River = this is referring to the Ganges River, the Hindus' most sacred river with a length of about 1,557 miles. (2)

Scorn = open or unqualified contempt; despise. (12)

Screen = guards or shields.

→ It is my opinion that here Jesus was stating that a master never shields himself, or separates himself from the people, especially those of ill conduct, for the sake of reputation or of fame. (7)

Shallow = lacking depth; superficial. (9)

Shallow Men = those who refuse to see deeper than the physical aspect of men and their faults, failing to realize that He who created him, also created them, that we all must pass through life and gain experience so that our God-Man may unfold. (9)

Shame = the painful feeling arising from the consciousness of something dishonorable, improper, ridiculous, etc., done by oneself or another. (32)

Shrewd = artful. "...*shrewd enough*..." means good and artful in the art of deception. (14)

Shun = to keep away from deliberately and especially consistently. (6)

Stalks = stems or main axis of plants; any slander supporting or connecting part of a plant, as the "petiole" of a leaf, the "peduncle" of a flower, or the "funicle" (stalk) of an ovele. (26)

Thieves = people who steal, especially secretly or without open force. (4)

Thistles = any of various prickly, composite plants having showy, purple flower heads, especially of the genera "Cirsium, Carduus," or "Onopordum." (24)

Thoughtless Think = the thoughts produced by those lacking in consideration for others. A lot of times this takes place when we become haughty in our ways. (9)

Tinseled = glittering due to a metallic substance, as copper or brass, in thin sheets, used in pieces, strips, threads, etc., to produce a sparkling effect cheaply.

→ *"tinseled coat of reputation…"* could be interpreted as one's holding to a false reputation established in a community where one is viewed as good in conduct and character, but their thoughts are meant to deceive, and they practice ought else in their thoughts. (23)

Upbraided = found fault with or reproached severely. (5)

Vile = morally low; highly offensive, unpleasant, or objectionable. (22)

NOTES:

JESUS SPAKE ON THE UNITY OF ALLAH AND MAN TO THE HINDUS

A Tiller of the Soil = a member of the Visya social class in Hindu society. The Visya were the tillers of the soil, herdsmen, and professionals. He/she fell below the Shatriya and above the Sudra in the caste system. (28)

Abode = to abide or stay. (28)

Ant = any of numerous black, red, brown, or yellow social insects of the family Formicidae, of worldwide distribution, especially in warm climates, having a large head with inner jaws for chewing and outer jaws for carrying and digging. They live in highly organized colonies containing wingless female workers, a winged queen, and during breeding seasons, winged males, some species being noted for engaging in warfare, slave making, or the cultivation of food sources. (8)

Awry = away from the expected or proper directions; wrong; amiss. (10)

Bee = any hymenopterous insect of the super-family Apoidea, including social and solitary species of several families, as the bumblebees, honeybees, etc. (8)

Benares = a former name for Varanasi. A city in SE Uttar Pradesh, in NE India, on the Ganges River. Hindu Holy city. (1)

Bound = tied; held with another element, substance, or material in chemical or physical union. (5)

Brahmans = members of the highest, priestly class among the Hindus, above the kshatriya (shatruya). (19)

Brahms = same as Brahmans. (1)

Brotherhood for Life = the ties that bind us all together with the rest of the living world. The Breath of ALLAH is what binds us to HIS creation. (3)

Causeless Cause = the One who caused all else yet was not Himself caused by anything; ALLAH. (19)

Comb = a honeycomb, or any singular group f cells. Honeycomb is structural rows of hexagonal wax cells, formed by bees in their hive for the storage of honey, pollen, and their eggs. (8)

Compassed = spaced within limits; enclosed within the limits of any area. (12)

Cruelty = the state or quality of being cruel. Cruel = willfully or knowingly causing pain or distress to others; enjoying the pain or distress of others. Cruel implies willingness to cause pain, and indifference to suffering. (10)

Deities = gods or goddesses; the estate or rank of gods; persons or things revered as gods or goddesses. (9)

Fancy Garbs = ornamental or decorative clothing, in this instance used by priests. (20)

Fiber = a slender, threadlike element or cell, as a nerve, muscle, or connective tissue; filaments collectively; a slender, tapered cell which, with like cells, serves to strengthen tissue. (5)

Generous Soul = a person free from meanness or smallness of mind or character. Generous stresses the warm and sympathetic nature of the giver. It could also be a member of the Visya caste system in Hindu society since the Visya were tillers of the soil, herdsmen, etc. (28)

Hebrew = in this instance, a Semitic language of the Afroasiatic family; the language of the ancient Hebrews, which, although not in a vernacular use from 100 B.C. to the 20th century, was retained as the scholarly and liturgical language of [modern] Jews and is now the national language of Israel; Hebraic. (19)

Hedged = enclosed with or separated by a hedge; any barrier or boundary. (12)

Hindu Priests = the Brahmans. (2)

Hinduism = the common religion of India, based upon the religion of the original Aryan settlers as expounded and evolved in the Vedas, the Upanishads, the Bhagavad-Gita, etc., having an extremely diversified character with many schools of philosophy and theology, many popular cults, and a large pantheon symbolizing the many attributes of a single God. Buddhism and Jainism (*infra*) are outside the Hindu tradition but are regarded as related religions. (See "Hindus" below).

Hindus = individuals who adhere to Hinduism (*supra*). In this instance, those living in India. (Heading)

Holy Brahm = The Creator, the first member of the Trimurti (trinity), with Vishnu the Preserver and Shiva the Destroyer. (27)

Ideal = a conception of something in its perfection; a standard of perfection or excellence; an ultimate object or aim of endeavor, especially one of high or noble character. An ideal is a concept or standard of perfection, existing merely as an image in the mind, or based upon a person or upon conduct. (16)

Insane = crazy; mentally deranged. (27)

Intercede = to act or interpose on behalf of someone in difficulty or trouble, as by pleading or petition. (22)

Jainism = a dualistic religion founded in the 6th century B.C. as a revolt against current Hinduism and emphasizing the perfectibility of human nature and liberation of the soul, especially through asceticism and nonviolence toward all living creatures. (See "Hinduism" above).

Jehovah = a name of ALLAH in the Old Testament. Yahweh (YHWH), which is "the conjectural pronunciation of one of the Hebrew names of God [ALLAH]. The name YHWH (the Tetragrammaton or "four-letter" name) occurs often in the Bible; out of reverence it was traditionally not pronounced except by the high priest when he entered the Holy of Hollies. 'Jehovah' represents another attempt to pronounce this name." (Oxford Concise Encyclopedia 2001 ed.) (19)

Love = the benevolent affection of God for His creatures, or the reverent affection due from them to God-ALLAH. (14, 15)

Meanest = inferior in quality, grade, character, rank, status, or dignity.

→ "*meanest worm…*" is used to imply that when men harm even that which is considered the most inferior, in this instance the worm since basically nothing can get lower into the ground in rank, we harm ourselves since all creation is bound by ONE. (6)

Middle Man = a person who acts as an intermediary. (22)

Might = superior in power or strength. (15)

Obsessed = having an obsession; dominating or preoccupying the thoughts, feelings, or desires of (a person). (27)

Parabrahm = a name used by the Hindus in reference to the Supreme Creator. (19)

Pray = to make petition or entreaty for. (11)

Priests = a group of people whose office it is to perform religious rites, and especially to make sacrificial offerings. (11)

Restrain = to hold back from action; keep in check or under control. (21)

Rootless Root = used to imply that all things have its origins here, yet that which created all things was not itself created nor does it have a beginning nor an end; ALLAH. (19)

Scribes = in Judaism, sophers, or sofer, of the group of Palestinian scholars and teachers of the Jewish law and tradition, active from the 5th Century B.C. to the 1st Century A.D., who transcribed, edited, and interpreted the Bible.

→ In this instance, since we are dealing with the Hindus and not Jews, a scribe here may have simply been a person who serves as a professional copyist, or a public clerk or writer of official status. (2)

Sheath = a case or covering for the blade of a sword, dagger, or the like. (6)

Service = an act of helpful activity; help; the servicing of God-ALLAH by obedience, piety, etc. (25)

Shrines = buildings or other shelters, often of a stately or sumptuous character, enclosing the remains or relics of a saint or other holy person and forming an object of religious veneration and pilgrimage; any structure or place consecrated or devoted to some saint, holy person, or deity, as an altar, chapel, church, or temple. (11)

Spider = any of numerous predaceous arachnids of the order Araneae, most of which spin webs that serve as nests and as traps for prey. (8)

Strove = past tense of strive. Strive = to contend in opposition, battle, or any conflict; to rival; fight. (26)

Temples = edifices or places dedicated to the service or worship of a deity or deities. (11)

Thoth = in Egyptian religion, the god of wisdom, learning, and magic, represented as a man with the head either of an ibis or of a baboon.

→ It is the contention of this writer that Thoth is simply used to represent different attributes of the Supreme Creator. It is suggested that we delve deeper into the ways of the ancients to gain a better understanding of their way of life and belief systems. Reading books written by individuals like Dr. Na'im Akbar, Anthony Broder, and Dr. Yosef ben-Jochannan will serve as a light in gaining this deeper understanding. We have allowed those who have a bias set of values define things for us and therefore most of what we've been trained to believe is based on fallacy. (19)

Thought = the capacity or faculty of thinking, reasoning, imagining, etc.; the product of mental activity.

→ A good view of what thought is, is offered by The Theological Science Society, International, Vol. 1, part 4 of "A Course of Training for Personal Development," in which they rightfully pointed out that "Thought is a spiritual activity, and spirit is the Creative principle," and furthermore that "Thought is mind-in-motion; Mind is Spirituality. Thought is therefore a form of Spiritual Power." (15)

Thrill = to affect one with a wave of emotion or excitement; to affect with a sudden wave of keen emotion or excitement, as to produce a tremor or tingling sensation throughout the body. (5)

Tremble = to shake involuntarily with quick, short movements, as from fear, excitement, weakness, or cold; to shake. (6)

Triune ALLAH = Triune means 3 in 1.

→ We must always bear in mind the ONE aspect of the ALL. We must also bear in mind the various attributes of ALLAH and so in Ch. 10 of our Moorish Holy Koran, there are specific attributes being pointed out. (15)

Udraka = master of the Hindu healers. (M.D. / Sis. Rashida-El). (2)

Unfolds = develops; to reveal or display; becomes clear, apparent, or known. (16)

Unison = in perfect accord; a process in which all elements behave in the same way at the same time; coincidence in pitch of two or more musical notes, voices, etc. (7)

Vibrate = to move rhythmically and steadily to and fro. (7)

Weaves = the act of interlacing (threads, yarns, strips, fibrous material, etc.) to form a fabric or material; to move or proceed in a winding course or from side to side. (8)

Will = the faculty of conscious and especially of deliberate action.

→ Will denotes fixed and persistent intent or purpose. Many of us think that we are exercising our Will when in actuality we have been programmed to follow the Will of someone else. A lot of us have a dormant Will which must be re-awakened. In order to re-awaken our Will, we must begin to submit to the "still small voice" within and place our Will in conjunction with that Will, the Voice of ALLAH who speaks within. (See Moorish Holy Koran, Ch. 8:7-9). (14)

Wisdom = knowledge of what is true or right coupled with just judgement as to action. (14)

Wrath = strong, stern, or fierce anger; vengeance or punishment as the consequence of anger. (21)

Zeus = the Supreme God in Greek and identified with the Roman Jupiter. He was usually portrayed as a bearded man, with thunderbolts and the eagle as His attributes. (19)

NOTES:

JESUS AND BARATA – TOGETHER THEY READ THE SACRED BOOKS

Absorbed = swallowed up; swallowed up in the identity or individuality of; incorporated; taken up or received by chemical or molecular action. (38)

Angel = one of a class of spiritual beings; a celestial attendant of God.

→ In medieval angelology, angels constituted the lowest of the nine celestial orders (seraphim, cherubim, thrones, dominations or dominions, virtues, powers, principalities or princedoms, archangels, and angels); an angel can also be a person who performs a mission of God or acts as if sent by God. (23)

Ape = any of a group of anthropoid primates characterized by long arms, a broad chest, and the absence of a tail, comprising the family Pongidae (great ape), which includes the chimpanzee, gorilla, and orangutan, and the family Hylobatidae (lesser ape), which includes the gibbon and siamang. (13)

Atmosphere = the gaseous envelope surrounding the earth.

→ Scientists divide the earth's atmosphere into five layers from the lowest to the highest: 1) the troposphere; 2) the stratosphere; 3) the mesosphere; 4) the thermosphere; and 5) the exosphere. The higher we travel in the atmosphere, the thinner the air gets. This means that our level of life within the atmosphere is dependent on the rate of atmosphere at the tropospheric level. (32)

Avesta = a collection of sacred Zoroastrian writings, including the Gathas.

→ The Avesta was "written in Old Iranian. The five books of Avesta contain prayers, hymns, ritual and liturgical instruction, and the main body of Zoroastrian law. Its surviving form dates from about the 6th Century A.D." (Oxford Concise Encyclopedia 2004 ed.). Zoroaster was an Iranian prophet believed to have lived around 628 B.C. and passing form 551 B.C. (2)

Barato Arabo = a Buddhist priest. (1)

Beast = any nonhuman animal, especially a large, four-footed mammal. (5)

Bird = any warm-blooded vertebrate of the class Aves, having a body covered with feathers, forelimbs modified into wings, scaly legs, a beak, and no teeth, and bearing young in a hard-shelled egg. (5)

Boundless = having no bounds; unlimited. (20)

Buddha of Enlightenment = this is referring to Brother Jesus. (44)

Buddhism = a "religion," originating in India, by Buddha (Gautama) and later spreading to China, Burma, Japan, Tibet, and parts of southeast Asia, and later to the Western Hemisphere, holding that life is full of suffering, caused by desire, and that the way to end this suffering is through enlightenment that enables one to halt the endless sequence of births and deaths to which one is otherwise subject.

Buddhist = a follower of the doctrines of Buddha. (1)

Cherubim = a member of the second order of angels. (31)

Coarser = of inferior or faulty quality; composed of relatively large parts or particles; lacking fineness or delicacy of texture, structure, etc.

→ Indeed, physical-man is inferior to Spirit-man. Man, himself is not the body nor the soul, but a spirit and a part of ALLAH. (29)

·····CHAPTER XI (11)·····
JESUS AND BARATA – TOGETHER THEY READ THE SACRED BOOKS

Composed = made or formed by combining things, parts, or elements. (24)

Conflict = to come into conflict, collision, or disagreement. (32)

Constitute = form. (24)

Consume = to eat or drink up, devour; to absorb. (34)

Creeping thing = something that moves slowly with the body close to the ground, as a reptile or an insect, etc. (9)

Crest = the highest point or level; culmination. "*...crest of time...*" The highest point of time, the culmination of something long awaited for. (41)

Deified = personified as a deity, or lesser God.

→ This is not to be misconstrued to mean that man or anything that has been created is God-ALLAH. But rather, all things in and of the creation have a part of the Supreme Creator within. ALLAH is the causeless cause and the rootless root from which all things have grown. (42)

Dense = having the component parts closely compacted together; difficult to understand or follow because of being closely packed with ideas or complexities of style. (29)

Earth = land; ground. (23)

Elohim = The Seven Creative Spirits of ALLAH. The Elohim are the architects of all that we see and all that is manifested and therefore are limited in existence. Knowing that there is a difference between those things created by ALLAH and those by Elohim is of great importance to all students and followers of Prophet Noble Drew Ali. Brother Nathaniel Chambers-El's "Moorish Questionnaire

Commentaries" covers this subject wonderfully. Within those pages of wisdom, Brother Nathaniel Chambers-El states, "the reader might ask, 'Is there a difference between the creations of ALLAH and those of Elohim?' Most definitely. For the creations of Elohim are finite, conditional, and vastly inferior to those of ALLAH. They are impermanent and will pass away, for time was when they were not. On the other hand, all things spiritual are creations of ALLAH; they are permanent, unchanging, and everlasting. 'Time never was when they were not'" (Brother Nathaniel Chambers-El, "Moorish Questionnaire Commentaries, pg. 205) (19)

Estate = interest, ownership, or property in land or other things; a period or condition of life.

→ Man's vast estate is above his ether plane. In this manifest, man was to be ALLAH'S vicegerent, but we lost this birthright when we submitted to our lower nature and began to abuse this right. When we debased ourselves via carnal thoughts, and words, and deeds, we lost this vast estate. However, it is the Will of ALLAH that man regains this lost vast estate and so HE has sent us prophets and/or messengers to show us the proper way so that we may unfold into the Breath and place our will in tune with the Will of ALLAH. Once we've accomplished this, we will begin to see ALL of LIFE in everything and begin to take steps in the direction. (35)

Evolution = any process of formation or growth. (33)

Experience = a particular instance of personally encountering or undergoing something. (6)

Fleshless = not of the carnal world; spiritual or mental. (15)

Formless Substance = that which lacks a particular form yet consists of or possesses atoms and/or a molecular structure in the physical world. (4)

Gautama Siddhartha = (circa b. 560 – d. circa 480 B.C.) Buddha was a prophet and the founder of Buddhism, the "religion" and philosophical system that produced a great culture throughout much of southern and eastern Asia. The very name "Buddha" means "the awakened one," or "enlightened one." (2)

Guess = to arrive at or commit oneself to an opinion about something without having sufficient evidence to support the opinion fully. (14)

Hebrews = a member of the Semitic peoples inhabiting ancient Palestine, and claiming descent of Abraham, Isaac, and Jacob. (19)

Jewish Psalms = any of the songs, hymns, or prayers contained in the Psalms.

→ Sister Rashida-El states "The Jewish sacred books containing the songs of praise used by the Jews in their worship in the Temple. It contains 150 praise psalms, or sacred lyrics, and was arranged by the Hebrews into five books, each having a particular superscription and terminating with praise to ALLAH. Some works or teachings of King Davis, King Solomon, and Aspha are contained in the Psalms." (M.D. / Sister Rashida-El). (2)

Living = having life; being alive. "...*living Oracle of ALLAH*," means ALLAH is now communicating directly to man through man and as we honor man, we honor ALLAH. We must cease bowing down to finite things and elevate our minds to the realm of the Spirit. (43)

Manifest = readily perceived by the eye or the understanding; evident. (38)

Marvel = wonder; an amazing, remarkable, or astonishing person or thing; a prodigy; a remarkable specimen or example of; the object of profound admiration for a particular person, age, etc. (3)

Mold = a frame on which something is formed or made. Barato Arabo believes that time existed before man and therefore, time molded man from a formless substance and then became a protoplast and so forth. (4)

Naught = nothing. (11)

Nourishment = something that nourishes, food. (27)

Oracle = an oracle in this sense is a person who delivers authoritative wise, or highly regarded and influential pronouncements. (43)

Plant = any member of the kingdom Plantae, comprising multi-cellular organism that typically produce their own food from inorganic matter by the process of photosynthesis and have more or less rigid cell walls containing cellulose. Some classification schemes may include fungi, algae, bacteria, blue-green algae, and certain single-celled eukaryotes that have plaint-like qualities, as rigid cell walls or photosynthesis. (23)

Prophets = the canonical group of books that forms from second of the three Jewish divisions of the Old Testament, comprising of Joshua, Judges, I and II Samuel, I and II Kings, Isaiah, Jeremiah, Ezekiel, Hosea, Joel, Amos, Obadiah, Jonah, Micah, Nahum, Habakkuk, Zephaniah, Haggai, Zechariah, and Malachi. (2)

Protoplast = the contents of a cell within the cell membrane, considered as a fundamental entity; the primordial living unit or cell. (See Ch. 1 for additional information). (23)

Rate = a quantity measured with respect to another quantity. (32)

Rate of Atmosphere = the speed at which the molecular structure in the atmosphere vibrates.

→ A profound aspect is shared by Brother Nathanial Chambers-El in which he states in his "Moorish Questionnaire Commentaries," "…when the rate at which the ether vibrated had slowed to the rate of the surroundings (atmosphere), the conflict came. What this means is that the ethers of the flesh had slowed to the point of becoming murky and dense." That there is an ether attached to the flesh can be confirmed by our Prophet when he quotes Elihu as saying, "The lower self, the carnal self, the body of desires is a reflection of higher self, distorted by the murky ethers of the flesh." (pg. 222). (32)

Redeemed = freed from sin and its consequences; brought back to its origin or place of origin. (38)

Regard Not = do not pay attention to; do not take into account. (15)

Reptile = any cold-blooded vertebrate of the class Reptilia, comprising the turtles, snakes, lizards, crocodilians, amphisbaenians, tuatara, and various extinct members, including the dinosaurs; used loosely for any various animals that crawl or creep. (5)

Restore = to bring back to a former, original, or normal condition. (35)

Rising Star = symbolic for Jesus. As a rising star brings forth a new day, as thus the sun, Jesus ushered in a new era in time. (42)

Sluggish = moving slowly or having little motion; indisposed to action or exertion; lacking in energy; not acting or working with full vigor, as bodily organs. (28)

Substance = that of which a thing consists; physical matter or material. (22)

Suited = appropriate; compatible or consistent with. (6)

Supplied = furnished or provided (a person, establishment, place, etc.) with what was lacking or requisite. (27)

Teeming = prolific or fertile; abounding or swarming; to produce offspring. (24)

Thrives = prospers; grows or develops vigorously. (34)

Utter = complete; total; absolute. "…*utter shamelessness*," implies the total disregard man had for his fellow creatures. (34)

Vedas = the entire body of Hindu sacred writings, chief among which are four books: the Rig-Veda, the Sama-Veda, the Atharva-Veda, and the Yajur-Veda; these four books, along with the Brahmanas and Upanishads. The very word Vedas is Sanskrit and means "divine knowledge." The Vedas is said to have been written around 1500 B.C. and these hymns, spells, mantras, and rituals were used during sacrificial worship of gods, representing various natural forces. (2)

Vibrate = vibration = a rapid motion of a particle or of an elastic solid about an equilibrium position. (28)

Vidyapati = the wisest of Indian sages, chief of the Temple Kapavistu. Without full knowledge, I point out (exercising my five senses) that "vidya" in Hinduism and Buddhism means transcendental knowledge leading toward Brahman; in Sanskrit "vidya" means knowledge. (40)

·····CHAPTER XI (11)·····
JESUS AND BARATA – TOGETHER THEY READ THE SACRED BOOKS

Will = power of choosing one's own action; the act or process of using or asserting one's choice. (31)

Wisdom of Guatama [Gautama] = wise sayings, writings, and/or teachings of Guatama [Gautama] Buddha [Siddhartha Gautama]. (2)

Worm = any of numerous long, slender, soft-bodied, legless, bilaterally symmetrical invertebrates, including the flatworms, roundworms, acanthocephalans, nemerteans, gordiaceans, and annelids; loosely used in reference to any of numerous small creeping animals with more or less slender, elongated bodies, and without limbs or with very slow ones, including earthworms, tapeworms, insect larvae, and adult forms of some insects. (6)

Yonder = at, in, or to that place specified, more or less distant; over there; being in that place or over there. (35)

→ Instruction 41 reads in part: "Six time ago a master soul was born who gave a glorious light to man." In exercising my senses, I believe that this statement is referring to Buddha, or Siddhartha Gautama. "Six time ago" could mean 600 years ago. The exact year of his birth has been the subject of debate among scholars. But, if we calculate from the date that has been widely accepted, 566 B.C., and calculate the age of Jesus at this time, which would have been around 25 years, we will come up with a total of about 591 years. Again, we must keep in mind that the exact year of Buddha's birth is open to debate as is the same with Jesus'. Some scholars mark Jesus' year of birth around 4 B.C., others at 3 B.C., while others may produce different calculations. In Ch. 13, instruction 2, it states that 5 and 20 years (25) had passed since Mary was taught by Elihu and Salome. Instruction 3

states that the last time Elihu, Salome, and Jesus met, he was a babe.

Also, further in this instruction (Ch. 11, instruction 42), the master soul that was born six times ago gave ("gave" is written in past tense form) a glorious *Light* to man. Again, the title "Buddha" means "enlightened one."

NOTES:

·····CHAPTER XII (12)·····
JESUS TEACHES THE COMMON PEOPLE AT A SPRING
TELLS THEM HOW TO OBTAIN ETERNAL HAPPINESS

→ Chapter 12 should be of great interest to all toilers, especially in this era of time where we are continuously moving at a rapid pace to unknown destinations and consequently, we seldom have the time to slow the mind down and look behind everything. When we look at toil with hope and love and know that there is something greater because of our toils, we open the way for a different way of life. In order to unfold the God-Man that is within, we must pass through trials and temptations, and so out of the worst the wise will find means of good and thus with hope and love behind out toils, we will embrace conditions and direct a proper course of action.

Amazed = greatly surprised. (11)

Aught = anything; whatever; at all. "*...that they can do 'anything' else.*" (21)

Barren = not producing or incapable of producing offspring; unproductive; unfruitful. A "*...barren field*" is an unproductive or unfruitful land.

→ When the mind of man is held captive by naught, it is unable to produce greatness until properly liberated. We must bear in mind that "the heart of man cannot attend at once to too many things." (16)

Boundless = having no bounds; infinite or vast. (10)

Brow = the ridge over the eye; also, the forehead. (2)

Caste = in Hinduism, any of the social divisions into which Hindu society is traditionally divided, each caste having its own privileges and limitations, transferred by inheritance from one generation to the next.

→ Hindu society's caste system consisted of a 4-tiered class: Brahman – priestly class; Kshatriya – royal and warrior class; Vaisya – professionals; Sudra – lowest class and the workers, or laborers. (1)

Cease = stop; discontinue. "*...cease to seek*" is directing the person(s) to stop looking for a heaven in the sky when it is already found within. (10)

City of the Dead = a cemetery. "*...city of the dead*" derives from the Greek word "necropolis": necro + polis. Necro = dead; polis = city, hence, "City of the Dead." (4)

Common = of low status as compared with upper or middle class in today's society.

→ It also means lacking rank, station, distinction, etc. The common people are those who in a society, like today's, are considered equal in a social platform. Most of the people belonging to the common class are considered more like proletariats, lumpen, peasants, etc. At this time, in Hindu society, it is referring to the social caste system. (Heading)

Delve = to carry on intensive and thorough research; to dig; excavate. (18)

Hope = the feeling that what is wanted can be had or that events will turn out for the best; to look forward to with desire and reasonable confidence. (6)

Imploring = begging urgently or piteously. (12)

Love = strong predilection, enthusiasm, or liking for anything; infused with or feeling deep affection or passion. (6)

Meditation = devout religious contemplation or spiritual introspection; continued or extended thought. (1)

Metes = limits or boundaries. "…*metes and bounds*" = the boundaries or limits of a piece of land. (8)

Naught = nothing. (18)

Parable = a short allegorical story designed to illustrate or teach some truth, religious principle, or moral lesson; a statement or comment that conveys a meaning indirectly using comparison, analogy, or the like. (13)

Pity = sympathetic or kindly sorrow evoked by the suffering, distress, or misfortunes of another, often leading one to give relief or aid to show mercy. (5)

Plow = to turn up (soil) with a plow. Plow = an agricultural implement used for cutting, lifting, turning over, or partly pulverizing soil. (17)

Reap = to cut (wheat, rye, etc.) with a sickle or another implement or a machine, as in harvest; to gather or take (a crop, harvest, etc.). (17)

Scanty = scant in amount, quantity, etc.; barely enough. (17)

Scarcely = barely; hardly; not quite. (4)

Servant = a person at the service of another. "… *servant caste*" = members of the sudra social caste system in Hindu society. (1)

Sow = to scatter (seed) over land, earth, etc., for growth; plant. (17)

Spring = an outlet of water from the earth, taking the form, on the surface, of a small stream or standing as a pool or small lake. (1)

State of Mind = a mental condition; particular condition of mind or feeling. (8)

Stirred = disturbed; to be emotionally moved or strongly affected. (5)

Toil = hard and continuous work; exhausting labor or effort; to move or travel with difficulty, weariness, or pain. (2)

Want = need; lack. (14)

Weary = physically or mentally exhausted by hard work, exertion, strain, etc.; fatigued; tired. (16)

→ Instruction 7 reads in part: "*Of heaven we have heard; but when it is so far away, and we must live so many lives before we reach that place!*"

I would like to think that the speaker is referring to the cycle of birth and rebirth or samsara. In order to break the cycle of birth and rebirth, one must begin to sow good seeds and let our good deeds outweigh our bad deeds, and only then can one gain nirvana. This is part of Buddhist philosophy, but also the law of Cause and Effect, or Karma, also known as the Law of Requital.

NOTES:

LIFE AND WORKS OF JESUS IN EGYPT AMONG THE GENTILES

Ages = having lived or existed long; elders. (5)

Babe = a baby or child. (3)

Buffeting = to force one's way by a fight, struggle, etc.

→ This is referring to the abuse, trials, etc., Brother Jesus had to experience throughout His journeys up to that particular time when He once again met His former teachers. (4)

City of the Sun = another name for Heliopolis.

→ In breaking down the word Heliopolis, we find that "helio-" comes from Greek for "sun," and the suffix "polis," which comes from Greek, means "city." Hence, Heliopolis combines to mean "City of the Sun." (9)

Convened = they came together; assembled. (10)

Crypts = subterranean chambers or vaults, especially those beneath the main floor of a church, temple, etc., used as a burial place, a location for secret meetings, etc. (14)

Delight = great joy or pleasure. (6)

Depths = a low intellectual or moral condition. "*Greatest Depths*" = the lowest degree one may reach in debasement, leading to extreme low intellectual or moral condition. (16)

Disappointment = disappoint; to fail to fulfill the expectations or wishes of. (13)

Dismal = causing gloom or dejection; melancholy.

→ "*Dismal Crypts*" = This may be making reference to the chambers that Brother Jesus had to travel through in order to unfold completely. Each chamber would deal with a specific issue, *i.e.*, lust, charity, etc., which hinders the growth of men and impedes his God-Nature from sitting on the throne. (14)

Egyptland = another name for Egypt. The land of Egypt. Egypt + Land = Egyptland. (2)

Elihu = a former teacher to Jesus' mother, Mary. (1, 6)

Five and Twenty Years = 25 years. At this time, Jesus was 25 years old. (2)

Garb = clothing. (17)

Grief = keen mental suffering or distress over affliction or loss; sharp sorrow; painful regret. (13)

Guide = a person who guides, especially one hired to guide travelers, tourists, hunters, etc. Guide implies continuous presence or agency in showing or indicating a course. (17)

Halls = large buildings or rooms for public gatherings.

→ "*Halls of men*," can be taken to signify knowledge of the material world, which would include physical suffering, as well as mental suffering due to the trials and temptations faced while we hold on to the finite world and limiting ourselves from unfolding into infinite wisdom. (11)

Heights = the highest point; utmost degree. Height denotes extend upwards, as well as any measurable distance above a given level. "*Highest heights*" denotes the highest point achieved and/or complete unfoldment. (16)

Heliopolis = Biblical name, On.

→ An ancient, ruined city in N. Egypt, on the Nile Delta. (See City of the Sun, *supra*). According to Anthony T. Browder's Nile Valley Contributions to Civilization (page 93), "Heliopolis, the On of the Bible, was considered the greatest university in the world. It had existed since much earlier times under the domination of the priests, of whom there were said to be 13,000 in the time of Rameses III, 1225 B.C. More than 2,000 years

LIFE AND WORKS OF JESUS IN EGYPT AMONG THE GENTILES

earlier, Moses was instructed at Heliopolis 'in all the wisdom of the Egyptians,' which included physics, arithmetic, geometry, astronomy, medicine, chemistry, geology, meteorology, and music." (9)

Hierophant = an official expounder of rites or worship and sacrifice; any interpreter of sacred mysteries or esoteric principles; mystagogue.

→ It is interesting and worth noting that the word "hierophant" is of Greek origin and the prefix "hiero-" signifies "sacred," or "priestly." It also demonstrates the impact of Kemetic philosophy on the Greek since their conquering and stealing the teaching of the Ancients, in particular the 332 B.C. invasion of Kemet by Alexander "The Great" of Macedonia. Another point of interest is that what we've called "hieroglyphics" was really called Medu Netcher by the Ancients of Kemet. The Greek word "hieroglyphics" translates to "sacred or priestly writing." (11)

Immanuel = "ALLAH in man." (8)

Journeys = one's traveling from place to place; passage or progress from one stage to another. (1)

Pupil = a person, usually young, who is learning under close supervision of a teacher at school, a private tutor, or the like. A pupil is one under close supervision of a teacher, either because of youth or of specialization in some branch of study. (1)

Rabbinate = the office, or term of office of a rabbi; a group of rabbis. (11)

Rabboni = according to the Vine's Complete Expository Dictionary, Rabboni "was an Aramaic form of a title mostly entirely applied to the president of the Sanhedrin, if such was a descendent of Hillel. It was even more respectful than Rabbi and signified 'My great master.'" During the time when Jesus was in the physical manifestation, we can see the God-Man coming

forth in Him. Others who had a discerning eye seeing this acknowledged Jesus as a great master and not just as a rabbi or a simple master. (11)

Reception = welcoming; the act of receiving. (5)

Salome = a former teacher of Jesus' mother, Mary. (1, 6)

Sore = causing great pain, distress, or sorrow; causing very great suffering, misery, hardship, etc. (13)

Stirred = affected strongly; excited. (4)

Succor = help; relief; assistance; a person or thing that gives help, relief, aid, etc. (13)

Tarried = remained or stayed. *"Tarried not"* means He did not remain in or stayed upon the coast. (2)

Temptations = enticement or allurement; the fact or state of being tempted, especially to evil. (13)

Thy Servants = the servants referred to here and Elihu and Salome. (6)

Vow = to enter a religious order or house; to pledge or resolve solemnly to do, make, give, observe, etc. (15)

Wisdom = knowledge of what is true or right, coupled with just judgment as to action.

→ the phrase *"wisdom of the gods,"* shows the depths Brother Jesus had gained on spiritual matters. It is an example of what we all must strive towards. (11)

Zoan = Tanis; an ancient city in the Egyptian Delta and seat of the 21 Dynasty. Zoan was an important port for over a millennium. (2)

NOTES:

THE MINISTRY OF JOHN THE HARBINGER
John The Harbinger, Returns to Hebron, Lives as A Hermit in The Wilds, Visits Jerusalem and Speaks to The People

Abode = an extended stay in a place; sojourn. (1)

Adulterers = persons who commit adultery. Adultery = voluntary sexual intercourse between a married person and someone other than his or her lawful spouse. (26)

Afar = from, at or to a distance; far away; from a long way off. (28)

Antagonist = a person who is opposed to, struggles against, competes with another.

→ Jesus did not come to compete for the finite (material) world, but for the minds of people, to elevate their minds to infinite wisdom, the realm of the Higher-Self. (14)

Bear = endure or tolerate. (23)

Bound = having something that limits, confines, or restrains. (23)

Burdens = things which are borne with difficulty. (23)

Carobs = the pods from a Mediterranean tree, Ceratonia siliqua, or the legume family, and the source of various foodstuffs, including a substitute for chocolate, as well as substances having several industrial uses, and sometimes used as food for animals. The pods contain hard seeds and sweet edible pulp. Also called St. John's bread, in reference to John the Baptist. (4)

Consume = to take in. (25)

Couriers = messengers, usually travel in haste, bearing urgent news, important reports or packages, diplomatic messages, etc. (12)

Cumberers = burdens; people or things that hinder the growth of someone or something; embarrassment; trouble. (24)

David's Cave = David's Cave is located in the wilderness of Engedi.

→ "This is the place where David, fleeing from King Saul, sought refuge. It is indeed an actual cave. As King Saul entered the cave to attend to his personal needs, David secretly cut a corner of his robe. It is believed that to touch a king's robe was to touch the king. By David cutting a corner of the robe, it is believed to have been done as a sign of loyalty, for David could have killed King Saul if he wished." (King James Study Bible). (2)

Defraud = deprived of a right, money, or property by fraud. (21)

Dens = rooms, often secluded, in a house or apartment, in this instance in sacred places. Designed to provide a quiet, comfortable, and informal atmosphere for conversations, reading, writing, praying, etc. (27)

Doctors = teachers of the Jewish religion. (24)

Engedi = "Engedi bears the name of a perennial spring that gushes from a small promontory about six hundred feet above Dead Sea. The remarkable water supply in the midst of such a desolate region led to the creation of a small community at the site."

→ Engedi was on the barren western shore of the Dead Sea about 35 miles from Jerusalem, 18 miles southeast of Hebron, and part of the allotment of Judah. Because Engedi lay on the eastern edge of the rugged wilderness of Judah, David himself lived in this area when he was fleeing from King Saul. It was watered by a hot spring that came forth about three or four hundred feet above the base of a large cliff and yielded an abundance of fresh water that

THE MINISTRY OF JOHN THE HARBINGER
John The Harbinger, Returns to Hebron, Lives as A Hermit in The Wilds, Visits Jerusalem and Speaks to The People

created an oasis which was rich in semitropical vegetation and vineyards. Engedi is a modern-day tourist attraction. (King James Study Bible). (3)

Extortioners = individuals involved in crimes of obtaining money or some other thing of value by the abuse of one's office or authority, or indulging in oppressive or illegal exaction, as of excessive price or interest. (26)

Fruits = the edible part of plants developed from a flower, with any accessory tissue, as the peach, mulberry, or banana. (4)

Heathen = an unconverted individual of a people that do not acknowledge the God of the Bible; a person who is neither a Jew, Christian, or Muslim; pagan, an irreligious, uncultured, or uncivilized person. Heathen is often distinctively applied to unenlightened or barbaric idolaters, especially to primitive or ancient tribes. (28)

Hebron = "one of the 'central' cities in the southern hill country of Judea some 20 miles south-southwestern of Jerusalem on the road to Beer-sheba. It is situated at one of the highest points (c. 3,040 feet above sea level) on the central mountainous ridge and is one of the oldest continually inhabited cities in Palestine. Originally, Hebron was called Kirjath-arba. Hebron was built seven years before Zoan (Tanis) in Egypt." (King James Study Bible). (1)

Hermit = a person who has withdrawn to a solitary place for a life of religious seclusion. (3)

Honey = a sweet, viscid fluid produced by bees from the nectar collected from flowers and stored in nests or hives as food.

→ Carobs, honey, nuts, and fruits, as in instruction 4, are indicative of brother John's dependence, not on man, but on nature which was brought forth by ALLAH. (4)

Lawyers = interpreters of the Mosaic law (law of Moses). (24)

Marts = markets; fair, trading centers. (25)

Palestine = Canaan, an ancient country in SW Asia, on the East coast of the Mediterranean. (18)

Pharisees = a member of a Jewish religious sect.

→ "The Pharisees flourished during the 1st Century CB.C. and 1st Century B.C. and differed from the Sadducees chiefly in its strict observance of religious ceremonies and practices, adherence to oral laws and traditions, and beliefs in an afterlife and the coming of a Messiah. They were associated more with the common people and so exerted a stronger influence over them. They accepted all of the Old Testament Scriptures but also much tradition, which they regarded as the Oral Laws down from the time of Moses. They did accept the supernatural: miracles and resurrection." (King James Study Bible). (6)

Ply = to carry on, practice, or pursuit busily or steadily; to address (someone) persistently or importunately, as with questions, solicitations, etc. (27)

Prophets = (See Ch. 11 for the proper definition). (8)

Proselytes = persons who have changed from opinion, religious belief, sect, or the like, to another; convert. (18)

Rage = angry; a fit of violent anger. (31)

THE MINISTRY OF JOHN THE HARBINGER
John The Harbinger, Returns to Hebron, Lives as A Hermit in The Wilds, Visits Jerusalem and Speaks to The People

Reform = the improvement or amendment of what is wrong, corrupt, unsatisfactory, etc.

→ To reform from our evil ways, we must begin to pay special attention to our thoughts. Once we are able to control our thoughts, we can begin to replace evil, negative thoughts with more constructive and positive thoughts. This will bring about a new way of living which will help the God-Man within unfold. (28)

Sadducees = a member of a Palestinian sect.

→ The Sadducees consisted "mainly of priests and aristocrats and flourished from the 1st Century B.C. to the 1st Century A.D. and differed from the Pharisees chiefly in its literal interpretation of the Bible, rejection of oral laws and traditions, and denial of an afterlife and the coming of the Messiah. Although they rejected the Old Testament Scriptures, they accepted the Pentateuch, the five books of Moses. Politically, they were liberal in order to win the favor of Rome. They were, therefore, able to control the office of the high priest, which was appointed by Rome." (King James Study Bible).

Scribes = one of the groups of Palestinian scholars and teachers of Jewish law and tradition, active from the 5th Century B.C. to the 1st Century A.D., who transcribed, edited, and interpreted the Bible; a public clerk or writer, usually one having official status. (6, 24)

Spin = to shape into a hollow, rounded form by pressure from a tool while rotating the metal on a lathe or wheel; to make by drawing out, twisting, and winding fibers. (25)

Strove = past tense of strive. Strive = to make strenuous efforts toward any goal, in this instance to follow Brother John. (17)

Thieves = plural of thief. Thief = a person who steals, especially secretly or without open force. (26)

Toil = hard and continuous work; exhausting labor or effort. (25)

Tumors = inflated pride; haughtiness; an uncontrolled, abnormal, circumscribed growth of cells in any animal or plant tissue; things that are harmful or of no advantage. (24)

Unrest = trouble or uneasy state; disturbance or turmoil. (11)

Veil = a piece of opaque or transparent material worn over the face for concealment, or protection from the elements, or to enhance the appearance. *"Drew a veil,"* means John concealed his form by pulling down a veil. (17)

NOTES:

Divine Ministry of Jesus – Jesus Goes to the Wilderness for Self-Examination,
Where He Remains Forty Days.
Is Subjected to Three Temptations – He Overcomes.
Returns to the Camps of John and Begins Teaching

Ambition = an earnest desire for some type of achievement or distinction, as power, honor, fame, or wealth, and the willingness to strive for its attainment. (15)

Bound = inseparably connected with; tied. (3)

Camps = groups of people favoring the same ideals, doctrines, etc.; places where an army or other group of persons are lodged in a tent or tents, or other temporary means of shelter. (17)

Carnal Self = the body of desires. (16)

Command = an order given by one in authority; demand. (6)

Consciousness of Holy Breath = spiritual awareness and operating in tune with the Will of ALLAH. (17)

David = son of Jesse and a prophet of ALLAH. Second King of Israel. Thought to have reigned from c. 1010-970 B.C. (11)

Deeds = acts that are done, performed, or accomplished; exploits or achievements; acts or gestures, especially illustrative intentions, one's character, or the like. (9)

Divine Ministry = the service Jesus had been bestowed with and appointed by ALLAH to bring to men. (Heading)

Fixed = set or intent upon something; steadily directed; not fluctuating or varying. (15)

Fame = widespread reputation, especially of a favorable character. (13)

Gentile = a non-Jewish person. *"Gentile Magicians,"* the magicians of the Pharaoh's court. (8)

Harbinger = a person who goes ahead and makes known the approach of another, John was the harbinger for Jesus and Marcus M. Garvey was the harbinger for Prophet Noble Drew Ali. (1)

Honors = evidence, as a special ceremony, decoration, scroll, or title, of high rank, dignity, or distinction. (13)

Introduced = presented (a person, product, etc.) to a particular group of individuals or to the general public for or as if for the first time by a formal act, announcement, series of recommendations or events, etc. (1)

Jerusalem = "a sacred city and well-known capital of Palestine."

→ The earliest known name for the city was Urushalem. Salem was a natural abbreviation for Jerusalem. David united the kingdom after Saul's reign and quickly made Jerusalem the political and religious capital of the kingdom. Jerusalem was chosen as the place for the capital because it was centrally located between the northern and southern tribes and because the topography of the city made it easy to defend. David gave the city the name 'Jerusalem' and it is also referred to as the "City of David." (10)

Logos = the divine word or reason incarnate in Jesus. Greek meaning "a word, saying, speech, discourse, thought." (1)

Messiahship = office, skill, or character of a Messiah, or one that has been appointed, or

**Divine Ministry of Jesus – Jesus Goes to the Wilderness for Self-Examination,
Where He Remains Forty Days.
Is Subjected to Three Temptations – He Overcomes.
Returns to the Camps of John and Begins Teaching**

chosen, to lead the people back to the path of ALLAH. (5)

Ministered = given services, care, or aid to; attended as to wants or necessities. (16)

Miracle = an effect or extraordinary event in the physical world that surpasses all known human or natural powers and is ascribed to a supernatural cause. (7)

Note = to take notice of; perceive; to observe carefully. (2)

Overcome = to get the better of in a struggle or conflict; conquer; to prevail over. (4)

Paved = *"paved the way,"* prepared for and facilitated the entrance of. (1)

Pharoah = Pharaoh, a title of an ancient Egyptian King. It is believed the title is Hebraic in origin and was used to refer to the palace of the king, or rule of ancient Egypt. (8)

Pleasures = worldly or frivolous enjoyments, usually referring to a carnal nature. (13)

Sacrifice = to surrender or give up, or permit injury or disadvantage to, for the sake of something or someone else. (4)

Spurn = to reject with disdain; scorn. (15)

Strength = the quality or state of being strong; mental power, force, or vigor. Strength is inherent capacity to manifest energy, to endure, and to resist. (2)

Taught = past tense of teach. Teach = to impart knowledge of or skill in. (17)

Temple Pinnacle = the highest peak or point of the temple in Jerusalem. According to Jewish historian Josephus (A.D. ?37-100) the peak was about 450 ft. (10)

Tempt = to put (someone) to the test in a venturesome way; provoke; test. Tempt is to attract by holding out the probability of gratification or advantage, often in the direction of that which is wrong or unwise. This was part of the way the devil (lower nature) worked against Brother Justice. (12)

Tempter = a person or things that tempts, especially to evil; the Lower-Self. (6)

Ties = things that confine, restrict, or limit one's growth. (3)

Uphold = to keep up or keep from sinking; support. (See Psalm 91:11). (11)

Vain = without real significance, value, or importance; foolish; excessively proud of or concerned about one's own appearance, qualities, achievements, etc. (15)

Wealth = a great quantity or store of money, valuable possessions, property, or other riches. (13)

Went Forth = moved from one place toward another, in this instance the wilderness. *"And he went forth,"* shows motion and dictates that Jesus set out to go to a specific place with a specific purpose. (2)

Wilderness = a wild and uncultivated region, as of forest or desert, uninhabited or inhabited only by wild animals. (2)

Divine Ministry of Jesus – Jesus Goes to the Wilderness for Self-Examination, Where He Remains Forty Days.
Is Subjected to Three Temptations – He Overcomes.
Returns to the Camps of John and Begins Teaching

<u>**Words**</u> = speech or talk. (9)

<u>**Worthiness**</u> = the state or quality of being worthy. Worthy = having adequate or great merit, character, or value. (2)

<u>**Wrestle**</u> = to contend, as in a struggle for mastery. (16)

<u>NOTES:</u>

Pilate's Final Effort to Release Jesus Fails
– He Washes His Hands in Feigned Innocence –
Delivers Jesus to the Jews for Execution – The Soldiers Drive Him to Calvary

Band = a body of armed men; gang; a group of persons, animals, or things. (5)

Barabbas = a robber and murderer.

→ It is believed that Barabbas may have been a member of the Zealots. Zealots were deeply opposed to and resented the Roman occupation of Jerusalem. It is also believed that Barabbas was an insurrectionist and had been behind revolts that led to bloodshed. It was a crime punishable by death to foment revolution or insurrection against Roman rule. (6)

Bear = carry. (4)

Boon = an order or command in the form of a request; benefit, favor, especially one that is specifically asked for or is given as the result of a request. (6)

Caiaphas = high priest of the Sanhedrin. The Sanhedrin were the supreme council and tribunal of the ancient Jewish nation consisting of 70 members and having jurisdiction over religious matters and important civil and criminal cases. (19, 25)

Calvary = the place where Jesus was crucified.

→ In the Aramaic language, Calvary is referred to as "Golgotha," meaning "Skull." This may be so because Golgotha was a place where criminals were executed, more in particular those found guilty of committing a capital offense, which included insurrection. Other scholars believe the place gained its name of Golgotha due to its shape being in the form of a skull. The actual place of Calvary has been an issue of debate amongst religious scholars and historians. Some believe it is located outside of the present-day northern wall of Jerusalem since

executions were not carried out within the city walls. (27)

Coming Feast = the "*coming feast*" is the Passover Feast. (See Passover Feast below). (6)

Consent = to permit, approve, or agree; comply or yield. "*Not give consent,*" Pilate would not approve or agree to the execution of Jesus. (18)

Cross = a structure consisting essentially of an upright and a transverse piece, upon which persons were formerly put to death. (24, 27)

Crucified = put to death by the nailing or binding of the hands and feet to a cross. This was usually done with nails, or something bound with rope. (24)

Crucify = the method of punishment used by the Romans.

→ It served as a deterrent against certain crimes, including insurrection. Individuals were forced to carry a cross to a certain area designed for this purpose. The person, or persons, were then bound by the hands and feet and forced to remain there until death, which wouldn't come for hours.

Custom = a practice so long established that it has the force of the law.

→ "*According to my custom.*" It is believed that the Romans practiced a religious rite called the "lectisternium" in which amnesty was granted to a prisoner during certain holidays. This may be what is being referenced to by Pilate. (8)

Cyrene = a city in North Africa. At the time of Jesus, it was a Roman province. (27)

Enraged = made extremely angry; infuriated. To enrage or to infuriate is to provoke wrath. (11)

·····CHAPTER XVI (16)·····
Pilate's Final Effort to Release Jesus Fails
– He Washes His Hands in Feigned Innocence –
Delivers Jesus to the Jews for Execution – The Soldiers Drive Him to Calvary

Exile = expulsion from one's native land by authoritative decree; to expel or banish. (11)

Fain = gladly or willingly. (4)

Frenzied = wildly excited or enthusiastic; violently agitated. (24)

Heap = to give, assign, or bestow in great quantity; accumulate. (2)

Imbue = to imbrue. Imbrue = to stain. (18)

Isaiah = a prophet of ALLAH believed to have lived in the 8th Century B.C. (22)

Jezia = a fellow prisoner of Barabbas who was also sentenced to death. (6)

Make Haste = to move fast in motion; to hurry or rush. (20)

Mangled = injured severely, disfigured, or mutilated by cutting, slashing, or crushing. (23)

Mob = a disorderly riotous crowd of people. (16)

Pharisees = the Pharisees were strict preservers of religious ceremonies and practices and staunch supporters to the adherence of oral laws and traditions. Unlike the Sadducees, the Pharisees believed in an afterlife and the coming of the Messiah. They also accepted the supernatural: miracles and resurrection. The Pharisees were associated more with the dealings of the common people. (18)

Place of Skull = another name for Calvary. (21)

Passover Feast = the Passover Feast celebrated by the Jewish nation.

→ It is during this holiday that the Jewish people celebrate the "passing over" of their household by the angel of death in Egypt when the first born of that land died. They smeared blood on their doorposts as commanded to protect their dwellings from death. It is also known as the Feast of the Pasch as referred to in Ch. 5 verse 1 of the Moorish Holy Koran. (4)

Rabble = a disorderly crowd; mob. (20)

Rapine = the violent seizure and carrying of off another's property; plunder. (5)

Scapegoat = a person or group made to bear the blame for others or to suffer in their place. (3, 6)

Score = 20; a lot; numerous. (9)

Seditious = of, pertaining to, or the nature of sedition. Sedition = incitement of discontent or rebellion against a government. (5)

Shed His Blood = to cause blood to flow; to kill by violence. (14)

Simon = inhabitant of Cyrene who was charged with helping Jesus carry the cross. (27)

Superstitious = of the nature of, characterized by, proceeding from superstition. Superstition = a belief or notion, not based on reason or knowledge, in or of the ominous significance of a particular thing, circumstance, occurrence, proceeding, or the like; irrational fear of what is unknown or mysterious, especially in connection with religion. (1)

Tiberius = (Tiberius Claudius Nero Caesar 42 B.C. – A.D. 37), the stepson of Augustus Caesar by way of adoption and recognized as Augusts' successor by the Roman Senate. Being that Tiberius ruled from A.D. 14 – A.D. 37, he is the Caesar repeatedly referred to during Jesus' ministry and crucifixion. (17)

·····**CHAPTER XVI (16)**·····
Pilate's Final Effort to Release Jesus Fails
– He Washes His Hands in Feigned Innocence –
Delivers Jesus to the Jews for Execution – The Soldiers Drive Him to Calvary

Took Council = gathered to decide the fate of Jesus. This was done by the Pharisees since Pilate did not want his soldier's hands "stained with innocent blood." (18)

Transgressions = acts of transgressing, violations of the laws, commands, etc.; sins. (22)

Trembled = shook involuntarily with quick, short movements, from fear. (16)

Vile = morally debased, depraved, or despicable; wretchedly bad. (5)

NOTES:

Jesus Appears, Fully Materialized, Before Apollo and the Silent Brotherhood in Greece – Appears to Claudas and Juliet on Tiber Near Rome – Appears to the Priests in the Egyptian Temple at Heliopolis

Ablaze = radiant with bright color. (33)

Acropolis = the citadel of Athens and the site of the Pantheon.

→ The citadel was a fortress that commanded a city and was used in the control of the inhabitants and in defense during attack or siege. In the citadel you would also find the religious and administrative body of Greece. Athens, or Athenai in Greek, is a city in and the capital of Greece, in the S.E. part. The Pantheon was the Temple of Athena Parthenos on the Acropolis at Athens, completed c. 438 B.C. by Ictinus and Callicrates and decorated by Phidias. At the time, it was regarded as the finest Doric Temple. (8)

Ambassadors = authorized messengers or representatives. (27)

Apollo = Greek sage and member of the Silent Brotherhood of Greece. (1, 8, etc.)

Arise = to get up or stand up. (19)

Arose = got up or stood up. (20)

Athens' Beach = a beach located within Athens, city and capital of Greece. (8)

Behold = to take into regard – (10)

Behold = to gaze upon; look; see. (26, 36)

Carnal Things = pertaining to the desires and appetites of the flesh; worldly or earthly; mundane. (25)

Chaos = the disordered state of unformed matter and infinite space supposed in some cosmogonic view to have existed before the ordered universe. (38)

Chemistry = any or all of the elements that make up something; the science of the composition, structure, properties, and reactions of matter, especially of atomic and molecular systems; the composition, structure, properties, and reactions of a substance. (41)

Clasped = gripped firmly in or with the hand. (13)

Claudas and Juliet = servants of King Tiberius; Jesus' ambassadors (representatives) to Rome. Husband and Wife. (16)

Consumed = completely destroyed. (2)

Creature = all living creation. (46)

Crete = large island southeast of Greece in the southern portion of the Aegean Sea.

→ Crete is about 156 miles long and ranges in width from about 7 to 35 miles. It is also the fifth largest island of the Mediterranean. In ancient times, two great civilizations existed on Crete: the Minoan, involving the semi-mythical King Minos, and later the Mycenaean. After about a one-thousand-year period of decline, it was conquered by the Romans in 67 B.C. It has also been postulated that the early inhabitants of Crete were descendants of the ancient Egyptians. The Philistines are believed to have migrated from Crete to Philistia, in the land of Canaan.

Deific Life = living according to the dictates of the Spiritual-self; living according to the Will of ALLAH; living in that which is of the Higher-self; when man and ALLAH are one. (41)

Delphian Grove = a small area in Delphi where meditation, teaching, and other religious activities took place.

·····CHAPTER XVII (17)·····
**Jesus Appears, Fully Materialized, Before Apollo and the Silent
Brotherhood in Greece –
Appears to Claudas and Juliet on Tiber Near Rome –
Appears to the Priests in the Egyptian Temple at Heliopolis**

→ Delphi was an ancient city in central Greece, in Phocis, site of an oracle of the Greek and Roman pagan god Apollo, "god of light, healing, music, poetry, prophecy, and manly beauty."

The Delphian Grove was discovered in 1890. The author believes that this is the same area that the late professor George G.M. James references in his scholarly work "Stolen Legacy." Of the Temple of Delphi Professor James states "the Temple of Delphi was burnt down in 548 B.C., and it was King Amasis of Egypt who rebuilt it for the brethren [fellow members of the Ancient Mysteries of Egypt] by donating three times as much as was needed in the sum of one thousand talents, and 50,000 lbs. of alum. According to information at hand, the temple had organized its members into amphictyonic [amphictyony = (in ancient Greece) any of the league at Delphi, united for mutual protection and the worship of a common deity,] league for protection against political and other forms of violence; but they were too poor to raise sufficient funds from the membership, and they decided upon a public contribution from the citizens of Greece.

"Accordingly, they wandered throughout the land soliciting aid, but failing their efforts. Having decided to visit the brethren in Egypt, they approached King Amasis who, as a Grand Master, unhesitatingly offered to rebuild the Temple and donated more than three times as much as was needed for the purpose." (George G.M. James, "Stolen Legacy," pg. 35.) (1)

Demigods = deified mortals; an inferior deity; partly divine and partly mortal. (23)

Demonstrate = to prove or make clear by reasoning or evidence. (32)

Disaster = a sudden misfortune; a sudden accident or a natural catastrophe. (3)

Disintegrate = decompose; to come apart; to separate. (37)

Divine = spiritual; not of the flesh; holy; supremely good; God-man. "*Love divine*' is love that is not directed by the flesh (it is not in flesh to think, nor is it in bones to reason) but comes from the essence of men, his Higher-self. (13)

Drama = any situation or series of events having valid, emotional, or conflicting interests or results. (44)

Essence = something that exists, especially a spiritual or immaterial entity; the inward nature, true substance, or constitution of anything, as opposed to what is accidental. Phenomenal, illusory, etc.

→ "*The essence of the body*," the real or ultimate nature of a person as opposed to its existence; permanent elements; the essential ingredients that are within the flesh. It is not in flesh to think, nor is it in bones to reason, so it is obvious that the true essence of men is not the flesh, for the body is measured by time and a time will come when it will be no more. The same is said about the soul. (37)

Estate = condition or circumstances with reference to worldly and spiritual prosperity; power over heaven (mind) and earth (body). (10)

Eternal = without beginning or end; everlasting; endless and impossible to measure. (12)

Everlasting = lasting forever; eternal, not susceptible to the finite. (25)

·····CHAPTER XVII (17)·····
**Jesus Appears, Fully Materialized, Before Apollo and the Silent
Brotherhood in Greece –
Appears to Claudas and Juliet on Tiber Near Rome –
Appears to the Priests in the Egyptian Temple at Heliopolis**

Evermore = forever; always. (6)

Fixed = put in order; established definitely.

→ "*the fixed is solved.*" The essence of the body cannot be quickened by the Holy Breath until things have taken place in a proper and meant fashion. Form follows function; therefore, the body must *first* disintegrate, then ALLAH breathes upon the plaint substances, etc. *And* life springs forth from death, the resurrection. (37)

Foes = people or things that oppose or impede; things that hinder growth.

→ Foes are also meant as something through which men can test his inner strength and manifest the strength of ALLAH that is in him/ her. Without a foe, a soldier never knows his strengths. (43)

Form = body. (46)

Galilee = an ancient Roman province in what is now N. Israel.

→ Galilee extends from the Esdraelon plain some 50 miles north from the Sea of Galilee about 30 miles to the west. Its primary feature is the 13-mile-long Sea of Galilee (seven miles wide at its broadest point). It lies 695 feet below sea level with the Jordan River flowing through it. Some towns of Galilee that were situated on the seashore were Capernaum, Bethsaida, Tiberia, and Magdala. Of these, only Tiberias exists today. Other significant Galilean towns include Nazareth and Chorazin. (16)

Gethsemane = "Oil Press" or "Olive Press."

→ Gethsemane was a garden on the western slope of the Mount of Olives where Jesus frequently went. The exact location of Gethsemane is unknown since it was destroyed during the Roman takeover in 70 A.D. Gethsemane is the place where Jesus spent his last hours before his betrayal by Judas and where he was eventually seized (arrested). It is believed that when Jesus stated in instruction 43 about his victories in Gethsemane, he was referring to the agonies he suffered during prayer when the time was near for his arrest. As in the wilderness, Jesus overcame the agonies of his human form. (43)

Gospel = something regarded as true and implicitly believed; a doctrine regarded as of prime importance.

→ Gospel translates to "good news" in the Greek language. It is indeed "good news" knowing that there is still redemption for humanity. Knowing that there is salvation for humanity demonstrates ALLAH'S mercy upon us. (12, 14, 28)

Greece = ancient Greek, Hellas. Modern Greek, Ellas. A republic in S. Europe at the S. end of the Balkan Peninsula. (15)

Greeks = natives or inhabitants of Greece; persons of Greek ancestry. (6)

Hail = a salutation of greeting or welcome; approve enthusiastically.

→ "*All hail*" was the greeting, or salutation, from the masters to Jesus in acknowledgement and approval. (33)

Heliopolis = an ancient city in N. Egypt in the Nile R. Delta.

→ Referred to as On in the Bible and Junu in Egyptian records, Heliopolis was famous for its obelisks. It was called Heliopolis by the Greeks

·····CHAPTER XVII (17)·····
**Jesus Appears, Fully Materialized, Before Apollo and the Silent
Brotherhood in Greece –
Appears to Claudas and Juliet on Tiber Near Rome –
Appears to the Priests in the Egyptian Temple at Heliopolis**

because it was the mecca for worshipers of the sun god Ra until the rise of Thebes c. 2100 B.C. It was from this ancient city that the obelisks found in London, New York and Rome were removed. (See "*Heliopolis*" in Ch. 13). (30)

Holy Breath = Spirit of ALLAH which animates all living things. (35, 37)

Idol = an image or other material object representing a deity to which religious worship is addressed.

→ "*Idol Worshipers*" are those who worship created things instead of the Creator of all, ALLAH. It was the worship of created things that caused the enslavement of the Asiatics who strayed after the gods of Europe of whom they knew nothing. (8)

Image = a reproduction of the appearance of someone or something, especially a sculptured likeness.

→ "*through image made by man*" refers to things made and worshiped by man; idolatry. (6)

Italy = modern day Italy is located in Europe and comprises a peninsula S. of the Alps, and Sicily, Sardina, Elba, and other smaller islands. The principal rivers of Italy are the Tiber and the Po. During the times of Jesus, Italy was part of the Roman Empire. (29)

Juliet = wife of Claudas and servant of King Tiberius. (16, 19, 27)

Kindred tongues = one's native tongue (language); many related languages. (6)

Like = of the same form, appearance, kind, etc.; in like manner with; similarly to; something of a similar nature. (36)

Manifest = appear; made visible. (13)

Manifest = appear in the flesh; made perceptible to the sense of sight. (17)

Manifest = "*the love of ALLAH made manifest to men.*" We must take into consideration the aspect of men's mind. Because men's inability to comprehend the spiritual aspect of himself, Jesus was appointed by ALLAH to demonstrate it to him. In Jesus, ALLAH'S love-divine was manifested and demonstrated to the world by the conduct of his character and his ability to become a mastermind and the God-Man of today. (12)

Manifest = "*I am the manifest of love raised from the dead.*" In this statement, Jesus is demonstrating ALLAH'S love-divine in that he was given the key (answer) to the resurrection of man. (26)

Masters = teachers. (33, 34, 46)

Nazarene = Jesus.

→ A Nazarene was a native or inhabitant of Nazareth. Nazareth was a town in Israel and childhood home of Jesus. (8)

Nazarite = "*brother Nazarite,*" "*The Nazarite,*" in both instances, it is Jesus who is being referred. (See "*Nazarite*" in Ch. 4). (30, 31)

Omnipotence = the quality or state of being omnipotent. **Omnipotent** = having unlimited or universal power, authority, or force; All Powerful.

→ "*Omnipotence of man,*" is man having unlimited power. The Prophet Noble Drew Ali teaches that the object of man's life according

·····**CHAPTER XVII (17)**·····
Jesus Appears, Fully Materialized, Before Apollo and the Silent Brotherhood in Greece –
Appears to Claudas and Juliet on Tiber Near Rome –
Appears to the Priests in the Egyptian Temple at Heliopolis

to Islam, is its complete unfoldment. He teaches that man is born with *unlimited* capacities for progress, growth. The conflict of the flesh is intended to aid in our unfoldment. (Reference "Moorish Literature," "What is Islam," pg. 10). (14)

Oracle = any person or thing serving as an agency of divine communication; a shrine or place at which an utterance, often ambiguous or obscure, is given by a priest, priestess, as the response of a God to any inquiry. (1, 2, 3)

Oracle = *"This Oracle will fail; the living Oracle of ALLAH, the One, will not fail."*

→ It is imperative that we understand that ALLAH speaks to man through man (His prophets and angels) and grasp the fact that ALLAH is not hedged about, limited as finite man is. We face a constant battle within and even though He speaks in a still small voice, we consistently submit to the lower nature. This is why He sends us prophets and angels, to show us how to better develop the strength that is within so that Love can sit on the throne as saviour. (7)

Oracle pedestal = a supporting structure or piece on which the Oracle was placed upon. (4)

Palatine = of or pertaining to the Palatinate; of or pertaining to a palace; palatial.

→ Since Claudas and Juliet were servants of Tiberius, they lived in the portion of the palace set aside for servants. (16)

Pattern = an original or model considered for or deserving of imitation; anything fashioned or designed to serve as a model or guide for something to be made.

→ In this instance, to use the example of Jesus' life as a pattern for our life, to show that we can do and accomplish the same things He accomplished. "What I have done all men can do, and what I am all men shall be." Prophet Noble Drew Ali is the Jesus of today and He came in the same spirit and so He has brought us the pattern that we are to follow. He informed His members to, "Imitate I, the Prophet." (44)

Perfect Man = God-Man; transmutation from human flesh into flesh divine. (23)

Pierced = made a hole in or through. To pierce is to perforate quickly, as by stabbing. (26)

Planes = levels of dignity, character, existence, development, or the like; a surface generated by a straight line moving at a constant velocity with respect to a fixed point.

→ According to the Kybalion, planes can also be degrees. The Kybalion states that "The Higher the degree of rate of vibration, the higher the plane, and the higher the manifestation of Life occupying that plane. So that while a plane is not 'a place,' nor yet 'a state of condition,' yet it possesses qualities common to both." ("The Kybalion," pg. 68). (13, 36)

Pliant = flexible; adaptable.

→ Pliant substances is matter that is no longer rigid because of its weakened atomic/molecular make up; something that is no longer rigid and is therefore flexible enough to accept or become something else when placed in a mold. A good example is the mind of man. When the mind is flexible, it means that it has not become rigid with a specific set of beliefs, or thinking

·····CHAPTER XVII (17)·····
**Jesus Appears, Fully Materialized, Before Apollo and the Silent
Brotherhood in Greece –
Appears to Claudas and Juliet on Tiber Near Rome –
Appears to the Priests in the Egyptian Temple at Heliopolis**

patterns, or hasn't been trained to operate in one fashion only. (38)

Priests = people having the authority to perform and administer religious rites. (30)

Quickened = accelerated; stimulated; given or restoring vigor or activity to; stirred up; restore life to. (37)

Rebuked = expressed sharp, stern disapproval of; reproved or reprimanded. (8)

Reserved = kept back or saved for future use. (32)

Resurrection = a rising above mortality through the understanding of spiritual life; to rise again; to return to an original state. (28, 30)

Rome = modern capital of Italy, in the W. central part of the Tiber River.

→ Traditionally, Rome is believed to have been founded by Romulus and Remus in 753 B.C. By around 275 B.C., Rome controlled most of the Italian peninsula. At its peak the Roman Empire controlled half of Europe, the countries of North Africa, and much of the Middle East. It was the capital of the Roman Empire until A.D. 323. (16, 22, 27, 29)

Sacred pedestal = a supporting structure of piece used to place a religious item on. (31, 33, 46)

Sanctuary = a sacred or holy place. (2)

Servants = people employed by another, especially to perform domestic duties; ones who serve a specific purpose. (16)

Silent Brotherhood = a religious order. (1, 9)

Spent = having come to an end; passed. (4)

Springs = to come into being, rise, or growth within a short time; to come into being, as if by growth. (39)

Substance = a particular make up of something; that of which a thing consists of. (35, 36)

Temple = a building dedicated to religious public and private worship. (33)

Tiber = a river in central Italy, flowing through Rome into the Mediterranean.

→ Tevere is its Italian name. The Tiber covers about 252 miles. (18)

Tiberius = (See "*Tiberius*" in Ch. 16). (16, 24)

Title = just cause of possession or control; a claim or right. (10)

Tone = a particular mental state or disposition; a higher form or quality. (35)

Trials = the determination of a person's guilt or innocence by judicial process.

→ "*my trials in the courts of men*" is referring to the times when Jesus was brought on charges before the state and eventually sentenced to death according to men's laws. (43)

Tune = to bring into harmony or agreement; to make One. (42)

Unto = to.

Vast = of very great area or extent; immense. (10)

Vast Estate = or inheritance from ALLAH.

**Jesus Appears, Fully Materialized, Before Apollo and the Silent
Brotherhood in Greece –
Appears to Claudas and Juliet on Tiber Near Rome –
Appears to the Priests in the Egyptian Temple at Heliopolis**

→ It is the opinion of this writer that part of the title of our vast estate that Jesus gives reference to is our kingdom on earth. The Prophet Noble Drew Ali states, "Seek ye first the kingdom of Heaven and all these things would be added unto you." In the teachings, we find that Man is the Lord of all the plane of manifest…" but he gave up his *birthrights* just to gratify his lower self, (Ch. 1). Further, in Chapter 11:35, we find "… the great work of master minds is to restore the heritage of man, to bring him back to his *estate* that he had lost, when he again will live upon the ethers of his native plane." We understand that heaven is a state of mind, thus we continue to strive to reach heaven while on the manifest. Man's native plane, the physical aspect of man, is this manifest, but Spirit-Man's native plane is the spiritual. Jesus states, "All power in heaven and earth are mine; to you I give all power in heaven and earth." (MHK 17:11). (10)

NOTES:

The Resurrection of Jesus
**– Pilate Places the Roman Seal Upon the Stone Door of the Tomb
– At Midnight a Company of the Silent Brotherhood March About the Tomb
– The Soldiers Are Alarmed – Jesus Teaches to the Spirits in Prison
– Early Sunday Morning He Rises from the Tomb. The Soldiers Are
Bribed by the Priests to Say That the Disciples Had Stolen the Body.**

Adon Mashich Cumi = Lord Jesus Arise; Hebrew, **Adon** = Lord, **Mashich** = Jesus, **Cumi** = Arise or above. These words are also Aramaic.

Aramaic = also Aramean; a northwest Semetic language that from c. 300 B.C. – A.D. 650 was a lingua franca (any language that is widely used as a means of communication among speakers of other languages) for nearly all of SW Asia and was the everyday speech of Syria, Mesopotamia, and Palestine. (26, 33)

Alert = fully aware and attentive; alert to danger. (9)

Arisen = to return from death to life. (44, 45)

Arose = got up or stood up. (37)

Arose = "*all this was before the sun arose,*" all this was before the sun came up; at dawn. (31)

Assemblies = the assembling or coming together of a number of persons, usually for a particular purpose. (20)

Assured = guaranteed; certain; sure. (2)

Behold = look. (32, 44)

Blanched = became white or pale. (30)

Blaze of light = a very bright light. (7)

Blazed = "*the heavens blazed with light,*" the skies shined brightly. (31)

Burial gown = a long, loose flowing garment, such as a robe that one is buried in. (36)

Caiaphas = a ruling high priest from A.D. 18 to 36. He was the high priest responsible for Jesus' death. (2, 45)

Cast = threw. (34)

Clad = "*white clad soldiers,*" soldiers dressed in white clothing. The Silent Brotherhood. (7, 10, 13)

Climes = regions or areas of the earth. (20)

Company = group. (2)

Council = an assembly of persons summoned or convened for consultation, deliberation, or advice. (19, 23, 45)

Countermarched = marched back over the same ground. (8, 10)

Cowardice = lack of courage in the face of danger, difficulty, or opposition. (30)

Descend = to go or pass from a higher to a lower place; move or come down. (32)

Disciples = followers of Jesus. (21, 48)

Faithfulness = true to one's word, promises, vows, etc.; steady in allegiance; loyal, reliable, trusted, or believed. (6)

Form = figure. (32, 34, 37)

Garb of flesh = man's physical body. (21)

Good Will to men = a kind of friendly attitude; benevolence; kindness. Benevolence = a desire to do good to others. (41)

Hail = "*All hail!*" in other words, "All welcome," a salutation of greeting or welcome. (35)

Hastened = hurried; to hurry. (43)

The Resurrection of Jesus
– Pilate Places the Roman Seal Upon the Stone Door of the Tomb
– At Midnight a Company of the Silent Brotherhood March About the Tomb
– The Soldiers Are Alarmed – Jesus Teaches to the Spirits in Prison
– Early Sunday Morning He Rises from the Tomb. The Soldiers Are
Bribed by the Priests to Say That the Disciples Had Stolen the Body.

Herald = signal the future arrival of. (31)

Holy Breath = Breath or Spirit of ALLAH that is within and throughout all His creation. (24)

Immortal = not subject to death; infinite. (39)

Jerusalem = a city in and the capital of Israel; an ancient holy city and center of pilgrimage for Jews, Christians, and Muslims. (43)

Joseph's home = this is not referring to Jesus' father. This is referring to Joseph of Arimathea. Joseph of Arimathea was from a small Judean town by that very name. He was also a member (counselor) of the Sanhedrin – the Jewish legislature and high court. According to some, he was a wealthy, just, and good man. It has been widely accepted that it was he who carried the Holy Grail (the cup used in the last Supper) to England. **Arimathea** = Arimathea; a town in ancient Palestine. (Matt. 27:26-27). (1)

Key = something that serves to reveal or solve a problem, difficulty, or mystery. (22)

Key of life = answer to life, real life which is Spirit life. (22)

Lord = Jesus.

Manifest = "*the body is manifest of soul, but soul is without its manifest*," meaning that the soul has shaken off the manifestation of flesh and it has traveled to the plane of soul. (15)

Masters = teachers. (20, 23)

Mighty = impressive or awesome in size. (34)

Mortal = subject to death; finite. (39)

Nazarene = they are speaking of Jesus.
Nazarene = a native or inhabitant of Nazareth.
Nazareth = a town in N. Israel; the childhood home of Jesus. (39, 44)

Olden times = ancient times; of or pertaining to the distant past or bygone times. (19)

Patriarchs = the male head of a family or tribal line; any of the very early personages regarded as the father of the human race, comprising those from Adam to Noah (antediluvian patriarchs). (19)

Pebble = "*a pebble from the brook*," a small stone from a stream of fresh water. (34)

Pilate = (please see definition of *Pilate* in Ch. 16). (4, 49)

Priests = persons having the authority to perform and administer religious rites. (43)

Prison = "*He opened up the prison doors and set the prisoner free*," shows that Jesus had a specific purpose in life. With the knowledge and wisdom that he had gained, he was able to impart it to those captive souls so that they may have ceased to be captives on the soul plane and achieve their complete unfoldment. "*He broke the chain of captive souls and led the captives to the light.*" As we take a deeper look, we see that chains are symbolic to restricted movement, and light symbolic to consciousness. Jesus traveled to the soul plane and taught those souls found there how they may be able to traverse the soul plane. (17)

The Resurrection of Jesus
– Pilate Places the Roman Seal Upon the Stone Door of the Tomb
– At Midnight a Company of the Silent Brotherhood March About the Tomb
– The Soldiers Are Alarmed – Jesus Teaches to the Spirits in Prison
– Early Sunday Morning He Rises from the Tomb. The Soldiers Are
Bribed by the Priests to Say That the Disciples Had Stolen the Body.

Prophets = persons who speak for God or by divine inspiration. (19)

Prophets = (not to get confused with the previous definition. This title is usually capitalized. This definition is simply additional information). The canonical group of books that forms the second of the three Jewish divisions of the Old Testament, comprising Joshua, Judges, I and II Samuel, I and II Kings, Isaiah, Jeremiah, Ezekiel, Hosea, Joel, Amos, Obadiah, Jonah, Micah, Nahum, Habakkuk, Zephanian, Haggai, Zechariah, and Malachi. (The *other two* of the Jewish divisions are the *Laws of Moses,* and *Hagiographa*). **Law of Moses** = the Pentateuch, (the first 5 books of the Old Testament),

containing the Mosaic dispensations, or system of rules and ordinances, and forming the first of the three Jewish divisions of the Old Testament, variously arranged, but usually comprising of Psalms, Proverbs, Job, Song of Solomon, Ruth, Lamentations, Ecclesiastes, Esther, Daniel, Ezra, Nehemiah, and Chronicles; also called the Writings.

Quake = to shake. (32)

Realm = the region, sphere, or domain within which anything occurs, prevails, or dominates. (16)

Realm of souls unmanifest = a kingdom of the soul. Any region, sphere, or province of the soul plane and is not seen by mortal eyes, and where there is no need for the physical body. Jesus went to the soul plane to teach. (Sister Rashida-El, D.M.) (16)

Resumed = to begin or take up again after interruption. (14)

Resurrection = the act of rising from the dead; revival; to bring back to spirit life. (22)

Righteousness = conformity to the divine or the moral law; the state of acceptance with God-ALLAH. (35)

Risen = returned from death or the grave. (42)

Sabbath day = the seventh day of the week, Saturday, as the day of rest and religious observance among Jews and now Christians. (25)

Saloam = a garden in Jerusalem. (1, 2, 25)

Scene = the place where an incident occurs or occurred. (25)

Scribe = an official or public writer usually as a clerk or keeper of accounts. (4)

Seal = an embossed emblem, figure, symbol, word, letter, etc., used as attestation or evidence of authenticity; to close by any form of fastening that must be broken before access can be gained. (4)

Silent Brotherhood = a religious order. (11)

Testimonials = statements in support of a particular truth, fact, or claim. (46)

Thunder = a loud rumbling or crashing noise heard after a lightening flash due to the expansion of rapidly heated air. (31)

Tomb = a vault or chamber for burial of the dead. (15)

The Resurrection of Jesus
– Pilate Places the Roman Seal Upon the Stone Door of the Tomb
– At Midnight a Company of the Silent Brotherhood March About the Tomb
– The Soldiers Are Alarmed – Jesus Teaches to the Spirits in Prison
– Early Sunday Morning He Rises from the Tomb. The Soldiers Are
Bribed by the Priests to Say That the Disciples Had Stolen the Body.

Tramped = to treat heavily or trample (usually followed by, on, or upon). **Trample** = to beat down with the feet so as to crush or destroy. (34)

Transmute = to change from one nature, substance, form, or condition into another. (39)

Unsheathed = to draw from a sheath (case), as in a sword, knife, or the like. (28)

Watch = to keep ground. (2)

Wonders of the night = the strange and unordinary events that took place during the night. (44)

NOTES:

Jesus Appears, Fully Materialized, to the Eastern Sages in the Palace of Prince Ravanna in India
– To the Magian Priests in Persia –
Three Wise Men Speak in Praise of the Personality of the Nazarene

Arose = got up; stood up. (13, 16)

Banquet hall = a building where people hold ceremonies, public dinners, especially one honoring a person, benefiting a charity, etc. (6)

Behold = to look at, examine closely. (11)

Behold = used here to call attention specifically to the point being made by Jesus, that what has taken place happened to a living physical being. (17)

Benediction = an utterance of good wishes, blessings, etc. (7)

Bethlehem = a town in the Judean highlands overlooking the principal highway leading from Jerusalem down to Beer-Sheba. It was the birthplace of David and Jesus. Occupied by Israel since 1967. (22, 33)

Borderland = an uncertain, intermediate district, space, or condition.

→ *"but I can cross the borderland at will"* shows the ability of Jesus to travel to the soul plane at his will. (17)

Brawn = strong, well-developed muscles.

→ Jesus was stating that He was made up of the same physical elements as any human, this being the flesh, bone, and muscle. (17)

Clime = a region or area of the earth. (15)

Confined = restricted; limited. (15)

Conquered = gained mastery over. (13)

Council = an assembly of persons summoned or convened for consultation, deliberation, or advice. (24, 25)

Dead = deprived of life; stagnant. (20)

Demonstrated = showed clearly. (33)

Demonstrator = a person who explains or teaches by physical demonstrations.

→ *"and I am here a demonstrator of the power of man"* explains the purpose of ALLAH sending the Spirit of Jesus to this earth. He was sent as a demonstrator to all, so that we may become spiritually conscious of the attributes of ALLAH that reside in each one of us. (15)

Dial plate of Heaven = prediction of time/events by observing Heaven.

→ Some consider the zodiac signs to be a dial plate of heaven as well. A dial plate is a plate, disk, fact, or other surface containing markings or figures upon which the time of the day is indicated by hands, pointers, or shadows, as of a clock or sundial. (See *"Time"* in Ch. 1 for further information). (32)

Eastern Sages = wise men, scholars, masters from the East, amongst them Mengste, Vidyapati, and Lamaas. (Heading)

Feast = a large meal marking a special occasion. (3)

Fleeting = passing swiftly; vanishing quickly; transient. Fleeting winds are brief gusts of winds which come and go. (17)

Fully Materialized = to appear in the physical form fully unfolded in the oneness of ALLAH. (Heading)

Goodwill to men = a kind or friendly attitude, kindness, or benevolence extended to humanity

Jesus Appears, Fully Materialized, to the Eastern Sages in the Palace of Prince Ravanna in India
– To the Magian Priests in Persia –
Three Wise Men Speak in Praise of the Personality of the Nazarene

in general. **Benevolence** = a desire to do good to others. (26)

Gospel = something regarded as true or implicitly believed; a doctrine regarded as of prime importance. Gospel in Greek means "good news." (20)

Groves = small wood or forested areas.

→ In this instance it would appear to be a place where meditation, teaching, and other religious activities took place. (34)

Hail = a salutation of greeting or welcome. (7, 25)

Halo = the aura of glory, veneration, prestige, or sentiment surrounding an idealized person; a circle of light surrounding the head of a holy person. (8)

Heritage = something transmitted by or acquired from a predecessor; birthright. (15)

Host = one who receives or entertains guests or strangers socially or commercially. In this instance, the royal host was Prince Ravanna. (16)

Immortality = the quality or condition of being immortal; endless life or existence; eternal. **Immortal** = not subject to death, never to be forgotten. (14)

India = a republic in S. Asia.

→ India is a union comprising 25 states and 7 union territories; formerly a British colony, gained independence on August 15, 1947. India has one of the oldest civilizations in the world. In the Indus Valley civilization can be traced back over 5,000 years. Jesus taught in Orissa, India. Buddha (Siddhartha Gautama, b. circa 566 B.C.) is amongst the many teachers to come from India. (Heading)

Jesus = Prophet of ALLAH, son of Joseph and Mary. (See "*Jesus*" in Ch. 46). (Heading)

Kaspar = one of the three Magian Priests believed to come from the East to visit the infant Jesus when He was born.

→ Kaspar is also spelled Casper. The three Magian Priests are also known as Magian Masters, the Three Wise Men, and Magi. As to the exact identity of the three Magian Priests who visited the babe, Jesus, were still a matter of debate amongst religious scholars. (22, 24)

Lamaas = a priest of Jaguanath. (4)

Magi = the Magi are also known as the Three Wise Men, Magian Priests, or Magian Masters. (32)

Magian Priests = the hereditary priestly caste of the Medes and Persians, who were regarded as the servants of ALLAH and the preservers and propagators of the sacred rites and traditions. These priestly caste had much influence in the affairs of individuals and of the state, and besides conducting religious worship, had charge of the educating of princes and nobles. In the time of Zoroaster, the Magi were reformed and disciplined, but later they declined in influence until they developed into magicians and fortune tellers. The name Magi is also given to the three wise men who came from the East to [honor] the infant Jesus. (M.D. / Sister Rashida-El) (Heading)

Mangste = Chinese sage and member of the Silent Brotherhood. (4)

Jesus Appears, Fully Materialized, to the Eastern Sages in the Palace of Prince Ravanna in India
– To the Magian Priests in Persia –
Three Wise Men Speak in Praise of the Personality of the Nazarene

Master = teacher. (24)

Masters = teachers. (22, 25)

Mission = an assigned duty or task.

→ *"His mission to the sons of men"* pinpoints exactly what Jesus was sent amongst the people to do by ALLAH. He came with a specific goal and His mission was assigned by ALLAH for the benefit of all humanity. (31)

Myth = an imaginary person; an illustration. (17)

Nazarene = Jesus.

→ A Nazarene was a native or inhabitant of Nazareth, the childhood home of Jesus. It was a town located in N. Israel. (Heading)

Needs = of necessity. (5)

Omnipotence = the quality or state of being omnipotent. **Omnipotent** = having unlimited or universal power, authority, or force; All Powerful.

→ *"Omnipotence of man,"* is man having unlimited power. The Prophet Noble Drew Ali teaches that the object of man's life according to Islam, is its complete unfoldment. He teaches that man is born with *unlimited* capacities for progress, growth. The conflict of the flesh is intended to aid in our unfoldment. (Reference "Moorish Literature," "What is Islam," pg. 10). (14)

Orissa = a state in E. India.

→ Known as Kalinga in ancient times, Orissa was once a Buddhist state and later a Jain region before being converted to Hinduism. Through the centuries, dozens of kingdoms, local and foreign, have ruled Orissa, and many have left their mark in huge temples and other structures. (1, 21)

Overcome = to prevail over; be victorious. (37)

Overthrown = defeated. (36)

Persepolis = an ancient capital of Persia; its imposing ruins are in S. Iran, 30 miles N.E. of Shiraz. (22)

Persia = also called Persian Empire.

→ The Persian Empire was an ancient empire located in W. and S.W. Asia; at its height it extended from Egypt and Aegean to India; conquered by Alexander "the Great" 334-331 B.C., and officially called Iran since 1935. (Heading)

Pierced = a hole made in or through something with a sharp object. (12)

Prophet = a person who speaks for ALLAH. (See *"Prophet"* in Ch. 48). (10)

Ravanna = a wealthy prince from India.

→ As a child, Jesus traveled to India with Ravanna where he learned the wisdom of the Brahms. (See Ch. 6:15). (Heading)

Resurrection = to bring back to life; revive; the act of bringing back from a spiritual death.

→ *"gospel of the resurrection"* is the Truth that man can attain to oneness with ALLAH and regain eternal life. This rests solely on men, for ALLAH changes not the conditions of people until they begin the changing process. (15)

Jesus Appears, Fully Materialized, to the Eastern Sages in the Palace of
Prince Ravanna in India
– To the Magian Priests in Persia –
Three Wise Men Speak in Praise of the Personality of the Nazarene

<u>**Roman Soldiers**</u> = soldiers under the leadership of Rome.

→ These particular soldiers served a specific purpose, they were the "execution squad" who were under the control of Pilate and responsible for carrying out the execution of those condemned to death. In this instance, Jesus. (12)

<u>**Shepherd**</u> = one who herds, guards, or tends sheep. (22)

<u>**Silent Brotherhood**</u> = a religious order. (24, 26)

<u>**Sore**</u> = suffering mental pain; causing great mental pain, distress, or sorrow.

→ "*sore temptation, buffeting, and woes*" is reflective of the suffering that Jesus had to endure at the hands of the enemy in order to be able to develop the attributes of ALLAH which were held deep within. The life and works of Jesus serve as an example as to what it is that we must do in order to develop that which we possess. The Prophet Noble Drew Ali suffered the same sore temptations, buffeting, and woes while he was on the manifest to bring us the Truth about ourselves. (35)

<u>**Sown**</u> = injected; planted.

→ "*He had sown the seed*" shows that by verbal expression Jesus threw forth thoughts into the minds of men that if properly guarded, guided, and nurtured would germinate into the very same message that Jesus was bringing. This message encompassed the omnipotence of men, the power of truth, and the resurrection of the dead. (21)

<u>**Speed of light**</u> = electromagnetic energy travels at 299,792.5 kilometers or 186,000 miles per second, which is thought to be the ultimate speed of light in the universe. (Reader's Digest III. Encyclopedia Dictionary.) (28)

<u>**Stamped**</u> = brought down forcibly or smartly to the ground; to extinguish, crush, etc. by striking with a forcible downward thrust; to stand upon triumphantly.

→ "*I stamped upon him and arose*" reveals the use of Jesus' spiritual force to suppress that which sought to hold him down, death, and rise to the level of eternal life in the Breath of the Holy One. After accomplishing this task, He returned amongst the people to demonstrate to them the possibilities of man when his (men's will) is in tune with that of the Supreme Creator. (13)

<u>**Thorny**</u> = full of difficulties, complexities, or perplexing.

→ "*thorny way of life,*" is basically the human drama that was faced by Jesus while on this manifest. Bear in mind that these events that Jesus experienced were meant to unfold, as they did. Jesus was divinely prepared for His mission. He wasn't any commoner, chosen out of the blue to fulfill the calling. ALLAH deemed Him worthy to give His life as a willing sacrifice for men. He faced a difficult life filled with complexities. But having His will in tune with the Will of ALLAH and having the spiritual force directing His life, He was able to defeat all His foes and gain strength. He became the one master of the human race whose flesh was transmuted into flesh divine, for Jesus was the master alchemist and had complete understanding on the operation of the soul and spirit of man and knew how to

·····CHAPTER XIX (19)·····
**Jesus Appears, Fully Materialized, to the Eastern Sages in the Palace of
Prince Ravanna in India
– To the Magian Priests in Persia –
Three Wise Men Speak in Praise of the Personality of the Nazarene**

overcome the limitations of the flesh. Thinking from a Spiritual perspective, as Spirit-Man, He was able to raise the substance of His makeup to that of a divine nature. (36)

Tomb = a vault or chamber for burial of the dead. Tombs may have been excavated graves on the ground or like in Jesus' instance a natural cave or a rock-cut vault. (13)

Transformed = changed in form, appearance, or structure; changed into another substance. (27)

Trials = tests (as of one's virtues, faith, patience, or stamina) by being subjected to affliction or temptation. (35)

Unannounced = unexpected. (7)

Unto = to.

Vacant = empty. (6, 9)

Vidyapati = a wise Indian sage. (See "*Vidyapati*" in Ch. 11). (4)

Wont = accustomed. (1)

NOTES:

HOLY INSTRUCTION AND WARNINGS FOR ALL YOUNG MEN

Allurements = actions intended to entice, especially with things that are desirable; fascinations; to allure. **Allure** = to attract or tempt by something flattering or desirable. (1)

Beware = to be on guard against; to be cautious and alert to risks; a warning. (1)

Bosom = the seat of affection; the human chest or breast.

→ *"Shut not thy bosom to the tenderness of love,"* means to not shun away sincere love. When true love has revealed itself to you, open your heart (mind) and allow the blessing that ALLAH has bestowed upon you to flow in. (10)

Decline = the period when something approaches an end; a downward movement or descent; the later years or last period of life. (5)

Delights = things that are meant to gratify the lower nature, or the carnal manifestation. Lewdness is one of these and so the harlot uses her physical appearance to entice you to submit to your lower nature. (1)

Delusions = false beliefs or opinions. (3)

Destruction = acts that lead to ruin.

→ *"thou shalt rush upon destruction"* is a warning. In this instance, the word "rush" implies a rapid, impetuous, or violent movement, that is, the unbridled desire that we allow to drive us, once reached, will have cost us more than what we think they are worth. In that sense, the cat was not worth the chase. It is a Pyrrhic victory. (2)

Dwell = abide or live; remain. (8)

Enchanting = charming; captivating.

→ *"neither suffer thy soul to be enslaved by her enchanting delusions,"* extends the warning to us not to allow our innermost part to be controlled by her deceptive machinations and charms. (3)

Enlighten = to give insight to; to inform or instruct. (6)

Ennoble = to elevate in degree, excellence, or respect; dignify; exalt. (10)

Enslaved = controlled. (3)

Enticements = deeds or acts that are intended to lead, especially to evil; to entice. **Entice** = to lead on by exciting hope or desire; lure. (3)

Excess = behavior or activities that exceed proper or lawful bounds; intemperance; overindulgence.

→ *"excess in her delights"* is to overindulge in that which give great physical pleasure. (1)

Exhausted = drained completely; depleted. (4)

Fairest = purest; free from blemish, imperfection, or anything that impairs the appearance, quality, or character. (10)

Fountain = the source of origin of something.

→ *"the fountain of health"* is that which produces or brings about soundness of body and/or mind. (4)

Harlot = a loose woman; a woman who is lacking in discretion and lives loosely; a prostitute. (1)

Heaven = firmament; the sky or universe. (6)

Impressions = memories; first and immediate effect of an experience or perception upon the mind. (10)

Influence = the capacity or power of persons or things to be a compelling force on or produce effects on the actions, behavior, opinions, etc., of others.

→ "*the influence of her power it is in vain to resist*" means it is futile to oppose her when she is decent and righteous in her ways because he knows there is no deception in her. (6)

Innocence = free from guile, cunning, or deceit. (8)

Lily = any scaly-bulbed plant of the genus Lilium, having white showy, funnel-shaped, or bell-shaped flowers.

→ I believe the Prophet is stating that the pureness of her heart (mind) is unmatched or unparalleled. (7)

Lustre = radiance of beauty, excellence, merit, distinction, or glory. (6)

Madness = intense excitement or enthusiasm; frenzy; rage.

→ "*the madness of desire shall defeat its own pursuit,*" when we lack control over the body and allow our loose desires to navigate the flesh, the outcome is always for the worst for we have gained the world but at the cost of the soul; again, a Pyrrhic victory of sorts. (2)

Modesty = having or showing a moderate estimation of oneself. (6)

Overtake = to catch up with. (5)

Prime = the most flourishing stage or state; the time of early manhood; the period or state of greatest perfection or vigor in human life.

→ "*prime of thy life*" is the age of ideal physical perfection and intellectual vigor. As we are fully aware, stress can cause a person to age drastically. A perfect example of this can be seen with presidential candidates. During the period of the primary races and main election the candidates appear energetic, young, and full of vigor. By the conclusion of the four years in office they have aged drastically. This is in part because of the amount of stress and responsibilities that come with such position. Therefore, we must make sure that in choosing a mate we do so not out of delusions, but in sincerity. (5)

Pursuits = actions or instances of chasing or pursuing. In this instance, it is referring to our loose desires. (2)

Rage = a violent desire or passion, (of feelings, opinions, etc.); to hold sway with unabated violence.

→ "*from the blindness of its rage*" is indictive of the times when our loose desires have grown so strong that we appear unable to restrain ourselves and our ability to reason is basically nil. This is one reason why the Prophet instructs us that to be just we are to hear without our passions. (2)

Shalt = shall; will. (2)

Simplicity = freedom from deceit or guile; sincerity; artlessness; naturalness. (8)

Tempt = to entice or allure; to get someone to do something wrong, unwise, or immoral; seduce. (1)

Thee = you.

Therefore = for that reason; consequently. (3)

Thou = you.

Thy = your.

Transcendeth = to rise above or beyond; bypass. (7)

Vain = not successful; futile. (6)

Virtue = moral excellence and righteousness; chastity in a woman. (6)

Wantonness = sexually lawless or unrestricted; loose; lascivious. (1)

NOTES:

MARRIAGE INSTRUCTIONS FOR MAN AND WIFE
FROM THE NOBLE PROPHET

Add = to attach to.

→ "*addeth wings to their feet*" means that her servants move quickly when given instructions. This phrase means that because she is kind when giving orders things are done swiftly and without resistance. Be mindful of the type of individual we are dealing with. The Prophet made a distinction when he stated, "and her kindness addeth wings to their feet." We are speaking of a reasonable and just woman. Not one who lacks in civility and behaves like a brute or tyrant when giving orders and demanding respect without just treatment of her servants. (22)

Adversity = a state of hardship or affliction; a condition marked by misfortune, calamity, or distress.

→ "*in adversity she healeth the wounds of fortune with patience,*" when things become difficult and she faces mental or emotional hurt because of mishaps, by having a calmness and ease of mind, she is able to figure out ways of properly dealing with such issues. By not allowing herself to get agitated, she has a clear mind for thinking things out. (23)

Affairs = private or personal concerns; matters of commercial or public interest or concerns; a particular action, operation, or proceeding; anything requiring action or effort.

→ "*she considers her affairs,*" she takes into account the things which must be done. (17)

Alleviated = made easier to endure; lessened the severity of; mitigated. (24)

Applieth = to devote or employ diligently or with close attention.

→ "*to that alone she applieth her study,*" she contemplates and considers the things that are best for her family's well-being. (18)

Appointeth = gives each person their assigned duties for the day. (17)

Ariseth = to get up from a night's sleep to start the day. (17)

Art = are.

Awe = an overwhelming feeling of reverence, admiration, fear, etc., produced by that which is grand, sublime, extremely powerful, or the like. (12)

Bloom = a flourishing, healthy, condition; the time or period of greatest beauty, artistry, etc. (1)

Bosom = a state of enclosing intimacy; the breast, conceived as the center of feelings or emotions.

→ "*he putteth his heart in her bosom,*" he shared with her his most intense intimate concerns and secrets. In other words, there is a relationship built upon trust. (24)

Brow = the forehead; the ridge over the eye.

→ When the forehead us used, it is metaphorical. By stating that "*discretion with a scepter sitteth on her brow,*" it is saying that she makes moves with discretion. When something is spoken of as being on the forehead, it is saying that something stands out since the forehead is a predominant area of the body. (11)

Caution = careful forethought to avoid danger or harm. (2)

Charity = tolerance in judging other people. (13)

Charms = attractiveness. (1)

·····CHAPTER XXI (21)·····
MARRIAGE INSTRUCTIONS FOR MAN AND WIFE
FROM THE NOBLE PROPHET

Commandeth = to order. (16)

Companion = partner. (3)

Councils = advice. (24)

Decency = conformity to the recognized standard of propriety, good taste, modesty, etc.; standards of morality or responsibility. (8)

Delight = great pleasure; joy. (2, 19)

Delight = enjoyment. (18)

Delighteth not = does not take pleasure in. (6)

Discretion = the power or right to decide or act according to one's own judgment. (11)

Dumb = mute; unable to speak. (12)

Dwelleth = lives; resides. (8)

Elegance = elegant; graceful, refined, and dignified, as in taste, habits, etc. (18)

Endearments = words expressing affection. (3)

Endearments = love or affection. (24)

Evil = morally bad or wrong. (14)

Fame = reputation; Archaic: rumors. (13)

Fashioneth = shapes. (20)

Form = physical body. (1)

Frugality = entailing little expense; inexpensive. (18)

Gadding abroad = gad; to move restlessly or aimlessly from one place to another. (6)

Gaze = to look steadily, intently, and with fixed attention. (2)

Give ear = pay close attention to. (1)

Glory = majestic beauty and splendor. (7)

Gratify = to give pleasure to or please; satisfy. (3)

Humility = the quality or condition of being humble; modest opinion of one's own importance. (7)

Informeth = gives facts or information to. (20)

Innocence = purity; freedom from guile, cunning, or deceit. (5)

Judgment = the ability to judge, make decisions, or form an opinion objectively, authoritatively, and wisely, especially in matters affecting action; good sense. (16)

Licentious = sexually unrestrained; unrestrained by law or general morality; lawless; immoral. (12)

Lo! = look! See! Used to attract attention or show surprise. (5)

Loose desire = unrestrained desires or passions, as of the carnal nature (lower instincts). (3)

Lustre = radiance of beauty, excellence, merit, distinction, or glory. (1)

Maiden = a girl or young unmarried woman. (5)

Mansion = dwelling place. (14)

Mansion = a large abode or dwelling. (18)

Marriage = the legal union of a man and a woman as husband and wife; the state of being married. Prophet Noble Drew Ali stated in the Moorish Literature: "We Moors cannot marry no one but we obligate you, according to our divine laws and covenant and the laws of the land. This must be proclaimed and made known to every Temple so that there will be no misunderstanding about I, the Prophet, and my teachings because ALLAH *alone* binds two hearts together as a unit." (Emphasis added). (Heading)

Meekness = meek; showing patience and humility. (7)

Merely = only as specified and nothing more.

→ *"not merely,"* means not only. The purpose of her life is not to satisfy her partner's base desires. She is worth more than that. She is his better half and should be respected and treated justly. (3)

Mildness = mild; amiably gentle or temperate in feeling or behavior toward others; kindness. (8)

Modesty = the quality of being modest; freedom from vanity, egotism, boastfulness, or great pretensions; free from ostentation or showy extravagance. (5)

Motion = movement.

→ *"the motion of her eye commandeth their obedience,"* this could imply that with her look we are advised to comply with whatever order has been given. She needs not to speak a word once she has given an order. It is a form of silent communication and at times a warning. Surely you can recall a time as a child when you were given an order and if failing to follow it the look you received from your mother, or father, would make you hurry up and do what you were ordered to do. It is the same in the instance spoken of here. (21)

Nature = the fundamental character or disposition of a person; temperament.

→ *"good nature,"* feelings of kindness or affection that are genuine, spontaneous, or unstudied in expression. (13)

Neatness = neat; in a pleasing, orderly, and clean condition. (7)

Obedience = the act or practice of obeying; dutifully complying with the commands, orders, or instructions of one in authority, in this instance from the wife to the husband. (9)

Obeyed = listened to. (16)

Passion = any powerful or compelling emotion or feeling, as love or hate; strong sexual desires. (3)

Persuasions = the act of persuading or seeking to persuade. **Persuade** = to prevail on (a person) to do something, as by advising or urging. (2)

Precepts = rules or principles prescribing a particular course of action or conduct. (1)

Presideth = exercises authority or control over; rules. (16)

Prosperity = a successful, flourishing, or thriving condition, especially in financial respects; good fortune; having success. (23)

Prudence = care, caution, and good judgment, as well as wisdom in looking ahead; wise or judicious.

→ *"to the instructions of prudence,"* to the lessons she has learned that are based on moral standard and good judgment. It is giving her a warning that she learns good judgment from an early age, be it a physical or spiritual lesson. (1, 10)

Prudence = *"The prudence of her management is an honor to her husband,"* the wisdom and careful management she displays economically demonstrates her respect towards her husband and the fact that he has labored hard to be able to provide for his family. In this wisdom is the fact that the wife is fully aware that things don't come easy and there are bigger things than selfish wants. (19)

Puffed up = inflated with pride, vanity, etc. (23)

Reasonable = fair and sensible; agreeable to reason or sound judgment; not exceeding the limit prescribed by reason. (3)

Recompense = reward. (3)

Reigneth = to predominate; be prevalent; to have control, rule, or influence of any kind.

→ "*and reigneth in his breast,*" implies that she is the only one for him. Beside her, there is no other. (4)

Resembleth = to look like or be similar to. (1)

Retain = continue to have; keep. (1)

Rose = any of numerous shrubs or vines of the genus Rosa, having prickly stems, pinnately compound leaves, and various colored, often fragrant flowers; the flower of any such shrub, of a red, pink, white, or yellow color. (1)

Scandal = talk that is damaging to one's character; malicious gossip. (13)

Sceptre = scepter: royal or imperial power or authority, a rod (staff) or wand held in the hand as an emblem of regal or imperial authority.

→ The prophet states that "*discretion with a sceptre sitteth on her brow,*" and I would think this to mean that when she gives an order, as someone in authority and power, she does so with discretion and this discretion reigns supreme and is noticeable to all. (11)

Seducing words = utterances, remarks, or comments intended to lead or draw away, as from principles, faith, or allegiance, often in a corrupt fashion. (2)

Seeketh = to go out in search of quest of; to try to obtain.

→ "*Her hand seeketh employment.*" It is very important that we understand this concept because today slothfulness is found everywhere. We must be sure that in deciding who our partners may be we don't end up with someone who only seeks to live off of others. It speaks volumes when we find a partner that enjoys working and if not working, doesn't sit around waiting for handouts but goes out to obtain what is needed. (6)

Servants = individuals employed to perform domestic duties in a household or for a person. (22)

Slave of his passions = one who is used to merely satisfy another's loose desires and/or longings. (3)

Soothe = to gently calm a person or their feelings. (3)

Spring = the first stage or the freshest period.

→ "*In the spring of thy youth,*" is referring to the first, or beginning stages of youth. This is one of the times in life when people are more vulnerable and/or naïve as to what actually takes place in the world. (2)

Subdueth = to conquer or subjugate; to bring under control. (4)

Submission = the state of being submissive or compliant; humble.

MARRIAGE INSTRUCTIONS FOR MAN AND WIFE
FROM THE NOBLE PROPHET

→ *"Submission and obedience are the lessons of her life,"* being compliant (not complaisant) and dutiful with the instructions which have been imparted to her displays an example for others to learn from and gain knowledge and wisdom. This does not mean that she must submit to her husband even if he's in error. This is if the husband is just and righteous in his ways. (9)

Temperance = moderation and self-restraint, as in behavior; self-control. (7)

Tenderness = marked by or expressing gentle emotions; loving. (3)

Thee = you.

Therefore = for this/that reason; consequently. (14)

Thine = your.

Thou = you.

Thy = your.

Thy being = your life; your living. (3)

Toils of life = times of strife in life; hard times. (3)

Virtue = moral excellence; conformity of one's life and conduct to moral and ethical principles. (10)

Virtue = moral excellence and righteousness; goodness. (12)

Wisdom = the quality of having experience, knowledge, good judgement; the ability to recognize or judge what is true, right, or lasting; insight; common sense. (20)

Withered = shriveled up; dried up, shrunk, wilted, faded, whether as a natural process or as the result of exposure to excessive heat or drought. (1)

Yonder = over there; one that is at an indicated place, usually within sight. (5)

NOTES:

DUTY OF A HUSBAND

→ The Prophet Noble Drew Ali makes it perfectly clear what our obligations are towards the individual that a man takes as his wife. He informs Moorish men in our Moorish Literature "your wives, brothers, must hear good words, kind words, and must know of your good deeds." In this chapter, he furthers his instructions and leaves no room for anyone to use any excuse as to why they mistreat their wives. The man has his responsibilities and moral obligations towards his wife. Use them to set you house in order.

Abideth = to remain; reside.

→ "*If her foot abideth not in her father's house,*" if she sleeps in other places instead of her father's home when she is young and single. (3)

Accomplished mind = having all the social graces, manners, and other attainments of polite society. (4)

Adornment = something that adds attractiveness; ornaments; accessory; to make more pleasing; enhancing the beauty of. (3)

Affliction = a state of pain, distress, or grief; the cause of continued pain or distress of body or mind (as illness or losses); suffering. (11)

Alleviate = to make more bearable; relieve. (11)

Allurements = things that attract or entice; fascinations. (3)

Assault = attack. (11)

Avail = help. (11)

Boldness = bold: the quality of being fearless; daring.

→ "*and her eyes with boldness rove on the faces of men,*" means if she is constantly looking at other men without regards for her self-respect or without regrets. (3)

Bosom = very intimate or dear; the seat of emotions. (4)

Cares = suffering of mind; sorrows. (7)

Charms = attractiveness; physical beauty. (3)

Cherish = to hold as dear; to treat with affection and tenderness; feel love for. (5)

Companion = partner; a mate. (4, 7)

Consider = bear in mind; remember. (12)

Counsels = advice.

→ "*her counsels are sincere,*" means that her opinions, instructions, and/or advice are genuine and honest. This implies a deep feeling for the cares of the partner in the marriage. (9)

Deceived = betrayed. (9)

Delighted = take great pleasure in.

→ "*and delighted with her own praise,*" means if she is full of herself, vain, or egotistical. (3)

Destroyed = rendered useless.

→ "*If much of her time is destroyed in dress and adornment,*" if she spends (wastes) too much time concerned about how she looks, her clothing, jewels, make up, etc. For someone to spend so much time indulged in such activities shows that they are concerned on how they appear to others and/or are full of themselves. Of course, this does not mean that she should not be proud of her appearance. On the contrary, she should strive to look her best. But, if she spends too much time in such activities, we should be careful. (3)

Duty = an act or course of action required by custom, law, or religion; one's responsibility or moral obligation. (Heading)

Enamoured = in love with. (3)

Endear = to make dear, esteemed, or beloved. (5)

Ensnared = captured or entrapped.

→ *"and suffer not they soul to be ensnared by the allurements of imagination,"* do not allow your soul, or mind, to suffer or be tortured by chasing or pursuing illusions, the charms, or seduction of such a woman. (3)

Exact = to call for, demand, or require.

→ *"exact not her obedience with rigour,"* do not demand and attempt to obtain her obedience by force or severity. (8)

Examine = to observe carefully or critically; to inspect or scrutinize carefully. (2)

Faithful = strict or thorough in performance of duty.

→ *"and become a faithful member of society,"* become a loyal or reliable member of the community. It is law that when the male becomes a man, he is to take a partner in marriage. It is not meant for men to be alone nor for him to jump from woman to woman. To become a faithful member of society entails the taking of a partner and becoming involved, as a unit, in the intricacies of said community to see it unfold. (1)

Fancy = liking; mental image or conception. (4)

Firmament = the sky; the vault of heaven. (3)

Fix = to become set.

→ *"and fix not suddenly,"* means not to act in haste (too quick) when searching for your companion. *"On thy present choice depends thy future happiness,"* take into consideration the fact that who you choose as your mate today will also dictate the happiness you will enjoy, or lack.

It is of great importance that in the search for a wife, the individual meets all requirements that the Prophet Drew Ali mentions in this chapter. (2)

Form = the physical body (outer) or shape. (4)

Frame = body. (12)

Grief = sorrow (mental suffering) or pain. (11)

Heaven = figuratively speaking the Supreme Creator, God-ALLAH. (5)

Husband = a man joined to a woman in marriage; a male spouse. (Heading)

Imagination = the faculty of imagining, or of forming mental images or concepts of what is not actually present to the senses. (3)

Imperfections = faults; failings; flaws; weaknesses. (12)

Inclinations = an attitude or disposition toward something; a liking or preference. (7)

Instigate = to cause by excitement; foment; to argue, provoke, or incite to come action or course. (11)

Mistress = a woman who has authority, control, or power, especially the female head of household. (6)

Oppose = to act against or provide resistance to; resist.

→ *"Oppose not her inclination without cause,"* do not go against your wife on what she favors or prefers without good, logical reason for doing so. Stand by her decision if they are just and righteous. (7)

Ordinance = an authoritative command, order, rule, or law from ALLAH; an established religious rite. (1)

Physicians = those skilled in the art of healing. (11)

Pity = a feeling of sadness and sympathy caused by the suffering of other people. (11)

Pleasures = delights; joyful times. (7)

Reprove = to criticize or correct, especially gently; to disapprove of strongly. (8)

Respect = a feeling of admiration; politeness. (6)

Rigour = rigor: strictness, severity, or harshness. (8)

Rove = to wander about; to wander over or through.

→ "*and her eyes with boldness rove on the faces of men,*" initially we must ask ourselves what is it that she is looking for by roaming over the faces of men. This would be a female who has no self-restraint and can be a downfall. (3)

Sensibility = mental susceptibility or responsiveness.

→ "*But when thou findest sensibility of heart,*" refers to a woman who has a refined awareness and ability to perceive and respond to other people's feelings and emotions, when such a woman is found, embrace her, first as a friend, then as a companion in life, you wife. (4)

Servants = persons employed by another, especially to perform domestic duties. (6)

Severe = unnecessarily extreme.

→ "*and be not severe to her weakness,*" don't be hard on her because she is weaker than you in certain areas, "*but remember thine own imperfections,*" and keep in mind that you have certain frailties, faults, and failings as well. (12)

Shalt = shall. (9)

Soothe = to please with soft or kind actions; to put the mind at ease with kind words and/or deeds. (11)

Tenderness = marked by, responding to, or expressing the softer emotions; fond, loving; showing care or thoughtful consideration; compassionate.

→ "*let thy tenderness soothe her affliction*" means when your companion is in pain or suffering, reach into the recess of yourself and let her suffering move you into saying kind words and doing righteous deeds, that it may aid in her healing process. Be kind to her and careful in protecting her from harm or injury. This is your obligation as a husband. The Prophet of ALI instructs us to protect our wife and children. This is the law, and the LAW must live. (11)

Thee = you.

Therefore = for that reason; consequently. (6)

Thine = your.

Thou = you.

Thy = your.

Thyself = yourself. (1)

Unto = to.

NOTES:

HOLY INSTRUCTIONS FOR THY CHILDREN

INSTRUCTIONS = imparted or acquired items of knowledge; lessons; imparted knowledge. (Heading)

→ This chapter is of great importance, not just to the students and followers of Prophet Noble Drew Ali, but to all those seeking to set their house in order. It is imperative that we heed these words of wisdom for they are for the uplifting of Our fallen humanity. The Prophet teaches us that our children are a reflection of us. No matter which way we cut it, the warning is clear. If we are to break the cycle in which our people are destroying each other, we must be sure to implement the 12 steps offered to us here that we may climb up this righteous ladder to the dome of purity which resides in each one of us. Then, and only then, will we be able to become useful members to our communities.

Art = are. (1)

Ashamed = feeling shame; distressed or embarrassed by feelings of guilt, foolishness, or disgrace. (8)

Attend = accompany; to be with. (10)

Being = a person; human. (1)

Benefits = things that are advantageous, or good; make improvements.

→ "*and he shall receive benefits,*" be teaching the child to be grateful and appreciative for the things he/she has, the laws of the Cosmos will continue to promote or enhance his/her well-being. (9)

Benevolence = a desire to do good to others; goodwill; charitable acts. (12)

Bent = course of action; leaning, bias, or inclination for. (4)

Bless = honor or glorify. (8)

Blessing = a gift bestowed (given) by God ALLAH, thereby bringing happiness or joy. (2)

Bosom = belly; very intimate or dear.

→ "*child of thy bosom,*" beloved child; the being you have produced and held closely in security. (2)

Cedar = any of several Old World, coniferous trees of the genus Cedrus, having wide, spreading branches. (5)

Charity = generous actions or donations to aid the poor, ill, or helpless; love for mankind; the act of giving or good will; generosity towards others. (9)

Community = the public; society. (2)

Consider = bear in mind; remember.

→ From the very beginning of the chapter, the first thing that it tells us is to "*Consider*" which means that we have to stop and think about something and think about it deeply. (1)

Cultivation = training or fostering; rearing. (7)

Curse = something bad or evil. (2)

Dependeth = to rely on; to be sustained by. (2)

Diligence = constant and earnest effort to accomplish what is undertaken; persistent; industrious. (12)

Doth = does. (6)

Duty = moral obligation. (1)

Evil = bad. (4)

Exalted = raised or elevated, as in character.

→ "*and his mind shall be exalted,*" his mental capacities will be raised, heightened, or elevated. (12)

Fortune = wealth; success; prosperity. (10)

Gratitude = the quality or feeling of being grateful or thankful. (See "*Gratitude*" in Ch. 33). (9)

Hast = have or has. (1)

Health = soundness, especially of body and mind; good health. (10)

Honor = great respect. (6)

Honored = respected (11)

Importance = the state or quality of being important. **Important** = of much or great significance or consequence.

→ Importance is assigning exceptional or notable value or influence to a person. When the Prophet is making us aware of "*the importance of thy trust*," he means to take into deep consideration the influence that you have when given the care or custody of another. (1)

Inclinations = attitudes or dispositions toward something.

→ "*watch the bent of his inclinations*," be aware of his attitude and mental disposition, tendencies, etc. "*set him right in his youth and let no evil habit gain strength with his years*," place him/her on the course of righteousness and if you see that which is unrighteous begin to show in his ways, help make the needed corrections then and there. The longer ones wait to correct bad habits and behavior the more difficult they will be to overcome. (4)

Increase = become greater or larger. (12)

Instruction = direction; guidance; supervision; knowledge or information imparted. **Imparted** = passed on; made known. (3)

Justice = the quality of being just; fairness; the principle of moral rightness; equity; just conduct, dealing, or treatment. **Just** = guided by truth, reason, justice, and fairness. (The fifth principle of moral life for the Moorish American Moslem. See "*Justice*" in Ch. 31 and 48). (11)

Maxims = a maxim is a fundamental principle; a primary rule of conduct. The 12 virtues we are instructed to teach our child(ren) (instructions 8-13) lays the lifelong foundation for proper conduct. (3)

Modesty = regard for appropriate behavior, speech, dress, etc.; freedom from vanity or boastfulness, etc. (8)

Obedience = the act or practice of obeying; dutifully complying with the commands, order, or instructions of one in authority. (8)

Prepare = to make ready before hand for a specific purpose, as for an occasion. In this instance, the child's future.

→ "*Prepare him early with instruction*." Impart knowledge to your seeds at an early age. It has been demonstrated that the ages between 2 and 5 are of great importance and it is during these ages where the child(ren) begin to retain what has been seen, learned, or taught, be it negative or positive. "*and season his mind with the maxims of truth*," improve or enhance the mind, or thoughts, of your seed(s) with truth and proper rules of conduct. (3)

Produced = you have created, brought into existence; give birth to. (1)

Prudence = care, caution, and good judgement, as well as wisdom in looking ahead; wise or judicious; careful management; economy. (10)

Religion = something one believes in and follows devotedly; a set of beliefs concerning the cause, nature, and purpose of the universe, especially when considered as the creation of a superhuman agency or agencies, usually involving devotional or ritual observances and often involving a moral code governing the conduct of human affairs. (See *"Religion"* in Ch. 35). (13)

Reproach = disgrace; bring shame upon. (6)

Science = systematic knowledge of the physical or material world gained through observation and experimentation; knowledge gained by systematic study; knowledge, as of facts or principles. (13)

Season = to render suitable. (3)

Seed = the germ or propagative source of anything. (7)

Soil = any place (mind) or condition providing the opportunity for growth or development.

→ *"The soil is thine own,"* the soil (breeding ground) is a place or a condition favorable for growth; it's yours – it is what you make it. *"Let it not want cultivation,"* let it not *lack* cultivation (refinement, nurturing, education). *"The seed which thou soweth, that also shall thou reap,"* whatever kind of seed you plant, that's the kind of person your child will grow up to be. You plant a good, strong, intelligent seed – cultivating it early – your child will grow up to be a good, strong, intelligent person. You sow or plant a bad, evil, weak seed…that is what your child will grow up to be. (7)

Support = this word is a transitive verb, which expresses an action carried from subject to the object, it shows action.

→ One the physical level, it demonstrates what must be provided for the child in order for him/

her to be able to grow physically well. This includes water, shelter, food, proper medical care, and finance where needed. On the spiritual level, it encompasses proper knowledge of the Supreme Creator and the gnosis (spiritual knowledge) that, within man, rests the ability for spiritual salvation and the steps needed to gain deific (paradise) life where we will unfold and become the God-Man of today. (1)

Temperance = moderation and self-restraint, as in behavior; self-control. (10)

Thee = you.

Thine = your.

Thou = you.

Thy = your.

Thyself = yourself.

Useful = being of use or service; serving some purpose; advantageous, helpful, or of good effort. (2, 13)

Wealth = possessions, assets, goods, property, money, etc. (12)

Wicked = evil; malicious or mischievous. (6)

Worthless = without worth; of no use, importance, or value. Good-for-nothing! (2)

NOTES:

·····CHAPTER XXIV (24)·····
THE OBEDIENCE OF CHILDREN TOWARDS THEIR FATHER

Obedience = the act or practice of obeying; to carry out or fulfill the command, order, or the instructions of your father.

→ Pay attention to the advice your father gives you and do as he says. Trust in him to know what is best for you. It is his duty to instruct you in life and set you in the proper course. The instructions that he gives you are rooted in his fatherly love, and he seeks only the best for you. (Heading)

Admonition = counsel; cautionary advice or warning; gentle reproof (criticism); reprimand firmly. **Reprimand** = a formal statement of disapproval. (5)

Aged = having lived or existed long; pertaining to or characteristic of old age. (2)

Aged Sire = in this instruction, it is referring to the father who has grown old and is supported and looked after by his seed, his son. (2)

Apply = to put to use; to put into action. (1)

Arabian = of or pertaining to Arabia. **Arabia** = a peninsula in SW Asia, including Saudi Arabia, Yemen, Oman, the United Arab Emirates, Qatar, and Kuwait; divided in ancient times into Arabia Deserts, Arabia Petraea, and Arabia Felix. (3)

Assist and Support = "*assist and support them in the decline of life*," to aid and assist (help) your parents in their later years of life, when they may not be able to do for themselves. (7)

Beareth = to carry; support; convey. **Convey** = to carry from one place to another; transport. (2)

Decline = the later years or last part of life. (7)

Delicious = highly pleasing or agreeable to the senses, especially taste or smell. (3)

Desert = a dry, often sandy area of land with little rainfall, extreme temperature, and with little or no vegetation, often marked by an annual rainfall of 10 inches at a single time or throughout the year. (2)

Ease = the condition of being comfortable. (6)

Filial = of, relating to, or appropriate for a son or daughter. (8)

Forwardness = the condition of being in advance; over readiness to push oneself forward,

→ "*nor the forwardness of thy youth*," refers to the times when in our youth we moved with eagerness and rashness. (7)

Grateful = warm or deeply appreciative; thankful. (4)

Hath = have or has. (6)

Hoary = greyish or white, as of the hair with age. (8)

Honor = deep respect. (6)

Incense = perfume or fragrance; an aromatic gum or other substance producing a sweet odor when burned, used in religious ceremonies, to enhance the mood, etc. (3)

Indulge = to engage or take part in; assist. (7)

Infancy = the earliest period of childhood.

→ "*forget not thy helpless infancy*," keep in mind that at one time you were helpless and as an infant dependent upon someone else. In this instance, your parents. (7)

Infirmities = physical weakness or ailments; frailty; feebleness; lack of strength. (7)

Instruction = lesson; an order; knowledge or information imparted. **Imparted** = passed on; made known.

→ In ancient times, Instructions were writings issued by Egyptians (Kemetic people) in the form of essays, based on good living. In our Holy Koran, we are given Instructions that if properly followed will set our house in order and our children will learn to love instead of hate. (1)

Irreverence = lack of reverence or due respect. (6)

Lodgeth = provided with temporary living quarters; to shelter. (2)

Observe = to watch carefully. (2)

Odors = aromas, redolence, or perfumes. (3)

Persia = also called the Persian Empire.

→ An ancient empire located in W and SW Asia: at its height it extended from Egypt to the Aegean to India. It was conquered by Alexander "the Great (Greek)" 334-331 B.C. It was the former official name of Iran until 1935. (3)

Piety = one's devotion (great love or loyalty) and reverence (deep respect) towards parents and family. (8)

Proceedeth = comes from; place or point of origin. "*Proceedeth from love*," informs us that the admonitions given to us as children were issued out of love and not based on ill intent. (5)

Reverence = a feeling or attitude of deep respect tinged with awe; veneration. **Awe** = a feeling of great respect mixed with fear.

→ "*in reverence of thy example, shall repay thy piety with filial love*," indicates that out of respect and love, your children will repay your loyalty towards your parents with the same love and compassion you displayed. This also indicates that you lead a good example, and your children witnessed your behavior and are now displaying it. (8)

Sire = a father (archaic). (2)

Stork = any of several wading birds of the Ciconiidea, having long legs and a long neck and bill.

→ In mythology, the stork was known as the mythical or symbolic deliverer of a new baby. (2)

Supplieth = provided. (2)

Sustained = supplied with nourishment and provided with other necessities of life, such as food, water, clothing, and shelter, as well as physical, mental, and spiritual guidance, etc. (4)

Thee = you. (4)

Therefore = for that reason. (6)

Thine = your.

Thy = your.

Toiled = labored.

→ "*toiled for thy ease*," informs you that your father's objective as he labored was to be able to supply you with the things needed for you to be able to grow up at ease and not having to worry about lacking the things needed for you to come up in life appropriately. (6)

Wafted = something, such as an odor, carried through the air. (3)

Welfare = health, happiness, and good fortune; well-being. (6)

Western Gales = a very powerful wind coming from a westerly course. (3)

THE OBEDIENCE OF CHILDREN TOWARDS THEIR FATHER

Wisdom = the quality or state of being wise; having experience, knowledge, and good judgement. Wise = the ability to discern (recognize) or judge what is true, right, or lasting; exhibiting common sense; judicious or prudent. (1)

Yea = yes. (3)

→ The Secrets of ALLAH are written and revealed in His creation. His creation declared His praise. The Prophet is instructing us to look upon creation and learn.

NOTES:

·····CHAPTER XXV (25)·····
A HOLY COVENANT OF THE ASIATIC NATION

A Holy Covenant = a divine agreement between ALLAH and the Asiatic Nation. (Heading)

Asiatic Nation = consists of Puerto Ricans, Cubans, Columbians, Dominicans, Mexicans, Brazilians, Chinese, Japanese, Korean, Arabians, etc., and all the Asiatic people or nations within the human race possessing the melanin that distinguishes those from Africa, Asia, North America, etc., from the pale skin nations of Europe. (Heading)

Adversity = a state of hardship or affliction; a condition marked by misfortune, calamity, or distress. (4)

Assist = help, aid, or support. (4)

Bindeth = to obligate or unite. (3)

Bonds of Affection = a unity of kind or warm (loving) feelings towards one another; fondness. (2)

Breast = either of two milk-secreting glandular organs on the chest of a woman. (1)

Care = protection, charge. (1)

Contribute = to be an important factor in; help to cause; to help bring about a result. (5)

Dwell = to live in or at a specific place; reside. (2)

Forsake = to abandon or give up on; to leave altogether; to desert. (4)

Fortunes = good luck; great wealth; ample stock of money, property, and the like; success. (5)

Hath = have or has. (1)

Prefer = to choose someone as more desirable or more valuable. (3)

Prefer not a Stranger = do not choose or side with an *outsider* over your *own blood*. Next to ALLAH and His Prophet, family comes in line of importance. (3)

Provide = supply or support with the necessities of life. (1)

Remember the Relation = is to always recall the bond…(3)

Separate = to part company; disperse; leave; to go your own way. (3)

Stranger = a person whom one does not know or with whom one is not familiar; an outsider. (3)

Suck = to draw something into the mouth by movements of the tongue and lips that create suction, especially to draw milk from a breast; to draw nourishment through or from. (1)

Support = to provide for or maintain by supplying with money, food, water, etc. (necessities of life). (5)

Thee = you.

Therefore = for that reason; consequently. (2)

Thy = your. (2)

Unite = to come or bring together as one, to form a whole. (2)

Whole Race = all Asiatics (Hue-Man family). (5)

Ye = you. Used when addressing a group of persons. (1)

→ Some people refer to this chapter in the usage of ALLAH as the *father*. I tend to disagree with this concept. For the most part, in almost every reference to ALLAH in our Moorish Holy Koran, the words *He, Him,* etc., are *capitalized*. This is not the case with this chapter. In addition, Chapter 24, instruction 4, verifies that the father and mother being referenced here is one's biological / adoptive parents.

CHAPTER XXV (25)
A HOLY COVENANT OF THE ASIATIC NATION

Noble Drew Ali teaches that Adam and Eve are the mothers and fathers of the human family, Asiatics and Moslems. This is a Holy Covenant of the Asiatic Nation. Meaning that this covenant was inspired by the Breath of ALLAH and is meant as an agreement between people to do something specified. In this case, to bring *UNITY* amongst the Asiatic Nation.

NOTES:

CHAPTER XXVI (26)
HOLY INSTRUCTIONS OF UNITY

→ This chapter of UNITY covers two aspects, or rather two types of individuals. The Noble Prophet of ALI begins this chapter by informing us that we are all on an equal basis when it comes to understanding, wisdom, and knowledge. This is very important to point out because it fortifies the point made in the Moorish Literature where we are informed that each individual has within him the seed of perfect development and it rests solely with himself to make or mar his fortune. After studying this chapter, we must pose the question as to whether we fall under the category of the wise or the ignorant. Whatever the answer may be, there is still much work for everyone to do. And in following these instructions, both the wise and ignorant can further unfold in the proper light.

UNITY = the state or quality of being ONE; being in accord and in harmony. (Heading)

Abomination = anything greatly disliked or abhorred; vile, shameful, or detestable action, condition, habit, etc.

→ *"The pride of emptiness is an abomination,"* could be taken to mean that it is a shame for ones to be proud in things that are truly of no spiritual worth. Ask yourself if ALLAH cares about the score of last night's game? Or who wrote this song or that song? How has the gathering of this information helped you spiritually? It is a misuse of what ALLAH has given us (knowledge, wisdom, and understanding) and we will be held accountable for such misapplication of these gifts. (4)

Absurdity = the state or quality of being ridiculous or wildly unreasonable; utterly opposed to truth or reason. (4)

Accounteth = to regard; consider as. (10)

Applause = approval or praise expressed by clapping; commendation. (6)

Appointed = assigned.

→ It was ALLAH who gave each individual the gift of understanding. It was also ALLAH who placed us in society to better unfold our gift of understanding. No other being has blessed us with this gift but ALLAH. The question is, what is it that we are feeding ourselves? With what type of understanding? Is it of the Spiritual nature or is it of the lower nature? We can get a glimpse as to what answer we may get by observing our daily activities. Are we carrying out deeds that are of the Higher nature, or are we misusing our gifts to harm ALLAH'S creation? (1)

Approbation = approval; commendation. (6)

Arts = science, learning, or scholarship; skill in conducting any human activity, e.g., a master at the art of communication. (9)

Attainments = personal acquirements; achievements. (7, 10)

Boast = to brag.

→ Brag implies vocal self-praise or claims to superiority over others. It is a sad sight to see boastful individuals who are wrapped up in the blindness and folly of human knowledge. All praise is due to ALLAH for from HIM comes all Understanding. (5)

Boasteth = talk with excessive pride and self-satisfaction about one's achievements, possessions, or abilities; the act or instance of bragging. (7)

Brethren = brothers; fellow members; individuals with which ones are closely related to. (6)

Clearest human knowledge = the most plain and obvious type of knowledge acquired here on this physical plane in human form.

HOLY INSTRUCTIONS OF UNITY

→ Human knowledge, carnal knowledge, or worldly knowledge, is actually minute in worth, insignificant, and next to nothing when compared to Divine and Spiritual Knowledge. I emphasize that in this instance we are speaking of HUMAN KNOWLEDGE. It does not mean that we are unable to attain Spiritual Knowledge within this physical plane. We must understand that human knowledge has a purpose. We gain human knowledge by way of the five senses. The problem comes when we make that type of knowledge the basis for everything. To gain Spiritual Knowledge, we must elevate our thoughts to infinite wisdom. It is not in flesh to think nor is it in bones to reason. (5)

Communicate = share information with (more in particular information on the knowledge of truth). (2)

Conceit = excessively high opinion of one's own abilities or worth; excessive pride in oneself; vanity. (5)

Crowneth = reward.

→ "*crowneth with honor*" means that the wise man gets his reward by not hearing praises from others but by seeing how what he has done has been of benefit to the community. He doesn't seek direct recognition from the community; therefore, he doesn't brag about what he has done. There is no need for that. To see the usefulness of what he has done is honor enough for him. (9)

Cultivates = to develop or improve one's mind with proper knowledge. (9)

Delight = enjoyment. (9)

Delighteth himself = to be pleased with oneself. (6)

Doubteth = to question the truth or fact of (something); a feeling of uncertainty about the truth, reality, or nature of something, or lack of conviction. (3)

Endowed = provided with a specific talent or quality such as wisdom. (2)

Enlightened = furnished with a spiritual understanding; made conscious. (2)

Folly = a lack of good sense, understanding, or foresight; an act or instance of foolishness; unwise conduct. (3, 5)

Foolishness = resulting from or showing a lack of sense; lacking forethought or caution.

→ "*foolishness of folly*," "folly" is the lack of understanding or sense. The statement "foolishness of folly" is a play on words to emphasize that the only reward of foolishness is additional folly. An individual with no sense or proper understanding who talks too much could lead others astray or may even bring harm to himself. He creates a terrible doom for himself. (4)

Gifts = contributions; special ability or capacity; faculty.

→ "*The gifts of the understanding*," are the benefits or blessings ones obtain from being able to understand and see things from a spiritual perspective. (1)

Hath = have; has.

Humbled = no longer arrogant or proud; made modest. (6)

Ignorance = lack of knowledge or information; the state or fact of being ignorant; lack of knowledge, learning, information, etc. (3)

Ignorant = lacking education, knowledge, or awareness about something in particular; uninformed. (2, 7)

Imperfections = faults, defects, or undesirable features; flaws. (6)

Impertinence = speech or deeds that are not relevant or are presumptuous. (4)

Improvement = a change or condition by which a thing is made better or improved; to make more desirable or excellent. (2)

Instruction = knowledge or information imparted; direction.

→ *"Communicate it to the ignorant, for their instruction,"* is to impart wisdom and knowledge to those who lack in the department to further their growth and guide them in the proper direction. (2)

Knowledge = the state or fact of knowing; facts, information, and skills acquired by a person through experience or study; the sum of what has been perceived, discovered, or learned; clear and certain mental apprehension.

→ *"the clearest human knowledge is but blindness and folly,"* that which most people think they know is generally inaccurate and based upon vicarious experience, so they accept "knowledge" based on blind belief or simply because that's what everyone is believing. (5)

Labor = something worked towards.

→ If one's mind is set on foolishness and folly, the rewards thereof will be foolishness and folly. What you sow, so shall you reap.

Laboreth in Vain = to work towards something to no avail.

→ To state that the wise man laboreth in vain for his own approbation shows a lot about the character of the wise man. The wise man fully understands that there are massive amounts of wisdom in this world. He frets not. Worldly wisdom is nothing when compared to True Wisdom. Even though he won't be able to obtain all that there is to obtain, he still moves forward in obtaining the appropriate wisdom, elevating his mind to infinite wisdom, and applying that for the benefit of humanity. (6)

Measure = a quantity, degree, amount, or proportion. (1)

Nevertheless = in spite of that; nonetheless; however. (4, 10)

Obstinate = stubborn; a person who refuses to change his perspectives and is set in his ways. (3)

Patience = tolerance; the ability to tolerate ignorance without becoming angry or upset. (4)

Pity = to show compassion for; to show mercy for; to sympathize. (4)

Portion = that which is allotted to a person by ALLAH.

→ To ALLAH belongs all Understanding, Wisdom, and Knowledge. From the inception we are equipped with these faculties. They have their origins with ALLAH, and we are all equipped with them. What we do with them is the story. (1)

Presuming = presumptuous.

Presumptuous = unwarrantedly or impertinently bold; forward.

→ *"True wisdom is less presuming than folly,"* could be taken to mean that when we are given true wisdom (wisdom of the spiritual nature), we begin to question it as though someone is attempting to deceive us. But when we are given folly, something that is an illusion, we accept it as though it were the truth. (3)

Puffed up = inflated with pride, vanity, etc. (5)

Reward = something given or received in return for good (or, more rarely, evil) perceived.

→ In this instance, we are taught that the rewards of the fool chasing after folly is shame and disappointment. If we were to examine our lives at this junction, what have our rewards been? Have we received shame and disappointment? We must make an honest assessment of ourselves and make the necessary correction where they need to be made. (8)

Science = knowledge, as of facts or principles; knowledge gained by systematic study.

→ In this instance, I believe that by using the word "science," the author is making reference to the true knowledge, the knowing of how to obtain true happiness in life. In the study of "happiness" we become more aware of its opposite, e.g., sadness, misery, etc., and how to avoid such emotions. (10)

Seemeth = fitting. Whatever measure ALLAH deems fitting for the individual.

→ "Seem" is applied to something that has an aspect of truth. We must bear in mind that understanding is actually the beginning state, or the foundation, on which man builds himself. We have it within us from the beginning. Through experience, we gain those things that are appropriate for further unfoldment. (1)

Superior understanding = understanding above all.

→ We are being cautioned not to become haughty because of the knowledge we've gained in this manifest. It is informing us that this knowledge is but blindness and folly. We have allowed ourselves to become so wrapped up in human knowledge that we've been blinded to the reality that human knowledge is but an illusion. The danger of this is that such blindness can be costly if not realized in time. (5)

Thee = you.

Thine = your.

Thy = your.

Toileth = hard, laborious work.

→ To toil after folly is to work toward frivolous or foolish things. It is the man with a sense of caution that avoids such mishaps. (8)

Treasures = things of great value that are bestowed upon another; things that are highly valued or precious. (1)

True Wisdom = consciousness of ALLAH and man (Spirit-man) (MHK 7:23). Of wisdom we read that it is the consciousness that man is aught, that ALLAH and man are one. That ALLAH is ALL. This is true wisdom. (3)

Truth = Truth is Aught, and Aught is ALLAH; conformity with fact or reality. (2)

Understanding = the ability to understand something; comprehension; to grasp mentally; perceive; the ability to discern.

→ Of UNDERSTANDING we read: "It is the rock on which man builds himself; it is the gnosis of the aught and of the naught, of falsehood and of truth. It is the knowledge of the lowerself; the sensing of the powers of man himself." (MHK 7:20-21). Understanding implies certain depth, or profundity, of the instructions imparted to us by ALLAH, through His Prophet Drew Ali. (1, 7)

Unto = to.

Utility = the quality or condition of being useful; usefulness. (9)

Virtue = moral excellence and righteousness; goodness. (10)

Wisdom = the quality of having experience, knowledge, and good judgement; the ability to recognize or judge what is true, right, or lasting, coupled with right execution. Wisdom is also the ability to use knowledge and understanding. All three of these qualities work hand in hand. But what makes all three effectual is proper application. (2, 4)

Wise = having or showing experience, knowledge, and good judgement; the ability to recognize or judge what is true, right, or lasting; judicious or prudent. (2, 3, 6, 9)

NOTES:

THE HOLY UNITY OF THE RICH AND THE POOR

UNITY = the state or quality of being one. (Heading)

RICH = having a great deal of money or property; material wealth. (Heading)

POOR = having little or no wealth and few or no possessions. (Heading)

In today's society, we have been trained to believe that the only way we can advance is by embracing the "dog-eat-dog" philosophy perpetuated for centuries by Western philosophers, politicians, religious leaders, etc. But Noble Drew Ali gives us an example of his profundity (great knowledge and insight) with Chapter 27. He informs us that something of a higher force has graced the rich men with his possessions. Instructions 1-8 demonstrates benevolence in the man with riches as it has afforded him the ability to serve humanity.

Instructions 9-14 are given as a warning to the rich and avarice. These instructions are signposts as to what should be avoided and the repercussions thereof.

Instructions 15-21 demonstrate the true riches which belong to the poor. We are instructed to find comfort in what we possess and why. But in order for comfort to be afforded to the poor, they must look upon what he has at present and be content.

The final instruction (22) shows "the Holy *Unity* of the Rich and the Poor" and that *Unity* is demonstrated in the providence of ALLAH, as He distributes His Divine Care and Guardianship to the righteousness of the rich as he does the works of ALLAH and the poor who is in a constant state of gratitude to ALLAH for what he has been given.

Abundance = a great or plentiful amount; a lot. (9)

Acquirements = something that is acquired especially an attainment. In this instance, wealth. (21)

Affordeth = allows; provides. (2)

Anxiety = distress or uneasiness of mind caused by fear of danger or misfortunes. (13)

Aright = rightly; correctly; properly. (1)

Assisteth = to give support or aid to; help. (5)

Benevolence = goodwill; desire to do good to others. (8)

Blameless = without blame or fault; free from or not deserving blame; guiltless.

→ *"and his joy is blameless,"* he doesn't have to feel guilty for experiencing joy. It is innocent and worthy of joy. (8)

Calamities = great misfortunes or distress; misery. (13)

Checked = measured. (8)

Clamours = clamor; a vehement expression of desire or dissatisfaction; a loud uproar, as from a crown of people. **Vehement** = showing strong feeling. (17)

Clamours of solicitations = outcries of discontent from those who may want handouts or better conditions – he is not teased, taunted, not burdened with the "Clamours of solicitations." (17)

Comfort = a state of ease and satisfaction of bodily wants, with freedom from pain and anxiety. (15)

Comparison = the act of comparing. (14)

Compassion = deep awareness of the suffering of another coupled with the wish to relieve it. (4)

THE HOLY UNITY OF THE RICH AND THE POOR

Contentment = a source of satisfaction; ease of mind. (21)

Continual fear = perpetual fear because of one's own ill will. (13)

Curse = the cause of evil, misfortune, or trouble. (13)

Dainties = pleasing to the taste and, often, temptingly served, or delicate. (18)

Debarred = shut out or excluded from a place or condition; prohibit.

→ *"Debarred from the dainties of the rich,"* to be debarred is to be excluded, from the dainties – the delicacies or refinements of the rich. Not having the spoils that the rich people possess also excludes you from the illnesses that may come with them. (18)

Defraudeth them not = does not cheat them. (7)

Dependents = persons who depend on or need someone or something for aid, support, favor, etc. (17)

Desires = wants; to wish or long for something; crave. (13, 21)

Despondence = to become discouraged; depression of spirits from loss of courage or hope. (22)

Devourers = one who swallows or eats up hungrily, voraciously, or ravenously. (16)

Dispenseth = to deal out or distribute in parts or portions; to administer. (22)

Distinguished = set apart as different; marked off as different.

→ *"highly distinguished,"* having extreme and above ordinary distinction so as to stand out from the rest of those around him. (1)

Distress = great pain, anxiety, or sorrow; acute (intense) physical or mental suffering. (12)

Downy = made of down; fluffy; soft. (20)

Draughts = draft; something that is taken in by drinking or inhaling; a drink. (19)

Embarrassed = made to feel self-conscious, or ill at ease; ashamed; discontent. (17)

Employ = to put to use or service; to put to work. (1)

Employed = hired or engaged in services; provided employment.

→ *"and the labor is employed,"* means that the working people are employed. (6)

Encourageth = to give support; promote. (5)

Flatterers = ones who try to please by complimentary remarks or attention; the act of praising or complementing insincerely, effusively, or excessively. (16)

Fortune = success. (8)

Gnawings = persistent, dull pains. (14)

Grandeur = the quality or state of being grand and impressive; nobility or greatness of character; high rank or social importance. (21)

Grief = strong mental suffering or painful state; misery, mental pain; torment. (12)

Grindeth = to oppress, torment, or crush. (9)

Hardened = made unfeeling, unsympathetic, or callous. (12)

Hath = have or has. (1, 15)

Heapeth up = to pile up. (9)

Humility = the quality or state of being humble; modest opinion of one's importance or rank; meekness. (21)

THE HOLY UNITY OF THE RICH AND THE POOR

Impression = a strong effect produced on the intellect, feeling, conscience, etc. In this instance, the suffering and grief faced by those less fortunate have no effect on his heart. (12)

Improvement = brought into a more valuable or desirable condition.

→ "*and the arts receive improvement,*" they will produce better and profitable results. (6)

Ingenuity = the quality of being cleverly inventive or resourceful; inventiveness. (5)

Iniquity = gross immorality or injustice; wickedness.

→ "*but the curse of iniquity pursueth him,*" iniquity is injustice, wickedness, or immorality and it follows him everywhere he goes. (13)

Injured = hurt; impaired. (3)

Inquireth = to ask information by asking questions; investigate. (4)

Joy = a cause of great pleasure and happiness; an emotion. (8)

Judgments = the ability to judge, make a decision, or form an opinion objectively, authoritatively, and wisely, especially in matters affecting action; good sense. (4)

Labor = working people; work force. (6)

Labor = physical or mental exertion, especially when difficult or exhausting; work. (20)

Liberally = liberal; freely; without restraints or prejudices. (5)

Luxurious = very comfortable; elegant and expensive; giving pleasure to the senses; rich. (19)

Means = available resources. (2)

Merit = a quality deserving praise or approval' virtue; demonstrated ability or achievement; an aspect of character or behavior deserving approval. (5)

Mighty = powerful or strong. (3)

Mind = the faculty of thinking, reasoning, and applying knowledge. (8)

Miseries = mental or emotional unhappiness or distress; suffering. (14)

Morsel = a small amount of food.

→ "*He sitteth down to his morsel in peace,*" he is able to enjoy his humble meal or his small possessions in peace, without schemers plotting to get a piece. (16)

Objects = persons to which thought, or action is direction. (4)

Oppress = treat in a very harsh and unfair way. (3)

Oppression = the exercise of authority or power in a burdensome, cruel, or unjust manner.

→ "*He driveth on oppression,*" the greedy and selfish urges on oppression. (10)

Orphan = a child who has lost both parents through death. (11)

Ostentation = pretentious display which is intended to impress others. **Pretentious** = trying to impress other people by showing off for their approval. (4)

Peculiarly = distinct from all others; special; unique. (1)

Peculiarly favored = one who is looked upon with grace and possesses a special quality that makes him/her stand out from all the rest. (1)

Pleasure = a feeling of happy satisfaction and enjoyment. (2)

Poverty = a condition of being poor; lack of the basic material goods. (14, 22)

Preserveth = to keep up; maintain. (20)

Presume = to take for granted; to take unwarranted advantage of. (22)

Procureth = to bring about; effect. (And brings about calmness or peace of mind). (20)

Promoteth = to contribute to the progress or growth of; further. (5)

Providence = divine care and guardianship; God, especially when conceived as omnisciently directing the universe and the affairs of humankind with wise benevolence. (22)

Rapacious = very greedy. (13)

Rejoice = to feel or show great joy or delight. (15)

Reliveth = to lessen or remove pain, distress, or difficulty; to free. (4)

Repose = the act of resting or the state of being at rest; freedom from worry; peace of mind; calmness; tranquility. (20)

Rewardeth = to make return for or requite (service, merit, etc.).

→ *"He assisteth and rewardeth merit,"* where he sees virtue and righteousness in a person, he takes special notice and promotes it for the benefit of all. (5)

Ruin = destruction. (10)

Schemes = a systematic plan for achieving a particular aim; a plan of action. (6)

Seeketh = to go in search or quest of. **Quest** = to search or seek for; pursue. (4)

Sloth = laziness. (20)

Solicitations = entreaty, urging, or importunity; a petition or request; to request. **Importunity** = to bother someone with persistent requests. **Entreaty** = an earnest or emotional request. (17)

Suffereth not = does not allow or permit; does not tolerate. (3)

Superfluities = an excessive amount. (7)

Teased = irritated or provoked with persistent petty distractions, trifling raillery, or other annoyance; trouble; disturb. (17)

Therefore = for that reason, consequently. (22)

Thereof = of the thing just mentioned; of that or it; from that. (9)

Vengeance = infliction of punishment in return for a wrong; retribution; the desire of revenge. (13)

Wants = wishes, desires, needs, etc. (4)

Wealth = a large amount of money, property, or possessions. (2, 12, 21)

Widow = a woman who has lost her husband by death and has not remarried. (11)

Woe = used to express sorrow or dismay; trouble. (But trouble unto him). (9)

NOTES:

HOLY INSTRUCTIONS FROM THE PROPHET
* MASTER AND SERVANT *

MASTER = an employer of workers or servants, **Employer** = a person that employs (hires) one or more people for wages or salary. (Heading, 3, 6)

SERVANT = a person employed to perform domestic duties in a household for a person. (Heading, 3, 6)

Admonitions = counsel; cautionary advice or warning; a gentle reproof. (8)

Advantages = benefits. (1)

Affairs = something done or to be done; personal business; concern. (4)

Appointment = the position to which one has been appointed. (1)

Art = are. (6)

Authority = the power to command, enforce laws, exact (demand or require) obedience, determine or judge. (8)

Cares = responsibilities; also, a state of mind in which one is troubled. (1)

Cheerfully = pleasantly; happily. (9)

Command love = to *make* someone love you, it can't be done! (7)

Create = give rise to; produce. (7)

Defraud = cheat. (5)

Diligence = constant and earnest effort to accomplish what is undertaken; persistent. (9)

Diligent = constant in effort to accomplish something; persistent; industrious.

→ *"be diligent in his affairs,"* be persistent and earnest (sincere) in the master's endeavors or work. (4)

Expecteth = require or demand something because it is appropriate or a person's duty. (6)

Fail = failure as to performance, accuracy, etc.

→ *"and fail thou not,"* this is directed to the master; reward the servant accordingly. (9)

Faithful = remaining loyal; worthy. (4)

Faithfully = steady in allegiance or affection; loyal; constant; reliable. (4, 9)

Fidelity = faithfulness to obligations, duties, promises, or observances. (2, 9)

Gratitude = the quality or feeling of being grateful or thankful. (9)

Hath = have or has. (1)

Honor = high respect; esteem; great privilege. (2)

Interests = involvement with or participation in something; a business, cause, etc., in which a person has a share, concern, or responsibility. (4)

Just = fair; impartial. (6)

Motive = something that causes a person to act in a certain way, do a certain thing, etc.; inventive. (9)

Obedience = the act or practice of obeying; dutifully complying with the commands, orders, or instructions of one in authority. (2, 6)

Obey = to carry out or fulfill the command, order, or instruction of; to behave obediently. (9)

Patient = the ability to accept or tolerate delay, trouble, difficulty, provocation, annoyance, or suffering without becoming angry or upset; understanding. (3)

Pleasure = enjoyment. (8)

Ready = complete. (6)

Reason = logical thinking; good judgments; intelligence. (8)

Reasonable = not excessive or extreme; fair and sensible. (6)

Rebuketh = to criticize or reprimand sharply; to express sharp, stern disapproval. (3)

Repine = to be discontented or low in spirits; complain or fret. (1)

Reposeth = places; to place your confidence or trust in a person. (4)

Reproofs = act of reproving, censuring, or rebuking. **Reproving** = to criticize, or correct someone; reprimand. (3)

Resignation = an accepting, unresisting attitude, state, etc.; compliance; submission. (3)

Rigour = rigor; strictness, severity, or harshness, as in dealing with people. (7)

Servitude = the state of subjugation to an owner or master. (1)

Severity = an instance of strict or severe behavior, punishment, etc.; harsh in treating others. (7)

Solicitudes = causes of anxiety, worries, or concerns in life. (1)

Spirit = "*The spirit of man is in him,*" the same spirit that is in the master is also in the servant, he is a human being and not a beast of burden. (7)

State = the condition of someone or something at a particular time; position. (1)

Studious = characterized by steady attention and effort. Pay close attention to the interest of the master. (4)

Submission = the act of submitting to the power or authority of another; the state of being submissive or compliant; humble. (2)

Thee = you.

Therefore = for that reason; consequently. (3)

Thereof = of the thing just mentioned; of that or it; from that. (5)

Thou = you.

Thy = your.

Unto = to

Virtues = moral excellence and righteousness; goodness. (2)

NOTES:

MAGISTRATE AND SUBJECT

MAGISTRATE = a civil officer with power to administer and enforce law; someone in a position of authority over others. (Heading)

SUBJECT = a person who is under the dominion or rule of a sovereign; a person under the control or influence of another. (Heading)

Abilities = skills or talents. (6)

Abound = well supplied; overflowing. (11)

Affection = a tender feeling toward another; fondness, devotion, or love. (16)

Art = are. (2)

Artists = a person who practices one of the fine arts, especially a painter or sculptor. (10)

Arts = the quality, production, expression, or realm, according to aesthetic principles of what is beautiful, appealing, or of more than ordinary significance. Also, a branch of learning or university study, especially one of the fine arts or the humanities, as music, philosophy, or literature. (8)

Begetteth = to cause to exist or occur; produce. (16)

Bosom = the chest of a human being; the chest is considered the source of emotion. (7)

Bounty = a premium or reward, especially one offered by the government; a generous gift. (10)

Business = work to be done or things to be attended to. (4)

Cause = a goal or principle served with dedication; the interests of one engaged in a struggle. (18)

Chaff = the husks of grains and grasses that are separated during threshing; worthless matter. (18)

Clothed in Purple = the color purple is symbolic for imperial, regal, royalty, or other high rank. Wearing clothes of this color represent such rank in ancient times. (2)

Colonies = a place where a group of people with a common interest live together. (11)

Commerce = the buying and selling of goods, especially on a large scale, as between different countries, or between different parts of the same country. (10)

Consulteth = to seek guidance or information from; to exchange views; confer. **Confer** = have discussions.

→ *"he consulteth among them with freedom,"* is to get advice from, or refer to. A good ruler will do this freely, openly, and often with the wise men of his kingdom, instead of making all decisions on his own without their input. (5)

Convenience = anything that serves or simplifies work, adds to one's ease or comfort, etc. (11)

Culture = special training and development; cultivate. "The sciences improve beneath the *'cultivation'* of his hand." (8)

Deceiveth him not = does not practice deceit. He keeps it real and sincere and is trustworthy. (7)

Delighteth = something that gives great pleasure or joy. (9)

Delivereth = saves; to set free. (14)

Dignity = elevated rank, office, or station.

→ *"the dignity and height of thy station,"* refers to the respect, the nobility, the honor, as well as the utmost prestige, of one's office; the respect and honor associated with an important position (station). (1)

Discernment = the act or process of exhibiting (displaying) keen insight and good judgment; to distinguish mentally; recognize as distinct or different. (6)

Dominion = a territory, usually considerable size, in which a single rulership holds sway. (3)

Dwelling = to live in or at a specific place; reside. (9)

Employeth = to hire or engage the services of; put to work. (6)

Emulation = effort or desire to equal or excel (surpass) others. (9)

Encircle = surround. (19)

Endanger = to expose to harm or danger. "Endanger not" means that the ill planning of enemies are not cause of danger to the wise ruler because the people of whom he rules over know him well and he has their support. (17)

Enemies = one who feels hatred toward, intends injury to, or opposes another; foe. (17)

Enricheth = to make fuller, more meaningful, or more rewarding; to add fertilizer to; to add nutrients to. (10)

Ensigns = a badge of office or power; a sign, emblem, or token usually representing an office or rank. (Crown, sceptre, purple clothing, etc., are ensigns). (2)

Equity = the quality of being just, fair, and impartial. (12)

Exalted = to raise in rank, character, or status; elevate. (9)

Extendeth = to stretch or spread (something) out to greater or fullest length. (10)

Evolveth = to develop gradually.

→ *"he evolveth high things,"* is to say he *devises* and *develops* benevolent and prosperous ideas for the welfare of his kingdom. (4)

Faithful = remaining loyal; worthy. (18)

Farmer = one who works on or operates a farm. (10)

Favor = friendly or well-disposed regard; goodwill; to aid or support. (10)

Favorite of his bosom = the one in whom the ruler has placed trust and confidence. (7)

Firm = constant; steadfast; stable; fixed; not subject to change. **Steadfast** = resistant to externally applied pressure; solid; immutable. **Immutable** = not subject to change or susceptible to change; not changing your attitude or aims. (18)

Flieth = to run away. (18)

Flourish = grow or develop in a healthy or vigorous way. (8)

Foundeth = to set up or establish on a firm basis or for enduring existence. (13)

Frameth = form, constitution, or structure in general; to contrive, devise, or compose, as a plan, law, or poem.

→ *"He frameth his statues with equity and wisdom,"* to frame is to shape, to contrive, to construct, to put together – his statues are the rules, law, or decrees that have the force of law. These rules/decrees, or laws are constructed, put together by the ruler with equity (fairness and impartiality) and wisdom (sound judgment, prudence). (12)

Glory = magnificence; great beauty. (19)

Grandeur = high rank or social importance; the quality or state of bring grand and impressive; nobility or greatness of character. (4)

Guardian = a person who is legally responsible for the care and management of a person or property of another person. In this instance, a guardian of the people. (15)

Harbors = a part of a body of water along the shore deep enough for anchoring a ship and so situated with respect to coastal features, whether natural or artificial, as to provide protection from winds, waves, and currents; any place of shelter or refuge. (11)

Heaven = *"the favorite of heaven,"* is a figurative phase in reference to the individual that most people in a society trust above all others to lead them. He is the favorite among Moors. (1)

Honoreth = to give recognition or glory to; respect. (10)

Impartial = treating everyone or everything equally; not biased; unprejudiced. (13)

Improvements = advancements; changes or additions by which something is improved.

→ *"the improvements of the scholar,"* a scholar is one who is well learned, knowledgeable, and schooled. In other words, the things that the scholar helps to improve with his enlightenment are his contributions to educate and better the kingdom. (10)

Increaseth = to become greater or larger. (11)

Ingenious = characterized by cleverness or originality of invention; cleverly inventive or resourceful. (9)

Ingenuity = the *quality* of being cleverly inventive or resourceful; cleverness or skillfulness of conception or design. (10)

Investeth = to cover, adorn, or envelop. **Adorn** = make more attractive or beautiful; decorate. **Envelop** = cover or surround completely. (2)

Just = fair. (7)

Kindleth = to stir up.

→ *"he kindleth in their breasts emulation,"* to "kindle" in one's breast, is to *ignite* or *arouse* or to stir up in somebody's heart the desire, the effort, and the ambition to excel, to do better and better: and the entire kingdom will shine more and more, the glory will be raised higher and higher by their work to excel. (9)

Kingdom = a territory or domain (area) controlled by a ruler. (2)

Labors = a job or task done or to be done; productive activity, especially for the sake of economic gain. (9)

Learned = connected or involved with the pursuit of knowledge, especially of a scholarly nature. (9)

Machinations = crafty schemes or plots, especially artfully or with evil purpose.

→ *"the machinations of his enemies endanger not the state,"* the evil plots or sinister schemes of his enemies are not a danger or a threat to the subjects of the ruler. Such machinations rarely exist. (17)

Magistrates = civil officers with power to administer and enforce law. (7)

Majesty = supreme power; supreme greatness or authority; impressive beauty. (2)

Merchant = a person who buys and sells commodities for profit; a store keeper or retailer. (10)

Mercy = compassion; kindness. (13)

Merits = demonstrated ability or achievement; worth. (6)

Ministers = persons appointed to some high office of state, especially to that of head of an administrative department. (7)

Murmurs = an indistinct, whispered, or confidential complaint; a quiet complaint; a mutter. (17)

Object = purpose. (16)

Observance = the act or practice of following, obeying, or conforming to. (12)

Offenders = one that breaks a law. (13)

Opinions = judgment based on special knowledge and given by an expert. (5)

Oppressors = one's seeking to keep down either politically, religiously, or economically another group of people or a nation by the use of force or authority. (14)

Principle of Mercy = showing kind and compassionate treatment to a person under one's power; a disposition to be kind and forgiving. (13)

Restraineth = he prevents oppressors from laying their hands down, and he pulls his subjects free from the oppressors' rule over them. (14)

Reverence = a feeling of *deep respect* tinged with awe; veneration. (15)

Rewardeth = something given or received in recompense (reward) for worthy behavior. (10)

Ruler = a person who rules or governs. (1)

Sceptre = scepter; a rod (staff) or wand held in the hand as an emblem of regal or imperial authority. (2)

Scholar = a learned erudite person, especially one who has profound knowledge of a particular subject. (10)

Science = a branch of knowledge or study dealing with a body of facts or truths systematically arranged and showing the operation of general laws; example: the mathematical sciences.

→ *"the sciences improve beneath the culture of his hand,"* sciences can be any of the various branches of learning as in literature, mathematics, arts, chemistry, etc. Under the care of a wise ruler, these sciences are improved. (8)

Searcheth = explore; look. (4)

Security = freedom from risk or danger; safety. (19)

Smileth = a pleasant or favorite disposition or aspect; to regard with favor or approval. (8)

Sovereign = having supreme rank, power, or authority; one with complete authority and say so. (1)

Statues = a permanent law or rule established by a government of a country, community, etc., to govern its internal affairs. (12)

Strict = characterized by or acting in close conformity to requirements or principles; stringent or exacting in or in enforcing rules, requirements, obligations, etc.; rigorous in discipline. (13)

Temples = in this instance, the "temples" is made in reference to the flattened region on either side of the forehead in human beings. (2)

Therefore = for that reason; consequently. (15)

Thine = yours; that which belongs to you. (2)

Thou = you. (1)

MAGISTRATE AND SUBJECT

Thy = your. (1)

Tyranny = undue (excessive) severity or harshness; rigor. (14)

Tyrant = a ruler who exercises power in a harsh cruel manner; an oppressive person. (18)

Unto = to.

Welfare = the good fortune, health, happiness, prosperity, etc., of a person, group, or organization.

→ *"The glory of a king is the welfare of his people,"* implies that pride, or the cause of a ruler's "shine" – his glory – comes from how well his tribe is doing; how they prosper; how they are educated; how their spiritual development is going; his power is based on how they feel about him in their hearts. (3)

Wisdom = the quality of having experience, knowledge, and good judgment; the ability to recognize or judge what is true, right, or lasting; insight; common sense. (12)

Wise = having or showing experience, knowledge, and good judgment; the ability to discern (recognize) or judge what is true, right, or lasting; exhibiting common sense; judicious or prudent. (5, 7)

NOTES:

SOCIAL = living or disposed to live in companionship with others or in a community, rather than in isolation; of or pertaining to the life, welfare, and relations of human beings in a community. (Heading)

DUTIES = things ones are expected or required to do by moral or legal obligations. (Heading)

→ First and foremost, it is imperative that we understand that society as it exists today is not of our own making. I am fully aware of the fact that since we are constantly bombarded with images of a decadent society, with people that phenotypically resemble us, we are led to believe that this is our true way of living. We fail to realize that in all actuality we are the outcome of something greater at work. We have been forced to live in a society of Western (European) principles that was formed for the benefit of those in power and to the detriment of those ruled. What we are doing is returning to our roots, by way of the Prophet of ALLAH. Church and state may be separate for Western-man, but for the Moorish-man, it is one and the same. To our ancient forefathers and foremothers, there was no such separation. That is a Western (European) concept and therefore we are returning it to its proper owners, while we are returning to our own. Before they were, we already existed and had blessed the world with civilizations before there was any such concept for them. It was us (Asiatics) who extended civilization into their realms and brought about order out of chaos.

We must bear in mind that every individual living in a society has responsibilities allotted to them and these responsibilities must be preserved if said society is to flourish. The springboard for a successful society is not based on the individual, per se, but on the collective, on each individual living accordingly and willing to make the needed sacrifices for the benefit of all. Sacrifice is the foundation of a society. ALLAH has blessed us by placing us within the bands of society. The purpose for this blessing was not that we become burdens upon one another, but rather that we may grow as a whole; a unit where every individual partakes in the benefit of the next: "It takes a village to raise a child." ALLAH sent His Prophet Noble Drew Ali to bring us back into the folds of society that we may live a righteous life. For us to live righteously, the Prophet brought us social duties, certain responsibilities, that as we look within ourselves, we may be able to note that our well-being, enjoyments, and our protection from injuries is co-dependent upon our society operating with a sense of guidance, that at the end, we can proudly shout "I am we," when asked for our identity. The Holy Koran of the Moorish Science Temple of America is our constitution, our cornerstone upon which we are to build our society. Let the light (consciousness) shine forth that all who have eyes to see may follow.

Acknowledge = to show or express recognition or realization of; to show or express appreciation or gratitude for. (1)

Assistance = support or aid; help. (1)

Bands = a company of persons joined, acting, or functioning together as a whole with a common interest. (1)

Beholdeth = regard; take into account. (1)

Benevolent = kindhearted; characterized by or expressing goodwill or kindly feelings; one who has the desire to help others. (3)

HOLY INSTRUCTIONS FROM THE PROPHET
* THE SOCIAL DUTIES *

Breast = figuratively speaking, the mind. (4)

Comforts = conditions or feelings of ease, well-being, pleasure, and contentment. (1)

Comprehendeth = understand; perceive. (7)

Confer = give; to bestow upon. (1)

Considereth = to think carefully about, especially in order to make a decision; contemplate, ponder, study, or examine. (1)

Desire = wish; a strong feeling that impels one to attain something that is seemingly within reach. (6)

Duty = something that one is expected or required to do. (2)

Ease = freedom from difficulty, pain, worry, distress; relaxation or comfort. (4)

Endeavoreth = to exert oneself to do or effect something; make an effort; strive. (7)

Endowed = provided or supplied with a talent, ability, faculty, or quality. (1)

Enjoyeth = to take pleasure in; experience joy. (4)

Enjoyments = feelings of pleasure and satisfaction; something that gives pleasure. (1)

Failings = acts or instances of falling short of success or achievement in something expected or desired; weaknesses. (5)

Faults = defects or imperfections; flaws; character weaknesses. (5)

Friend = a person whom one knows, trusts, and has a bond of mutual affection; supporter. (2)

Friendly = kind and pleasant; warm, comforting, or helpful. (2)

Generosity = kindness; amplitude; freely giving or sharing; unselfishness. (7)

Goodness = kindness, moral excellence. (1)

Honored = the privilege of receiving a favor from a respected person, group, organization, etc.; shown a courteous regard for. (1)

Humanity = the human race.

→ *"O son of humanity,"* is directed towards the individual but at the same time is letting him/her know that it is much bigger than him/her. It is about the relationship between the individual and humanity. (1)

Imperfections = flaws. (1)

Injuries = wrong or injustices; harm.

→ Injury denotes a wrong done or suffered, and is used for any kind of evil, impairment or loss, caused or sustained. (1)

Interest = benefit; advantage; self-interest. (2)

Largeness = being broadminded, understanding, and tolerant. (7)

Mankind = the human race. (2)

Mutual = having the same relationship each to the other; directed and received in the equal amount; reciprocal. (1)

Nature = the particular combination of qualities belonging to a person, animal, *thing*, or class by birth, origin, or constitution; native or inherent character. In this instance, the inherent constitution of the rose. (3)

Obligations = acts of binding oneself by a social or moral tie; a binding sense of duty. (1)

Occasions = particular times, especially marked by certain circumstances or occurrences; opportunities. (6)

Oppression = cruel and unjust treatment. (6)

Oweth = to have a moral obligation to do; to be under the obligation to do. (1)

Pleasures = feelings of happy satisfaction and enjoyment. (1)

Produceth = to bring forth or into existence; give rise to; cause; exhibit. (3)

Promote = to contribute to the progress or growth of; further; support or actively encourage. (7)

Prosperity = a successful, flourishing, or thriving condition. (4)

Protection = the act of protecting or the state of being protected. **Protect** = to defend or guard from attack, insult, injury, etc.; to shield. (1)

Receive = to have (something) bestowed, conferred, etc. (1)

Reciprocal = given, performed, experienced, or felt by both sides; mutual. (1)

Rejoiceth = to feel or show great joy or delights. (4)

Relieveth = to alleviate the pain of (in this instance, from the heart (mind) of the benevolent man). (6)

Researcheth = investigate or inquire; careful study. (6)

Rose = any of the wild or cultivated, usually prickly-stemmed, pinnate-leaved flowered shrubs of the genus rosa; the flower of any such shrub, of a red, pink, white, or yellow flower. (3)

Slander = defamation; a malicious, false, and defamatory statement or report. **Defamation** = to attack the good name or reputation of someone; slander or libel. (5)

Society = a group of individuals living as members of a community and possessing the same objective. (1)

Speech = the faculty or act of speaking; ability to express one's thoughts, feelings, or perceptions by the articulation of words. (1)

Sweetness = the quality or state of being pleasing or fresh to the sense of smell. (3)

Thee = you.

Therefore = for that reason; consequently. (2)

Thereof = of the thing just mentioned; of that or it; from that. (6)

Thou = you.

Thy = your.

Tranquility = the quality or state of being tranquil; free from commotion or disturbance; peacefulness of mind; calm. (4)

Wants = areas in which one is deficient in; to be lacking or absent. **Deficient** = lacking some element, characteristic or quality. (1)

NOTES:

JUSTICE = the principle of moral righteousness; equity; the quality of being just; fairness; conformity to moral rightness in action or attitude; the upholding of what is JUST, especially fair treatment and due reward in accordance with honor, standards, or law. (Heading)

Advantage = to benefit; gain or profit from someone who does not know better. Even if a person does not know better, you're not supposed to take advantage of him because *you* know better. (Always be fair and just in your dealings). (11)

Allure = to attract or tempt by something flattering or desirable; entice. (4)

Aright = rightly; correctly; properly. (2)

Assured = sure; certain; guaranteed. (9)

Atone = to make up for a wrongdoing or error one has committed (done). (7)

Bear = to support; spread. Don't support lies, rumors or falsehood against people, and don't initiate it. (5)

Betray = to be unfaithful or disloyal to someone especially a friend; to be a traitor; to lead astray (mislead); to deceive. To reveal a secret told in confidence. **Traitor** = a person who betrays a friend group, organization, country, etc. (a sellout). Be assured, it is *less* evil in the sight of ALLAH to *steal* than to *betray*! (9)

Bosom = the chest of a human being. The chest is considered the source of emotion. (6)

Bounds = within reasonable limits; limit or boundary; something that limits, confines, or restraints. (2)

Cast = do not direct your eye on someone else's property with bad intent. (3)

Character = a person's good reputation; the qualities he has, such as morals, principles of Honor and Integrity.

→ "Defame him not in his character," do not slander a person's name or their reputation. (5)

Conscience = moral guidance; the inner feeling or voice of what is right or wrong in one's conduct or motives urging you to choose *right* over wrong! Awareness. (11)

Corrupt = to cause to be dishonest or disloyal, especially by bribery. (6)

Credit = a sum of money owed to a person; loan. (If someone *lends* you something, they *expect* it back). (12)

Debts = something owed, such as money, good, or services. (12)

Deceive = to cause someone to believe something that is not true by misleading them; to mislead by a false appearance or statement; trick. **Trick** = an act or scheme intended to deceive or outwit someone. (9)

Defame = to attack the good name or reputation of someone; slander or libel. (5)

Defraud = to deprive (withhold) someone's money; to take something by fraud or swindle. Don't cheat anyone out of their money, property, etc. (2)

Desires = longing or craving, as for things that bring satisfaction or enjoyment. (2)

Due = something that is owed or deserved; something that is owed or naturally belongs to someone. (12)

Enjoyment = a feeling of pleasure and satisfaction; delight or gratification; something that gives pleasure. (1)

Evil = morally bad or wrong; wicked; harmful; malevolent; sinful. (3)

Examine = to observe carefully or critically; inspect; to study or analyze. (13)

Excite = to arouse or stir up (emotion or feeling). To excite a person to anger. (4)

Faithful = worthy of trust or belief; reliable, consistent with truth; loyal. (9)

Forsake = to quit or leave entirely; abandon (someone or something). (7)

Grief = strong mental suffering or painful state; misery, mental pain; torment. (7)

Hath = have or has. (13)

Hazard = danger. (4)

Honor = personal Integrity; high respect; good name; reputation. He relieth on your word. (Word is Bond). **Integrity** = the quality of being honest and having strong moral principles; moral uprightness. (12)

Ignorance = lack of knowledge or information, or awareness in general; uneducated. (11)

Impartial = the act of treating everyone equally; fair and just. (Also see the definition of "*Just*" in this chapter). (8)

Injury = a form of hurt, damage, or loss. A wrong or injustice done or suffered. (7)

Just = honorable and fair in one's dealings and actions; consistent with what is morally right and fair. The word "*Just*" also implies to the

following words in this chapter: Impartial and Justice. (8)

Justice = righteousness, equitable, or moral rightness; just conduct, dealing, or treatment.

→ "*The peace of society dependeth on justice*," in order for any society to experience any degree of peace, there must be justice; law, order, fairness. (1)

Laboring = the act of working or striving towards a goal; the working man. (10)

Mean = offensive, selfish, unkind, spiteful, or cruel. (12)

Moderation = the act of being moderate; being within reasonable limits; not excessive or extreme. (2)

Oppress = to persecute or subjugate by force; to keep down by severe and unjust use of force or authority. **Persecute** = subject to harassment or cruel treatment, because of religion, race, or beliefs. **Subjugate** = to bring under complete control; conquer, master, or enslave. (10)

Peace = a state of harmony between people; freedom from quarrels and disagreement; quiet and calm; serenity. (To maintain law and order). (1)

Possessions = things owned or possessed. Things that belong to you; personal property that you own. (1)

Power = ability to do or act; capability of doing or accomplishing something.

→ to the most of your ability. "*To the utmost of thy power*," do the most you can possibly do that is within you to get something done. In this instance, to correct your wrongs. (13)

Provocation = the act of provoking; to stir up; instigate; urge on; to anger. (4)

Relieth = to depend on someone with full trust or confidence. (12)

Relieve = to free from pain or distress. (7)

Remembrance = the act of recalling or remembering something; memory. (13)

Reparation = the act or process of correcting a wrong one has committed (done); compensation or restitution for a loss, damage, or injury of any kind. (7)

Sacred = secured from violation; free from danger or harm; safe from your touch. (3)

Satisfied = pleased; content; satisfied with what you have, and not wishing for more. (11)

Servant = one who labors (works) for or serves another; a person employed by another, especially to perform domestic duties. (6)

Society = a group of individuals living as members of a community; human beings collectively. (1)

Speedy = fast, quick, promptly. (13)

Tempt = to entice or allure; to get someone to do something wrong, unwise, or immoral; seduce; test. (6)

Temptation = a desire to do something wrong, unwise, or immoral; to tempt or entice; allurements, enticements which draws one away from *righteousness*. (4)

Thee = you.

Thine = your.

Thou = you.

Thy = your.

Transgressed = to act in violation of the law; offend; to go beyond or above a limit or boundary; to sin. (13)

Unjust = violating the principles of Justice or Fairness; unfair, faithless, or dishonest. (The opposite of Just). (12)

Unto = to. (8)

Utmost = do the most that you can possibly do. The greatest or most extreme extent or amount. (13)

NOTES:

CHARITY = generous actions or donations to aid the poor, ill, or helpless; love for humanity; the act of giving or good will. (Heading)

Admonition = gentle reproof; cautionary advice or warning. (6)

Alleviate = to make easier to endure; lessen the severity of. (7)

Animosity = a feeling of strong dislike, ill will, or enmity that tents to display itself in action; active hatred. (8)

Anxieties = distress or uneasiness of mind caused by fear, danger, or misfortune; worries. (7)

Assisteth = to give support or aid; help. (3)

Benediction = an utterance of good wishes. (9)

Benefit = for the "good" of humanity. (2)

Benevolence = a desire to do good to others; goodwill; charitable acts. (1)

Breast = mind; the heart (symbolic for the mind). (1)

Censureth = an expression of strong disapproval or harsh criticism; to criticize severely; reprimand. (4)

Compassion = a feeling of deep sympathy and sorrow for another who is stricken by misfortune, accompanied by a strong desire to alleviate the suffering. (7)

Endeavoreth = to exert oneself to do or effect something; make an effort; strive; to attempt earnestly; try. (7)

Envy = a feeling of discontent or covetousness with regard to another's advantages, success, possessions, or qualities, etc. **Covetousness** = having or showing a great desire to possess something belonging to someone else. (4)

Excite = to arouse or stir up emotions or feelings; awaken. (7)

Fountain = point of origin. (2)

Fury = wild or violent anger; rage. (8)

Goodness = kindness; generosity. (2)

Grief = strong mental suffering or painful state; misery, mental pain; torment. (7)

Hath = have or has. (1)

Healeth = to bring to an end or conclusion, as conflicts between people or groups, usually with strong implication of restoring former amity; settle; reconcile. (8)

Injuries = wrong or injustices done or suffered; to treat unjustly or unfairly. (5)

Injustice = a wrong; an unjust or unfair act. (6)

Labor = efforts. (7)

Malevolence = the ability, state, or feeling of being malevolent; ill will towards others; malice; hatred. (See "*Malice*" below). (4)

Malice = a desire to inflict injury, harm, or suffering on another, either because of a hostile impulse or out of deep-seated meanness; ill will. (5)

Mankind = humanity. (2)

Mischief = a cause or source of harm, evil, or annoyance. (8)

Misfortunes = afflictions. (7)

HOLY INSTRUCTIONS FROM THE PROPHET
* CHARITY *

Produce = outcome; something that is produced; product or yield. (1)

Promoteth = to contribute to the progress or growth of; further; support or actively encourage. (9)

Prosperity = successful, flourishing, or thriving conditions; good fortune. (3)

Quarrels = angry arguments or disagreements, typically between people who are usually on good terms; a cause of dispute, complaint or hostile feelings. (8)

Rejoiceth = displaying great enthusiasm; to feel or show great joy or delight. (3)

Remembrance = memory; the act of recalling or remembering something. (5)

Requiteth = to repay an injury or insult.

→ *"but requiteth their injustice with a friendly admonition"* means that the wise man does not return injury for injury, or insult for insult, but rather as an individual who truly desires the best for others he returns a friendly admonition, or a gentle reproof even though a wrong has been done to him. (See *"Admonition"* above). (6)

Revenge = the act of inflicting hurt or harm on someone for an injury or wrong suffered at their hands; retaliation. (5)

Slanders = malicious, false, and defamatory statements or reports; defamation. **Defamation** = to attack the good name or reputation of someone; slander or libel. (4)

Sown = to sow, implant, introduce, or promulgate. (1)

Strife = violent or bitter conflict; lack of harmony; active hostility; competition or struggle between rivals; contention. (8)

Thereof = of the thing just mentioned; of that or it; from that. (1)

NOTES:

GRATITUDE = generous actions or donations to aid the poor, ill, or helpless; the quality of being thankful; readiness to show appreciation for and to return kindness. (Heading)

Acknowledgeth = to recognize (one's obligation towards another). (2)

Admiration = respect and warm approval; a feeling of wonder or pleasure. (5)

Amiable = having or showing pleasant, good-natured personal qualities; easy to get along with; friendly. (5)

Arose = originate (come from/out of); occur as a result of. (1)

Avarice = extreme greed for wealth or material gain; greedy. (6)

Avaricious = having or showing an extreme greed for wealth or material gain; very greedy. (6)

Benefactor = a person who gives a form of help or aid to a person or cause; kindly helper. (2, 5)

Benefit = something that is advantageous or good; an act of kindness, charity, or a kind deed. (1, 5)

Bosom = the deepest part of something.

→ The bosom (the mind) in this instance, symbolizes the one who takes in all manners of goodness extended to him/her but gives nothing in return. (4)

Branches = limbs of a tree. (1)

Breast = figuratively the mind. (3)

Cheerfulness = to deserve and receive (respect, sympathy, attention, etc.). (5)

Conceal = to hide; keep secret. (5)

Conferred = bestowed upon as a gift, favor for honor; contribute to. (5)

Delighteth = to find joy in. (1)

Envy = despise or be jealous of. (5)

Esteem = to regard highly or favorably with respect or admiration. (2)

Generosity = kindness; the quality of being kind and generous; freely giving or sharing; unselfishness. (5)

Grateful = warmly or deeply appreciative of benefits received; thankful. (1, 4)

Greediness = an excessive desire to acquire or possess more than one needs or deserves, especially possessions or wealth. (4, 6)

Heart = figuratively speaking the soul or mind. (4)

Herbage = non-woody vegetation; the succulent parts, leaves and stems, of herbaceous plants; the fleshy, often edible parts of plants. (4)

Humility = the quality or state of being humble; modest opinion of one's own importance or rank; meekness. (5)

Kindness = the state or quality of being kind; a friendly feeling.

→ *"he nourisheth the memory of it in his breast with kindness,"* means that if the recipient of a favor is unable to return said favor, he is forever mindful that there was one who extended his/her hand in his direction to assist him/her. The importance of this is that when ones are mindful of receiving favors, even though they may not be able to return said favor at the time, by the deed being kept fresh in the mind ones wouldn't hesitate to do for others as was done for them. (3)

CHAPTER XXXIII (33)
HOLY INSTRUCTIONS FROM THE PROPHET
* GRATITUDE *

Nourisheth = to cherish and keep alive; to promote the growth or development of.

→ If we are unable to reciprocate a favor we nourish it, sustain it, and hold it in our minds with a feeling of gratitude. (3)

Obligation = the act of binding oneself by a social, legal, or moral tie; a binding promise or sense of duty. (2, 6)

Oblige = to place under a debt of gratitude for some benefit, favor, or service. (5)

Obliged = to be the recipient of a service or favor. (5)

Pride = arrogant or disdainful conduct or treatment; conceit. (6)

Produceth = to bring into existence; give rise to; cause or bring forth.

→ *"produceth nothing"* is pointing out the characteristics of the selfish who are always willing to be the recipients of favors, blessings, and the likes, but refuse to extent the same favors upon others. Of these individuals we must stay clear from, for they are only out for self. (4)

Proud = feeling deep pleasure or satisfaction as a result of one's own qualities, possessions, or achievements; having or showing a very high opinion of oneself or one's importance. (6)

Root = a part of the body of a plant that develops, typically, from the radicle (root) and grows downward into the soil, anchoring the plant and absorbing nutriment and moisture. (1)

Sap = the watery fluid that circulates through a plant, carrying food and other substances to the various tissues. (1)

Satisfied = fulfilled.

→ *"the greediness of avarice shall never be satisfied,"* in a basic way, it is informing us that avarice is itself an illness. To have an insatiable greed for riches, or a desire for gain, is a pathological disorder. As we have seen countless times in our society, ones with such disorder as greed are never content. They have this weakness that even though they've gained much, still want more. Once they've gained more, they yet yearn for more. This is why we are instructed in our Moorish Holy Koran "that to be content [satisfied], is to be happy." (6)

Selfish = caring only or chiefly for oneself; concerned with one's own interest, welfare, etc., regardless of others. (6)

Shame = a painful feeling of humiliation or distress caused by the consciousness of wrong or foolish behavior; sense of guilt, embarrassment, unworthiness, or disgrace. (6)

Strive = struggle; try hard; to struggle in opposition. (5)

Ungrateful = not displaying gratitude; unappreciative. (4)

Vanity = lack of real value; hollowness; worthlessness. *"the vanity [worthlessness] of pride shall expose thee to shame."* (6)

Whence = from where; from the place, source, origin, cause of, etc. (1)

NOTES:

SINCERITY = the quality of being sincere; freedom from deceit, hypocrisy, or duplicity; probity (honesty) in intention or in communicating; truthful; pure in purpose. **Duplicity** = dishonest behavior that is intended to deceive. (Heading)

Adviseth = to offer counsel; give advice to or offer suggestions; recommend. (8)

Art = are. (14)

Betrayed = revealed or disclosed; to make known unintentionally. (11)

Blundereth = blunder: to make a gross mistake, especially through carelessness or mental confusion; to move or act blindly, or without direction or steady guidance; to utter thoughtlessly. (11)

Blusheth = to redden (in the face), as from embarrassment or shame; to feel shame or embarrassment. (3)

Business = the activities or endeavors of one's life. (9)

Caution = careful forethought. (7)

Character = having good qualities such as principles of honor, integrity, honesty, fortitude; good morals. (4)

Character = trait; an account of the qualities or peculiarities of a person or thing.

→ "*he laboreth for the character of a righteous man*," means that the hypocrite toils to display the qualities of a righteous man, all to no advantage, because there are those (children of wisdom) who see straight through the facade. (1, 3)

Charms = attracting or alluring characteristics; attractiveness; beauty. (1)

Consistent = constantly adhering to the same principles, course, form, etc. being steady and regular. (5)

Constancy = the quality of being unchanging or unwavering, as in purpose, love, or loyalty; firmness of mind; faithful and dependable. (1)

Courage = the quality of mind or spirit that enables a person to face difficulty, (in this instance to face the TRUTH), without fear. (5)

Crown = to reward; an exalting or chief attribute; the distinction that comes from a great achievement. (1)

Cunning = skill employed in a shrewd or sly manner, as in deceiving; cleverness. (13, 14)

Deceit = the act or practice of deceiving someone by concealing or misrepresenting the truth for the purpose of misleading; dishonesty. (2)

Deceive = to cause someone to believe something that is not true by misleading them; to mislead by a false appearance or statement; trick. **Trick** = an act or scheme intended to deceive or outwit someone. (9)

Derision = ridicule; to laugh at or make fun of. (14)

Dignity = bearing, conduct, or speech indicative of self-respect; the quality or state of being worthy of honor or respect; a sense of pride in oneself; self-respect. (4)

Discretion = the quality of being discreet, especially with reference to one's own actions or speech; judicious in one's speech.

→ The sincere will speak only when it is the opportune time to do so. And when he speaks, he uses discrimination on what is said. "The thoughtless man bridleth not his tongue; he speaketh at random and is entangled in the foolishness of his own words." ("Unto Thee I Grant," p. 4) "In all labor there is profit; But idle chatter leads only to poverty." (Proverbs 14:23). (7)

Disguise = something that serves or is intended for concealment of identity, character, or quality.

→ *"when in the midst of security, thy disguise is stripped off"* is referring to the time when the hypocrite thinks he is safe, in a false sense of security, his facade is revealed and is exposed for the hypocrite that he is. One thing we can rest assure, the hypocrite has it fixed in his heart that he can deceive anyone. It is at that time, when he relaxes his guard that he blunders into the light and is exposed for his true nature. (14)

Dissimulation = to conceal or disguise (one's thoughts, feelings, or character) under a false appearance; concealing one's true feelings or intentions.

→ *"He is far above the meanness of dissimulation,"* is informing us that the sincere man is beyond the smallness of mind (pettiness), or petty act of deception. As a man, he can stand tall and speak the TRUTH. His words are the thoughts of his heart (mind). There is no need for him to say one thing while meaning something else with the intent to deceive the hearer. There is no variance (conflict) between his words and his thoughts. (6)

Embarrassed = caused (someone) to feel awkward, self-conscious, or ashamed. (5)

Enamoured = enamored: to be in love with; filled or inflamed with love; charmed or captivated by.

→ I think it is important to note one specific point in instruction 1. When it states, *"O thou who are enamoured with the beauty of truth,"* it is making reference to someone already set apart. That individual is the sincere at heart who has an open mind and is willing to be the receptacle for the Truth. He is willing to open his mind and allow TRUTH to rush in unmolested. (1)

Exposed = uncovered; made visible to the eye; brought to light; revealed. (11)

Falsehood = the act of lying or making false statements, etc., intended to mislead the ignorant; something that is false. (3)

Fancieth = to imagine; to believe without being absolutely sure. (11)

Fidelity = faithfulness to obligations, duties, observances, or a person, demonstrated by continuing loyalty and support. In this instance the loyalty is to TRUTH. (1)

Fixed = set; clearly determined; established. (1)

Forsake = to give up (something held dear); renounce; leave entirely; abandon or desert. (1)

Founded = set up or established on a firm basis or for enduring existence. (3)

Hast = have.

Hath = have or has.

Honor = distinction; high respect.

→ *"the consistency of thy virtue shall crown thee with honor,"* means that one will be distinguished, or set apart from the hypocrite due to his holding firm and remaining strong to the virtue of TRUTH. (1)

HOLY INSTRUCTIONS FROM THE PROPHET
* SINCERITY *

Hypocrisy = a pretense of having a virtuous character, moral or religious principles, etc., that one does not really possess; pretending to be what one is not with the objective to deceive.

→ *"arts of hypocrisy,"* means the methods, skills, or craft of deception. In other words, the cunningness, or trickery of hypocrisy. There is an art form for all aspects of life, both negative and positive. Here it is the arts of hypocrisy. (4)

Hypocrite = a person who feigns some desirable or publicly approved attitude, especially one whose private life, opinions, or statements belie his or her public statements; a person who pretends to have virtues, moral or religious beliefs, principles, etc., that one does not actually possess, especially a person whose actions belie stated beliefs.

→ Of the hypocrite the Holy Qur'an reads, "They have taken their oaths for a protection, and they turn others aside from the way of God [ALLAH]: it is surely evil which they do. This is testified of them, because they believed, and afterwards became unbelievers: wherefore, a seal is set on their hearts, and they shall not understand." (63:2-3). To deal with a hypocrite one must use extreme caution. The hypocrite knows what the TRUTH is but attempts to conceal it and/or mislead others away from it. It is best to avoid any dealings with a hypocrite lest we fall victim to his/her games. (9)

Interpretation = explanation; explication; elucidation.

→ *"the words of his mouth have no interpretation,"* meaning that what he speaks is ambiguous, open to having several possible meanings or explanations. What he states is difficult to understand because he sets it to be

so. He doesn't want to be accountable for his words, so he speaks with a forked tongue. He is a snake in the grass that must be trampled upon. (10)

Joy = the emotion of great delight or happiness caused by something exceptionally good or satisfying. (10)

Laboreth = to act, behave, or function at a disadvantage; to struggle or work hard for; toil. (13)

Meanness = small-mindedness.

→ Dissimulation is for the trivial (petty) individual. The sincere sees no purpose for deception, which belongs to the hypocrite and indicates pettiness in character. (6)

Midst = in the middle of. (14)

Mock = to treat, tease or laugh at in a scornful or contemptuous manner; ridicule; scoff or jeer. (14)

Mole = any various small (insect-eating) mammals, especially of the family Talpidae, living chiefly underground, and having velvety fur, very small eyes, and strong forefeet. (11)

"O" = the letter "O" is used here before a name in direct address, especially in solemn or poetic language, to lend earnestness to an appeal. In this instance, the appeal is directed to those who are enamoured (entranced/charmed) with the beauty of TRUTH in instruction 1, and in instruction 14 is calling to attention the fool to warn him/her of his/her actions. (1, 14)

Perpetual = constant.

→ *"He passeth his days in perpetual constraint,"* means that the hypocrite is in a continuous state

HOLY INSTRUCTIONS FROM THE PROPHET
* SINCERITY *

of having to restrict his/her actual nature for fear of being exposed. It is an endless effort to refrain from showing his/her nature as a hypocrite. They must forever be on guard lest they be revealed for what they are. (12)

Prudence = wise and judicious; care, caution, and good judgment, as well as wisdom in looking ahead. **Judicious** = having and exercising good judgment; discreet. (7)

Reproveth = to criticize or correct someone; reprimand.

→ "*he reproveth with freedom*," the sincere at heart will correct another with frankness of manner or speech because he lives a life accordingly and will not reprimand another while he does the opposite of what he tells him not to do. (8)

Rooted = firmly planted or established. (2)

Scorn = to detest, despise or loath. (14)

Scorneth = reject or refuse. (4)

Security = safety; freedom from danger, risk, etc.

→ Here it is referring to the illusion of the hypocrite wherein he thinks he is safe in his disguise (facade) which will eventually be stripped off him. He has a false sense of security, and it is only a matter of time before he is revealed for his true nature. (14)

Semblance = a resemblance; outward aspect or appearance; a likeness, image, or show of TRUTH. If it's an unreal appearance, it is falsehood. (9)

Simplicity = freedom from deceit or guile; sincerity. (1)

Sincere = genuine and honest; one who is free from deceit, hypocrisy, or falseness; honest and truthful. (2)

Sorrow = a feeling of deep distress; mental suffering; grief. (10)

Steady = firmly placed or fixed; free from change, variation, or interruption; firm. (3)

Stoop = to lower one's moral standards; to descend from one's level of dignity. (4)

Supporteth = to maintain or preserve; to uphold (the dignity of his/her character); to maintain or support. (4)

Thou = you.

Truth = ALLAH. Truth is the ultimate reality. It is Permanent, Unchanging, and Everlasting. Truth is the actual state of something, as opposed to what seems to be.

→ Truth is not restricted to "not lying." It is not fully encompassed in 'Just being honest," or "admitting to a wrongdoing or destructive act." When Jesus stated, "Truth will make you free" in the scriptures, He meant that you must be in TRUTH, not simply tell the truth. We are not speaking of truth as convenient men, but rather the Ultimate TRUTH. TRUTH is AUGHT and AUGHT is ALLAH. Being TRUTH entails manifesting those Divine attributes in our sacred principles of Love, Truth, Peace, Freedom, and Justice through our thoughts, words, and deeds, on a perpetual basis. Truth means being the strength of ALLAH made manifest – and TRUTH is the only thing that changes not. TRUTH means to be in the Spirit of the Almighty ALLAH instead of merely being the son of man. The only Son of ALLAH is man - Spirit-man, which is ALLAH'S highest

Love (Love Divine) thought. The Spirit-man is that divine seed that comes from the heart of ALLAH. (1)

Unto = to.

Variance = conflicting; inconstant; the state of being different or in disagreement. (12)

Virtue = moral excellence and righteousness. (1)-

Weepeth: to express emotion, such as grief or sadness, by shedding tears; cry. (10)

Whatsoever = whatever. (8)

Wisdom = ALLAH. (See Ch. 1, p. 4). Children of Wisdom are the children of ALLAH who operate as Spirit-man. (14)

Wouldst = would or will. (14)

NOTES:

HOLY INSTRUCTIONS FROM THE PROPHET
* RELIGION *

Religion = a set of beliefs concerning the cause, nature, and purpose of the universe, especially when considered as the Creation of ALLAH usually involving devotional and ritual observances to HIM and often incorporating a moral code governing the conduct of human affairs.

→ The actions mentioned above allows for individuals to bond (re-ligion), or unite, with others who share the same purpose (the oneness of ALLAH and Man), moving in the same direction (Righteousness). Today, man has corrupted religion. They have hijacked "faith" to serve their selfish motives. But in following the Prophet Noble Drew Ali we are placed on the path of righteousness for we are following the dictates of the One True God, ALLAH, who is everlasting and not subject to the mere ideas of men. The Holy Qur'an of Mecca teaches that "To those who worship other things than ALLAH, hard is the way to which thou callest them." (42:13) ALLAH speaks to man through man and today He speaks to us through His Divine Love Thought Prophet Noble Drew Ali. We are taught that religion should serve to reconnect, or to relink us to God-ALLAH who is the Most Wise and Beneficent. HE (ALLAH) has sent us an Angel to warn us to repent from our sinful ways and return to the divine ways of our ancient forefathers. We are further taught in the Moorish Holy Koran that religion was instituted amongst men to teach us of our infirmities, to remind us of our weakness, and to show us that from Heaven (ALLAH) alone are we to hope for good.

This chapter informs us that there is but ONE GOD, ALLAH, and gives us various attributes of the Supreme Being. We are further given a more profound insight concerning the Creation period. Between instructions 2-7, we find the creation of the sun, stars, worlds (planets), etc. Instruction 18 details the creation of the world (earth) of which we inhabit with the hills, fields, rivers, etc. Between instructions 19-22 we are informed about the creation and formation of ALLAH'S crowned jewel; Man. Meditate on this chapter that you may be better established in ISLAMISM. It is imperative that we heed the words of the Prophet for they are the words of ALLAH. The coming of Prophet Noble Drew Ali was a blessing bestowed upon us as ALLAH heard our suffering and blessed us with the Prophet to guide and direct us back to our religious creed, that we may learn to love instead of hate. (Heading)

Acknowledgment = acceptance of the truth or existence of ALLAH; the act of expressing or displaying gratitude or appreciation to ALLAH for the blessings HE has bestowed upon men. (22)

Admire = to regard with wonder or pleasure the sun for providing the ideal climatic conditions for life on earth. However, it is only by ALLAH'S leave that the sun is able to do so. Therefore, the glory belongs to ALLAH, the Creator and not the sun, the created. (2)

Admonish = guide, direct, advise, warn or caution (the reader). (29)

Adoration = the act of paying honors, worship, and fervent devoted love to ALLAH. (3)

Adore = to regard with utmost esteem, respect, and love to ALLAH. (20)

ALLAH = the Supreme Being; the TRUE GOD of whom there is no other. ALLAH is the Source, the Author, the Governor, the Originator, the Creator - that is, the Father of all virtues and divine ideas, including the principles of Love,

Truth, Peace, Freedom, and Justice. ALLAH is the Creator and Sustainer of the entire Universe, and all life forms are dependent on HIM. The Supreme Creator is known throughout the lands by various names, but He remains the Causeless Cause and Rootless Root from which all things have grown. (1, etc.)

Almighty = All powerful; having unlimited power; an attribute of ALLAH; Omnipotent. (1)

Anger = a strong feeling of displeasure and belligerence aroused by a wrong.

→ When we speak of ALLAH'S anger, we are referring to ALLAH'S divine chastisement upon an individual or humanity as a whole. ALLAH'S anger is caused by men and is not without justification. It is of our own doing as to whether we call down the love of ALLAH, or His punishment. (8)

Author = the Composer; The One who made everything by creating and combining parts or elements; The Originator or Creator, ALLAH. (1)

Beneficent = ALLAH as being the Most Kind. (3, 16)

Benevolence = a desire to do good to others; goodwill. (29)

Bold = daring.

→ "*O think not bold men,*" do not be fearless and/or daring in doing that which ALLAH condemns. Bold suggests impudence, shamelessness, and immodesty. At all times be mindful that ALLAH is always vigilant and what we put out will be attributed to us as our reward and to no one else. (25)

Bounds = limits. (5)

Cast = a turning of the eye in a particular direction.

→ In this instance, it is by casting our eyes to the earth that we see ALLAH'S blessings shine forth just as we do when we lift them up to the heavens. From above to below ALLAH'S glory shines forth. (18)

Conception = the act of conceiving; the act or power of forming notions, ideas, or concepts.
Conceive = to form (a notion, opinion, purpose, etc.). No finite mind can comprehend things infinite. (14)

Conformeth = to make like; to bring into agreement, accord; comply.

→ "*and each, by his nature conformeth to His will.*" Everything in creation serves a purpose. We don't embrace the thought that things simply appeared or unfolded from one species to another as Barato Arabo (Moorish Holy Koran, Ch. 11). ALLAH'S Creative Spirits created all things to receive nourishment from their native planes. As thoughts of ALLAH change not, we understand that the manifests of life on every plane unfolds into perfection of their kind. Stars, sun(s), moon(s), planets, the ocean, earth, stormy winds, and lightnings all conform to ALLAH'S Will by their very nature. Animals conform to the nature that ALLAH gave to them by way of the Elohim. Earth conforms to its will accordingly. The flesh has a nature as does the soul. Each will carry out that nature. But the Spirit of man is exalted above all else in creation for it is given directly by ALLAH. Man's essence is the Spirit-Man, not the soul, nor the flesh. In 'The Meaning of The Holy Qur'an,' by Abdullah Yusuf Ali, he states in footnote #3541, "As turned out from the creative hand of ALLAH, man is innocent, pure, true, free, inclined to right and virtue, and endued with true understanding about his own position in the Universe and about ALLAH'S goodness, wisdom, and power. That is his true nature, just as the nature of a lamb is to be gentle and of a horse is to be swift. But man is caught in the meshes of customs, superstitions, selfish desires, and false teachings. This may make him pugnacious, unclean, false, slavish, hankering after what is wrong or forbidden, and deflected from the love of his fellow-men and the pure worship of the One True God." (pg. 1016). By embracing this fact, we can further our cause of uplifting fallen humanity and better demonstrate the God-Man that lies within each and every one of us. (10)

Contemplate = to look at or view with continued attention; to consider thoughtfully or thoroughly; think deeply about. (20)

Contingent = happening by chance or without known cause.

→ "*nothing is contingent*" implies that there is no happenstance, everything that takes place has a cause and a reason. (13)

Counsels = counsel: plan or purpose; design.

→ "*His counsels are inscrutable*," ALLAH'S plans and purpose are based on His Infinite Wisdom and beyond the understanding of finite-man. Mental elevation into the Infinite Will of ALLAH is to be our objective if we are to glimpse at His Divine Beauty. Men plans, and ALLAH plans, and ALLAH is the best of Planners. His prudence is incapable of being analyzed, or understood, by the finite. (14)

Course = a direction or route taken or to be taken; the path, route, or channel along which anything moves. (4)

Creator = ALLAH; the Originator of everything in existence. The Creator of the heavens and earth and everything between, above, and below. (1)

Creatures = animals. (17, 19)

Cumbrous = cumbersome; troublesome, burdensome, hindering or overloading; difficult to handle or manage because of weight or bulk.

→ "*the cumbrous shackles of this mortal life,*" would be those things which are burdensome, hindering, or overloading - holding us down or keeping us (our soul's attention) stuck to this mortal life. The Soul must conquer its foes in order to be free of these hindering burdens. (27)

Depth = deepness; profundity. (11)

Described = to trace the outline of; to set in a specific course.

→ ALLAH, being the Omniscient Force, knows the course of all things for it was He who set it to be so. Therefore, once something is placed in a course by ALLAH it must follow said course, for there is none who can supersede ALLAH'S Might or Authority. (4)

Determination = the act of coming to a decision or of fixing or settling a purpose. (12)

Devotion = profound dedication; earnest attachment to a religion, cause, person, etc. (29)

Discretion = way.

→ "*bow down thyself in humble and submissive obedience to His [ALLAH'S] supreme discretion*" is to be a Moslem; it is fruition in the ladder of salvation. ALLAH'S way is the best of ways. The Holy Qur'an of Mecca states, "The Way of ALLAH, to whom belongs whatever is in the heavens and whatever is on earth. Behold (how) all affairs tend towards ALLAH." Yusuf Ali furthers this point by stating in footnote #4603 that "The most comprehensive description of the Straight Way is that it is the Way of ALLAH, the Way of the Universal Law; for ALLAH is the source, centre, and goal of all things in heaven and earth. Everything goes back to Him. According to our own understanding we make our own laws, our own standards, and our own institutions. But the ultimate test of their validity or authority is ALLAH'S Will, as revealed to us by His Revelation." (15)

Dismayed = a sudden or complete loss of courage in the face of trouble or danger; to frighten; make afraid. (6)

Distinguished = anointed; set apart as different made prominent or eminent. **Eminent** = high in station or rank; greatest; utmost. (19)

Dominion = territory; the plane of things made manifest. (20)

Economy = the management of the affairs of life, of an individual, a group, community, or establishment with a view involving its proper maintenance or productiveness.

→ "*true economy of human life,*" is the proper application of life according to the Divine Plan of ALLAH. ALLAH'S Creation is equipped with a Divine Plan. From creation to redemption to final beatitude, everything unfolds according to ALLAH'S Divine Plan. Everything conforms to His Will. But in the flesh finite man has inconsistency. This (man's will) causes the Divine Plan to be delayed. ALLAH gave us a will and it rests solely on us to prolong or expedite our unfoldment. Economy of human life is the proper management (application) of life in accordance with the Divine Plan of ALLAH. "Take from the period of thy life the useless part of it, and what remaineth? Take off the time of thine infancy, thy second infancy of age, thy sleep, thy thoughtless hours, thy days of sickness; and, even at thy fullness of years, how few seasons hast thou truly numbered!" (Ch. 39, instructions 13-14). (30)

Endued = provided with a quality trait, or gift; endowed. (20)

Enlighteneth = illuminate or lighten up.

→ The brightness of the sun serves to illuminate our path; the moon at night also helps to illuminate our path in the cover of darkness amongst other functions. The light from the moon is but a reflection of the light from the sun. (2)

Equally = in an equal or identical manner according to Divine Law.

→ The good and the bad, high and low, rich and poor, at the time of judgment will receive their reward according to their deeds and nothing more. We must sow good seeds so that at the time of judgment we can reap our reward. (27)

Equity = the quality of being just, fair, and impartial.

→ ALLAH "*will judge the earth with equity and truth.*" ALLAH will judge us not according to what someone else did for this would not be fair and impartial. He is consistent with His Laws and will judge each of us according to our deeds. (23)

Established = founded, built, or instituted (in goodness and mercy). (24)

Eternal = without beginning or end; everlasting; always existing; endless and impossible to measure; not measured or concerned with time. (1, 29)

Ever = continuously; at all times; always. (9)

Exalted = raised or elevated; placed above, as in rank. (19,20)

Exalted thy mind = raised or heightened our mental capacities in comparison to the rest of the created beings. (19)

Exalted thy station = raised our place in creation above all other creatures; the Lord of the planes of things made manifest. (19)

Favor = a gift.

→ Peculiar favor, or unique gifts given to men by ALLAH include the ability to reason, meditate, and communicate (language). (19)

Fear = reverential awe, especially toward ALLAH.

→ Fear has many definitions, mostly taken with negative connotations. However, the above given definition seems to fit in a more meaningful way. We fear that which we don't understand and tend to respect those things we think we understand better. Electricity serves as a good example here. For a long time, many had feared electricity. However, when man was able to harness electricity to better assist humanity in their way of life, we began to respect its power. We have a negative fear of ALLAH because we see ALLAH as a foe. This fear has been the means by which others have kept humanity as slaves. "When man sees ALLAH as one with him, as Father ALLAH he needs no middleman, no priest to intercede." In the Holy Qur'an we read, "O ye who believe! Fear ALLAH as He should be feared and die not except in a state of Islam." (3:102) In footnote #427, Yusuf Ali states "Fear is of many kinds: (1) the abject fear of the coward; (2) the fear of a child or an inexperienced person in the face of an unknown danger; (3) the fear of a reasonable man who wishes to avoid harm to himself or to people whom he wishes to protect; (4) the reverence, which is akin to love, for it fears to do anything which is not pleasing to the object of love. The first is unworthy of man; the second is necessary for one spiritually immature; the third is a manly precaution against evil as long as it is unconquered; and the fourth is the seedbed of righteousness. Those mature in faith cultivate the fourth; at earlier stages, the third or the second may be necessary; they are fears, but not the fear of ALLAH. The first is a feeling of which anyone should be ashamed." (pg. 153) Yusuf Ali further states in footnote #740 that, "fear of ALLAH" does not mean "fear" in the ordinary sense, which would make you avoid the object of fear. On the contrary, the "Fear of ALLAH" is the intense desire to avoid everything that is against His Will and Law. It is in fact duty to ALLAH, for we are told to seek ardently the means by which we may approach Him, and that can only be done by striving with might and main for His cause. (29)

Felicity = Spiritual happiness; happiness that comes from Spirit-man, not the flesh; the state of being happy, especially in a high degree.

→ *"eternal felicity"* is a state of perpetual happiness which comes only when ALLAH and man are one. (29)

Fitted = provided; furnished; equipped or prepared. (20)

Flatter = to feel satisfied with oneself as though one has gotten away with something. (25)

Futurity = future time. (11)

Generation = offsprings.

→ *"from generation to generation"* could also be taken to mean supported perpetually within that species. (17)

Goodness = moral excellence; virtue; kindness; generosity; the best or most valuable part of anything; essence. (17, 18, 22, 24)

Government = direction; control; management. (10)

Governor = ALLAH as the Supreme Being in charge of the direction or in control of His creation. ALLAH is the Executive Head of all that there is. (1)

Gracious = kind, benevolent; merciful and compassionate. (16)

Gratitude = the quality of being thankful; readiness to show appreciation for and to return gratitude. (See "Gratitude" in Ch. 33). (22,29)

Guide = to steer in the right direction. (29)

Hath = have or has.

Humble = not proud or arrogant; modest. (15)

Ignorant = lacking education, knowledge, or awareness about something in particular; unaware. (27)

Image = a physical likeness or representation of a person, thing, etc., made visible. Image can also be a mental representation, idea, or conception. (2)

Incomprehensible = impossible to understand or comprehend. Archaic: having no limits; boundless. (1)

Infinite Wisdom = Spiritual Wisdom; limitless sagacity and prudence; Spiritual consciousness; Spiritual awareness. (9)

Inimitable = incapable of being imitated or copied; surpassing imitation; matchless or unmatchable by anyone or anything.

→ *"Adore His inimitable perfections,"* to have the utmost esteem, and pay Divine Honors to ALLAH'S unmatchable creation, e.g., the universe and all it is composed of, which cannot be imitated or duplicated by the hand of men. (20)

Inscrutable = beyond the comprehension of finite-mind; incapable of being investigated, analyzed, or scrutinized; not easily understood. (14)

Inspire = to encourage to do right. (29)

Instituted = set up; established. (10)

Instrument = a tool or implement; a means by which something is effected.

→ The sun is the tool that feeds energy to the earth. The human body receives vitamin D from the sun which is essential for the formation of normal bones and teeth. (2)

Judge = to try; to decide or settle authoritatively. (23)

Judgments = wise or sagacious decisions; discernment. (28)

Just and righteous = impartial, fair, and correct without fault.

→ ALLAH is Most Prudent and Most Wise and will not judge wrongly but based upon our way of life, e.g., words, actions, and deeds. (23)

Language = a body of words and the systems for their use common to a people who are of the same community or nation, the same geographical area, or the same cultural tradition; communication by voice in the distinctively human manner, using arbitrary sounds in conventional ways with conventional meanings; speech. (20)

Lest = so that (one) should not; that; "lest [that] you be destroyed." Do not try (tempt) ALLAH'S hand by doing wrong unless you want destruction cast upon you. (8)

Lightning = a brilliant electric spark discharge in the atmosphere, occurring within a thundercloud, between clouds, or between a cloud and the ground. (6)

Maintain = to keep in existence; to keep up or carry on; continue to preserve. (26)

Majesty = Supreme Power; Supreme Greatness and Authority; Impressive Beauty. All of these are attributes of the Most High God-ALLAH. (8)

Mansions = Archaic: dwelling places.

→ "the mansions of eternal felicity," the final abode of Man – The House of Peace described in the Moorish Literature of The Moorish Science Temple of America, "What Is Islam," (pg. 10). This is the Paradise of ALLAH. (20)

Meditate = to engage in thought or contemplation. (22)

Meditation = continued or extended thought; contemplation. (20)

Mercy and Love = Mercy: compassion and kindness. Love: Divine embrace; affection; ALLAH.

→ ALLAH created the world in Love and Mercy. We must be careful not to misconstrue these attributes of ALLAH in comparison with

human frailty. The attributes of ALLAH are within each and every one of us and operates through the Spirit-man. Mercy and Love are Divine, Holy, and Spiritual attributes found in the essence of men. (16)

Nations = large bodies of people, associated with particular territories that are sufficiently conscious of their unity to seek or to possess governments, usually for their own improvement and furtherance of their cause. (6)

Nature = the instincts or inherent tendencies directing conduct, motion, behavior, movement, etc. (10)

Nature = characteristic disposition; the original and natural condition of someone or something. (21)

Noblest = elevated in rank or position; of high rank; most honored; most respected; Highly Esteemed. (2)

Obedience = to carry out or fulfill the command, order, or instruction of. (21)

Omnipotent = having unlimited universal power, authority, or force; All Powerful. (8)

Ordained = destined or predestined; ordered by virtue or superior authority; decree or enact; to confer Holy order upon. (21)

Paradise = a place, mental state, or the like, where there is absolute peace, tranquility, and harmony. (29)

Paths = a route, course, or track along which something moves; a course of action, conduct, or procedure.

→ "*walk in the paths which He hath opened before thee,*" is instructing us to follow the examples, instructions, and laws which ALLAH has given us through His prophets. There are no strange happenings in the course of human events. All things and events are established by ALLAH, and we must discern what "appears to be" from the "true essence of things," and follow that which is right. (29)

Peculiar = distinct from all others; especial; unique. (19)

Perfections = perfect embodiment or example of something; of the highest or most excellent quality. (20)

Persons = individuals of distinction or importance. (26)

Pierceth = to penetrate with the eye or mind; see into or through something. (26)

Pleasure = a feeling of happy satisfaction and enjoyment. (17)

Praise = the act of expressing approval or admiration; commendation; the offering of grateful homage in words or song, as an act of worship to ALLAH. (3, 17, 18)

Precepts = rules or principles prescribing a particular course of action or conduct. (21)

Prescience = knowledge of things or events before they happen; foreknowledge; foresight. (13)

Preserveth = to keep alive or in existence. (17)

Products = things produced.

→ Products can be persons or things seen as a result of something, or the process of something. In instruction 2, "products" refers to all things produced on earth, i.e., all life on earth. The sun

is a by-product of the creation and is not to be confused or attributed the Creator of Life but is a sustainer and generator of the creation of ALLAH. (2)

Providence = divine care and guardianship; ALLAH, especially conceived as omnisciently directing the universe and the affairs of humanity with wise benevolence. (9, 13)

Prudence = wise and judicious; care, caution, and good judgment, as well as wisdom in looking ahead.

→ "*Let prudence admonish thee*," is to follow the course of wisdom; heed the still small voice that speaks within. (29)

Reason = logical; rational.

→ Reason refers to giving man a rational mind, capable of thinking logically, instead of being illogical, irrational, and operating from instincts. (20)

Rejoice = to feel or show great joy or delight. (18, 28)

Respecteth not = disregard.

→ ALLAH judges according to one's words, actions, and deeds, regardless of what position, rank, title, or reputation one's may have. It is not about the title or rank you hold that you will be judged by, but according to what you did in life. (26)

Restrain = to holdback or keep in check; control. (29)

Resound = to give forth or utter loudly; to proclaim loudly (praise, etc.); to echo or ring with sound. (18)

HOLY INSTRUCTIONS FROM THE PROPHET
* RELIGION *

Retribution = the distribution of rewards or punishments in a future life.

→ *"just and everlasting retribution,"* is the final judgment in which one's will receive from ALLAH according to their works. It is retribution based on fairness and according to one's deeds. (27)

Reverence = honor. (8)

Revolveth = revolve: to cause to move in a circular or curving course, as about a central point.

→ *"In the depths of His mind, He revolveth all knowledge."* If to revolve is to proceed or occur in a round or cyclical motion, to say that ALLAH revolves all or cyclical motion, to say that ALLAH revolves all knowledge, it could be meant that He (ALLAH) knows all knowledge. When something rotates in a circular motion, when it returns to the beginning point the individual should be aware of all that it consisted of. All knowledge comes from ALLAH and all things are known by Him since He is the originator of all. (11)

Righteous = the good, benevolent, charitable, sincere, and just people; morally right; virtuous; those who stand for TRUTH. (28)

Smiteth = smite: to inflict a heavy blow upon; to afflict. (7)

Stars = glowing bodies of gases that also emit heat and other forms of energy that derive ultimately from thermonuclear reactions taking place in their interior. (4)

Stations = positions, in a scale of estimation, rank, or dignity. (26)

Stretched forth = caused to be spread out; disseminate. (4)

Submissive obedience = unresisting and humble compliance; to humbly obey.

→ This submissive obedience can only come from us placing trust in ALLAH and submitting to His dictates. This is what a Moslem is, and this is what Prophet Noble Drew Ali has taught and is teaching us to do. (15)

Sun = the star and central body of our solar system around which the planets revolve and from which they receive light and heat.

→ The sun is about 93 million miles from the earth. It has a circumference of about 865,000 miles with a surface temperature of about 11,000 degrees Fahrenheit. It is placed perfectly where we receive just the proper amount of energy and heat to sustain life on earth. Because of the wonders of the sun, ancient religions would worship the sun as though it were ALLAH, the Most High. In this there was errors for there was One greater who created the sun. (2)

Supporteth = to furnish or provide for; supply. (17)

Supreme = Greatest in Power, Authority Rank, or Force: ALLAH. (3)

Temperance = moderation and self-restraint, as in behavior; self-control. (29)

Tempt = call on, stir up, or cause to rise; to try or test. (8)

Thanksgiving = the act of giving thanks; an expression of gratitude towards ALLAH. (3, 22)

Thee = you.

Therefore = for that reason; consequently. (15)

Thereof = of the thing just mentioned. (24)

Thou = you.

Thy = your.

Thyself = yourself.

Transcendeth = to rise above or go beyond; surpass, exceed, etc.; to be independent of or prior to the universe and time.

→ "*transcendeth thy conception,*" ALLAH'S knowledge is beyond, or exceeds anything man can conceive, imagine, or think of within the flesh. (14)

Transgressors = people who willfully violate the laws or commands of ALLAH; sinners. (24)

Tremble = quake; to be affected by vibratory motion. (6)

Unto: to.

Varied = characterized by or exhibiting variety; various. (10)

Veneration = a feeling of deep respect or reverence, etc. (15)

Wicked = evil or morally bad or low in principle or practice; sinful; operating from the lower-self. (6)

Winketh = to show indirect approval of.

→ "*winketh at thy doing,*" means to think that simply because we have not yet received punishment for a misdeed, that ALLAH approves of our actions. In this, there is error and punishment will be distributed accordingly. When we have yet to receive punishment for a wrong committed, it is because we have been granted an opportunity to make the necessary corrections. (25)

Wise = having or showing experience, knowledge, and good judgment; the ability to discern (recognize) or judge what is true, right, or lasting; exhibiting judicious or prudent behavior. (27)

Wise = ALLAH being the Most Wise and having All Knowledge; Omniscient. **Omniscient** = having complete or unlimited knowledge, awareness, or understanding. (3)

Wonders = miraculous deeds or events; remarkable phenomenon; something that causes astonishment and reverent admiration.

→ "*wonders of His love,*" refers to ALLAH'S miraculous creation, all that is found in creation. (22)

Worship = the ceremonies, prayers, or other religious forms by which love is expressed to ALLAH; ardent devotion to ALLAH; adoration; homage. (3)

Worship him not = do not worship the sun because by doing so we place the created above the Creator. (2)

NOTES:

CHAPTER XXXVI (36)
HOLY INSTRUCTIONS FROM THE PROPHET
* KNOW THYSELF *

→ KNOW THYSELF: To "Know Thyself" means to become aware of one's true and actual nature. The prophet teaches us that the key of civilization was and is in the hands of the Asiatic Nations. From our natural state, we, as thoughts of ALLAH made flesh must conform to the laws dictated to us from ALLAH through His prophet Noble Drew Ali. As living beings, we tend to connect more with the physical aspect of self and many of us get stuck in the soul of things. It is because of this that ALLAH sends messengers and prophets to direct our course to the Oneness of ALLAH and man. Our nourishment must come from the Higher-Self since that is the eternal part of men. To "Know Thyself" is to know ALLAH in man, evolving in life and reaching deific life (paradise), the will of man conjoined with the Will of ALLAH. A good perspective is shared by Brother Nathaniel Chambers El in his work "Moorish Questionnaire Commentaries" in which he states: "Know Thyself. Remember who you are, who made you, and the vast powers you possess. You are not your body, nor your soul but a spirit and a part of ALLAH. And as such you have within you the very potencies and attributes of ALLAH. When we as a people internalize the meaning of who we are, we'll know that we have the power to uplift our families, our communities, our nation, and the world." (Heading)

Accountable = responsible for; having to answer for something; to be responsible or held liable for certain actions. (7)

Admire = to regard with pleasure or approval; to have a high opinion of; respect; to look at with pleasure. (3)

Adore = to regard with utmost esteem, respect, and love; extend Divine honors to. (3)

Art = are (you are made). Archaic: be. (1)

Ass = a long-eared, slow moving, sure-footed domesticated mammal, Equus asinus, related to the horse, used chiefly as a beast of burden; any wild species of the genus Equus, as the onager.

→ "*Knoweth the ass the use of food, because his teeth mow down the herbage?*" In other words, does the donkey truly understand the use of food simply because it feeds? Is it conscious of its true value or is it simply following its instincts? "*. . .nor be thou like to the horse and the mule, in whom there is no understanding.*" (Ch. 38:4) (8)

Awe = an overwhelming feeling of reverence, admiration, fear, etc., produced by that which is grand, sublime, extremely powerful, or the like. (2)

Behold = look; see; discern. **Discern** = to distinguish mentally; recognize as distinct or different. (6)

Behold = to observe; see.

→ "*that thou shouldst behold His works?*" The reason that man is made erect, (being able to stand straight), is so that he may better see ALLAH'S creation, or admire all that ALLAH has created. (3)

Behold = to be cognizant of; to make mentally aware of something in particular.

→ "*behold a part of ALLAH Himself within thee*" is informing man that he is to be aware that in him, his true essence, is his Higher-self. (10)

Clay = physical body; earth, especially regarded as the material from which the human body was formed during creation. (6)

Consciousness = the state of being conscious; awareness; aware of one's own existence, sensation, thoughts, surroundings, etc.; the spiritual awareness of ALLAH and man. (4)

Contemplate = to observe or study thoughtfully and thoroughly; think deeply about; study.

→ *"Contemplate thine frame,"* is to think or take into deep consideration your form (physical body) and those things that accompany it. Study the body and how perfect it has been made and then ask yourself who else, but the Supreme Creator could create such perfection? It is by ALLAH'S leave that Elohim was able to create the things they did, therefore the glory belongs to ALLAH! (1)

Creator = ALLAH. (2, 3)

Derived = to trace from a source or origin; to come from. (4)

Descend = to move from a higher to a lower level of behavior, consciousness, etc.; debase.

→ *"nor dare descend to evil or to meanness,"* is to be mindful that man is ALLAH'S greatest creation and that in us there is that part of ALLAH that sets us apart from the rest of the creation. Because of this, we should always be proud (not haughty) and not debase ourselves to the sense of brutes (beasts). Man, not beast/animal, is the Lord of the plane of things made manifest. (10)

Dignity = elevated in rank, office, station, etc.; nobility or elevation of character; worthiness. (10)

Divinity = being of a higher nature, or spiritual form; that which makes the difference between man and beast. (10)

Dust = earth or other matter in fine, dry particles.

→ With the phrase *"O child of the dust,"* we are reminded where this flesh derived from and where it will return. (1)

Erect = standing straight; upright. **Upright** = erect or vertical, as in position or posture. (3)

Eternal = not measured by time or limited to the confines of the flesh. (7)

Evil = morally wrong or bad behavior; immoral; wicked; opposite of what the Higher-self is. (10)

Fearfully = extreme in size, intensity, etc.; full of awe or reverence. (2)

Fled = left ("after it has *left*"). (7)

Formed = molded; given shape to; developed. (9)

Herbage = nonwoody vegetation; the succulent parts, leaves and stems, of herbaceous plants; the fleshy, often edible parts of plants; grass. (8)

Humble = not proud or arrogant; modest. (1)

Ignorant = lacking education, knowledge, or awareness about something in particular; unaware. (1)

Immaterial = having no material body or form; not composed of matter; bodiless; not subject to time in relation to the flesh. (7)

Infinite Wisdom = Spiritual Wisdom; limitless sagacity and prudence; spiritual consciousness; spiritual awareness.

→ There is a difference that must be pointed out when dealing with "Infinite Wisdom" and "human wisdom." Human wisdom is never absolute, but relative. It is void of spiritual wisdom. By applying Spiritual Wisdom to human wisdom ALLAH enhances our wisdom to manifest His Will. The Wisdom of ALLAH is not only displayed in the creation but is also revealed through His prophets, messengers, religious texts, etc., in our case Prophet Noble

HOLY INSTRUCTIONS FROM THE PROPHET
* KNOW THYSELF *

Drew Ali and The Moorish Holy Koran and other teachings by the Prophet.

Human wisdom is gained through the physical senses and human experience. It can be used for good or evil, hence "the pretended wise." Spiritual (Infinite) Wisdom is the Will of ALLAH made manifest and breeds Justice, Mercy, Love, and Right. (1)

Informs = to animate or inspire; to give information; supply knowledge or enlightenment.

→ "*something informs thy clay*," something animates, or inspires the body to move or take action. (6)

Instructed = informed; directed; furnished with knowledge.

→ Instruction 11 is speaking of ALLAH.

Know Thyself = to become aware of one's true essence; to be that which one should be, the Higher-self.

→ "know thyself and the pride of His creation," knowing thyself is a fundamental law of knowledge. Before you know anything or anyone else, you must first know self. The pride of ALLAH'S creation is man who is imbued with unlimited knowledge and the consciousness of Him who created him, which makes him ALLAH'S pride. (10)

Matter = the substance or substances of which any physical object consists or is composed of. (10)

Mayest = may. (3)

Meanness = the state or quality of being mean.

→ Mean suggests pettiness and smallness of mind (small-mindedness). We are to be mindful that a part of the Supreme Creator is within each one of us and that we are to strive to unfold into the Oneness of ALLAH and not debase ourselves morally and/or spiritually, but rather elevate into Infinite Wisdom. (10)

Mow = to cut down with the teeth (grass, grain, etc.). (8)

Object = something perceived; perception; purpose; a thing, person, or matter to which thought, or action is directed; anything that may be apprehended intellectually.

Perceive = to become aware of, know, or identify by means of the senses.

→ "*higher than all is the object of thy senses*." The "*all*" in "*higher than all...*" is referring to all creatures in creation (See Instruction 3 above). Because of man's ability to perceive and mentally discern what is being conveyed by the physical senses, he is placed in a higher status than all other creatures in creation by the Father of the Universe. Even though animals have senses (See Ch. 38:15), man is blessed with thinking, understanding, reasoning, and willing as the actions of the Soul. But above all else, he has the consciousness of who he is and who the Supreme Creator is. (6)

Omnipotence = the quality of being omnipotent. **Omnipotent** = having unlimited or universal power, authority, or force; All Powerful.

→ "Wouldst thou see omnipotence displayed before thee?" If men were to remain in a weak and ignorant state, would he be able to recognize the glory of ALLAH in all His creation? Emphatically no! To be able to discern the beauty of ALLAH'S creation men must first elevate their thoughts to infinite wisdom. By doing thusly they are better equipped to see beyond the veil of what seems to be. (1)

Oughtest = as obligated to; obliged. (1)

Perceiveth = to become aware of through the senses; understand. (5)

Praise = the offering of grateful homage in words or song, as an act of worship to ALLAH. (2)

Principle of Knowledge = Principle: fundamental law (an essential quality).

→ *"and of His own breath did He communicate to thee the principle of knowledge,"* could be taken to mean that ALLAH has endued us with the fundamental law (principle) of knowledge. He has established within us a knowledge of the preeminence of virtues (Moorish Holy Koran 42:23). By knowing self, we become aware of these virtues and move in the direction of living according to them instead of the vices which are of the lower self. (9)

Rejoice = to feel or show great delight. (2)

Reposed = to put (confidence, trust, consciousness, etc.) in a person; to instill. (4)

Reverence = a feeling or attitude of deep respect tinged with awe; veneration. (2)

Serpent = in a general sense, any snake.

→ Serpent can be used in the general sense here. However, because it first states in this instruction that the serpent has terror planted in its tail, it could be referring to a rattle snake, since a rattle snake has a series of horny, interlocking elements at the end of the tail. This series of horny, interlocking elements at the end of the tail of a rattle snake produce a rattling sound. This rattling sound causes terror to the hearer since it foretells danger, and the individual imagines the consequence of being the recipient of the snake's bite. (11)

Shouldst = shall. (3)

Superiority and command = Lordship and mastery over creation; Vicegerent. (9)

Tame = to change from a wild and savage state to a domesticated one; trained. (11)

Terror = intense, sharp, overmastering fear; honor sound; fearful sight; something feared. (11)

Thee = you.

Therefore = for that reason; consequently. (2)

Thine = your. (10)

Thou = you.

Thy = your.

Weak = lacking in bodily (physical) strength, or healthy vigor, as from age or sickness; feeble; infirm; lacking in mental power, intelligence, or judgment; lacking firmness or character or strength of will. (1)

Wert = were. (9)

Whence = from where; from what place, source, origin, or cause. (4)

Wherefore = for what purpose or for what reason; why? (3, 4)

Wonderfully = excellent; great; marvelous; amazing. (2)

Wouldst = would or will. (1)

NOTES:

HOLY INSTRUCTIONS FROM THE PROPHET
* THE BREATH OF HEAVEN *

BREATH OF HEAVEN = the Breath of Heaven is Holy Breath, TRUTH, The Breath of ALLAH, which animates all in creation. It is ALLAH speaking to man through man; It is EVERLASTING LIFE. (Heading)

Actuate = to put into motion or action; impel; motivate.

→ "so let thy spirit, O man, actuate and direct thy flesh," the Spirit (Spirit-man) is a thought and a part of ALLAH and to let it actuate, which is to put in motion or activate, and direct, lead, or guide the flesh by way of the Soul, is to do the Will of ALLAH, who lives within. The Spirit will not lead you astray for it is of the Higher-self; ALLAH in man. (3)

Assistance = the act of assisting; help; aid; support. (10)

Attentive = giving careful or attention to; to be observant; to be mindful. (9)

Aught = anything. (10)

Avoid = to keep away from; to prevent the occurrence of; to refrain from.

→ *"avoid guilt, and thou shalt know that fear is beneath thee,"* guilt plays on the conscious of the guilty. It is the responsibility that comes from doing wrong. Fear is the emotion that is caused by the expectation or awareness of danger. By avoiding guilt, we avoid any fear for there would be no purpose for it. Therefore, do nothing that would cause you to feel guilty. Live a humble life according to the dictates of the Prophet of ALI. (12)

Basis = the bottom or base of anything; the part on which something stands or rests. (4)

Behold = acknowledge. (6)

Billows = a great wave or surge of the sea. (3)

Blushing = to redden (in the face), as from embarrassment or shame; to feel shame or embarrassment. (11)

Canst = can. (14)

Channel = a route through which anything passes or progresses. (7)

Conveyances = vehicles; a means of transportation.

→ "conveyances of truth," means that by teaching the soul moderation and the spirit (human spirit) to be mindful of its good, the senses evolve to grasp the higher meaning of things. We will no longer use taste, sight, smell, hearing, and feeling to satisfy the flesh. We will now penetrate all things and see the Truth behind them. (9)

Countenance = the face; appearance especially a look or expression of the face indicative of encouragement or of moral support. (12)

Course = route, path, or direction. (6)

Delicacies = delicacy: something delightful or pleasing, especially a choice food considered with regard to its rarity, costliness, or the like. (7)

Direct = to take charge of; control. (3)

Dismay = a sudden or complete loss of courage in the face of trouble or danger; to frighten. (12)

Distinguish = tell the difference between. (8)

Fear = to be afraid or frightened of something; an unpleasant often strong emotion caused by expectation or awareness of danger. (12)

Furnace = a structure or apparatus in which heat may be generated, as for smelting ores, heating clay or pottery etc. (2)

Fury = unrestricted or violent anger, rage, passion, or the like. (3)

Globe = the earth. (4)

Glorious = magnificent; characterized by great beauty; delightful. (14)

Honorable = in accordance with or characterized by principles of honor; upright; worthy of honor and high respect. (1)

Instructing = directing. (14)

Loins = the part of the human body between the hips and the lower ribs, especially regarded as the seat of physical strength and generative power; the genital area. (14)

Master = one having authority or control.

→ "is not the master of the house more honorable than its walls?" The answer to this question is an emphatic yes. I like to visualize this instruction from a different perspective, yet in conjunction with the teachings of the Prophet. From a simpler view, we can look at this tri-personality from this aspect: **Master** = Spirit-man; **House** = Soul; **Walls** = Flesh. We can clearly deduce from this chapter, as well as from the teachings of the Prophet, that the honor goes not to the house or its walls, but to its Master. As stated in Chapter 36:5, "It is not in flesh to think; it is not in bones to reason." And in Chapter I, pg. 4, "But man himself is not the body, nor the soul; he is a spirit and a part of ALLAH." And as master of the house, we are further instructed to "let the spirit, O man, actuate and direct thy flesh." Our thoughts must be elevated to those of Infinite Wisdom. (1)

Ministers = things that serve as agents; envoys. (9)

Moderation = the quality of being moderate, that is, having the discipline of keeping within reasonable and proper limits, as to avoid excessiveness.

→ "*Keep thy soul in moderation*," is to be moderate in regards to what you feed the soul as to good and bad, worthy and unworthy. In other words, be conscious of the grade of thoughts you feed the soul; "*teach thy spirit to be attentive to its good*," is to focus on the good that is within the spirit, human spirit. Bear in mind that the more we focus on the good, the more we manifest the good that is within us. The middle ground for all of this is the soul. The soul is the battle ground where we fight the good fight. (9)

Offspring = one's descendants collectively; children. (14)

Ordained = destined; invested with ministerial functions; decreed; authorized. (6)

Perfumes = a substance, extract, or preparation for diffusing or imparting an agreeable or attractive smell, especially a fluid containing fragrant natural oils extracted from flowers, woods, and spices. (7)

Piety = dutiful respect or regard for parents.

→ In instruction 14, we are informed as to the proper usage of our gift of speech. We are instructed to use our ability to speak to give praise to ALLAH. By thus doing, we extend our wisdom to our children since our children mimic our behavior. (14)

Pillars = upright shafts or structures, made of stone, brick, or other material, relatively slender in proportion to its height, and of any shape in section, used to support buildings or other structures. The bones of the body serve the purpose of holding the body erect allowing us the proper motion to accomplish what we will. (4)

Porcelain = a hard white translucent ceramic made by firing a pure clay and then glazing it with fusible materials. (2)

Potter = a person who makes pottery. **Pottery** = ceramics, pots, dishes, and other materials made of earthenware or baked clay. (2)

Prepared = made ready before hand for a specific purpose. (2)

Prerogative = an exclusive right, privilege, etc.; a right, privilege, etc., in this instance the gift of speech exclusively extended to men by ALLAH. (14)

Rational = reasonable; wise or judicious. (14)

Repress = to keep under control, check, as desires, feelings, actions, etc. (3)

Resideth = dwell; abides. (1)

Retain = to keep; maintain. (6)

Reverence = respect; honor; regard. (13)

Ruddy = having a fresh, healthy reddish color.

→ *"ruddy splendor,"* every human possesses a ruddy appearance in the face. Some individuals may be too "swarthy" to make it visible, but it is there. This ruddy appearance is a sign of good health. (12)

Sentinel(s) = a person or thing that keeps watch; guard. (8)

Shadows = suggestions; faint ideas; faint representations; prophesies; a hint or faint, indistinct image, or idea; also, soul(s).

→ *"Wherefore to thee alone speaks shadows in the vision of the pillow?"* For the meaning of "shadows" we have given the definition we think best fit within this context. "Shadows" could be taken to be faint ideas or suggestions we receive during our period of sleep. By these ideas or suggestions being faint it informs us that it takes a person with a discerning mind to arrive at the conclusion or meaning behind the dreams. There is a specific message being converted and it is up to the recipient of said dreams to either follow or ignore what is being converted. Of these dreams, (shadows, *e.g.*, faint ideas, prophesies, suggestions, etc.), it is said that Prophet Muhammed had once stated, "A good dream (that comes true) of a righteous man is one of forty-six parts of (Prophethood)." (Narrated by Anas bin Malik, hadith of Prophet Muhammed).

As for the last given definition, Soul(s), it is based upon the following. In the Oral Statement and Prophesies of Prophet Noble Drew Ali #48, it is stated that "The Holy Prophet Mohammed said, 'If you dream of me, it is like seeing me for true, because the devil cannot steal my appearance. (So, if one dreams of seeing the Holy Prophet Noble Drew Ali take heed to what you see and hear in that dream).'" Abu Huraire narrated a hadith from Prophet Mohammed in which he stated of dreams, "I heard the Prophet saying, 'Whoever sees me in a dream will see me in his wakefulness, and Satan cannot imitate me in shape.'" Abu Said al-Khurdi narrated that the Prophet said, "Whoever sees me (in a dream) then he indeed has seen the truth, as Satan cannot appear in my shape."

Another aspect that must be covered is the *"Reverence them, for know that dreams are from on high,"* of the same instruction. It is of great importance that we recognize the types of individuals that have the dreams because there are different types of dreams and different places where they come from. First it must be stated, to avoid confusion, that the ability to have dreams is extended to all of humanity. It is a gift, from ALLAH to all. But the types of dreams had is the issue addressed herein. Dreams are truly from on high, as it was a gift bestowed upon us by the Creator. But we must also keep in mind that a lot of our dreams (natural dreams) could be based on several experiences. They could be based on certain impactful thoughts that we may have during the day (wakeful hours), or before our placing our heads on the pillow; emotions that have had an effect on us during the day; or even from certain anxieties experienced.

Dreams from on high (from ALLAH or Spiritual realm, lofty, etc.), can serve as warnings to individuals to change a certain way of life; prophesies extended for the benefit of humanity as ALLAH speaks to man through man to grant a chance at redemption before the wrath of ALLAH touches them. Dreams in which we see someone we know, or that has passed form could also serve as motivation in life. To say that we are to reverence dreams for they are from on high, is to say that we are having good, positive dreams. The righteous have righteous dreams for ALLAH is Righteous. The wicked have their dreams (nightmares) because that is what they've created but even then, these could also serve to warn the dreamer. But when a warning is extended to a wicked person, it is from ALLAH for ALLAH is all Mercy and forgiving. Abu Said al-Khurdi narrated that the Prophet Mohammed said, "If anyone of you sees a dream that he likes, it is from ALLAH, and he should thank ALLAH for it and narrate it to others; but if he sees something else,

i.e., a dream that he dislikes, then it is from Satan, and he should seek refuge with ALLAH from its evil and he should not mention it to anybody, for it will not harm him." (13)

Shalt = shall. (12)

Shame = a painful feeling of humiliation or distress caused by the consciousness of wrong or foolish behavior; sense of guilt, embarrassment, unworthiness, or disgrace. (11)

Shameful = anything that brings about a cause of shame; an act that is humiliating, indecent, or offensive. (11)

Splendour = splendor; brilliant or gorgeous in appearance, coloring, etc. (12)

Sustain = support or maintain. (4)

Thee = you.

Therefore = for that reason; consequently. (11)

Therein = in that place. (1)

Thine = your.

Thou = you.

Thy = your.

Unnamely = unknown; foreign. (12)

Unto = to. (3, 10)

Vault = to boast of; brag.

→ To brag is to place the thing being bragged about in a higher standard above all else. When we brag about the body or the brain because of what they have therein, we place these things above that which is truly worth value, the essence of men. We waste energy that could go towards awakening the God-man that is within. (1)

Wherefore = for what reason?; why? (10, 13)

Wilderness = wildness; unrestricted; undisciplined or unrestrained; lacking reason or prudence; uncultured. (3)

Wonder = to marvel at; be in awe of. (14)

NOTES:

·····CHAPTER XXXVIII (38)·····
HOLY INSTRUCTIONS FROM THE PROPHET
* THE SOUL OF MAN *

THE SOUL OF MAN = The Soul is an independent principle of life. A garb for the Spirit in order to function independently on the Soul plane. The essence of the Soul is the Spirit. The Soul possesses actions. These actions are: "thinking, understanding, reasoning, and willing." The Soul is influenced by our thoughts, so we must be careful of what and how we think, because our Soul is shaped (molded) by these thoughts, and as we expand our thought environment, we give the Soul greater expression. The Soul is also here to gain perfection, so we must begin this process by becoming aware (conscious) of our spiritual aspect and letting the Spirit actuate and direct the flesh, in other words, let the Higher-Self take its course. (Heading)

Actions = acts that one consciously wills and that may be characterized by physical or mental activity; an exertion of power. (3)

Advantage = benefit. (14)

Agility = the power of moving quickly and easily; the ability to think and draw conclusions quickly. (23)

Anointeth = to put oil on during a religious ceremony.

→ To anoint someone was to set them apart for some specific purpose. Figuratively oil symbolizes prosperity. In this instance true prosperity would be the outcome of wisdom. (9)

Answer = to be or declare oneself responsible or accountable. (11)

Application = the act of putting to a special use or purpose.

→ *"and application anointeth her with the oil of wisdom"* can also mean that the application

of honesty (sincerity) elevates her (the Soul) into the realm of Spiritual Wisdom. (9)

Arabia = The Arabian Peninsula in modern days. Bounded by the Persian Gulf and the Gulf of Oman on the E., and the Arabian Sea and the Gulf of Aden on the S., followed by the Red Sea on the W.

→ The Arabians were at one time a very superstitious people. It wasn't until the coming of Prophet Muhammed that the Arabs were civilized and brought into the belief of ONE GOD (ALLAH). *"Think not with Arabia,"* is instructing us not to embrace the way of thinking of the foreign Arabs, their superstitions, which included the belief that one soul was parted amongst all of humanity. There is error in this thinking for each one has their own and we are each accountable for it. Our vices and/or our virtues are what molds the soul.

Attain = to arrive at; to reach; to accomplish or achieve. (26)

Aught = anything. (24)

Avail = to be of use or value to. (15)

Behold! = to observe; look at; see. Used to attract or call attention to. (28)

Brutes = nonhuman creatures; characteristics of animals; lacking or showing a lack of reason or intelligence. (4)

Canst = can. (19, 22)

Clay = earth; mud. (7)

Cock = a male chicken; rooster. (13)

Contraries = opposite directions or positions.

→ Depending on what is being thought the Soul can do what we consider good or bad. It is imperative that we become conscious of our thoughts. (7)

Corruption = decay; to falling apart of the flesh. (12)

Created = brought into existence. (10)

Debase = to lower in character, quality, or value; degrade. (4)

Deformed = having the form changed, especially with loss of beauty; disfigured. (11)

Delight = a high degree of pleasure or enjoyment; joy. (23)

Despised = to regard with corrupt, disgust, or disdain; scorn; to look down on. (14)

Didst = do. (15)

Dignity = high rank or position; the quality or state of being worthy, honored, or esteemed.

→ *"Remember thou its dignity forever,"* is calling to mind the fact that the Soul we possess is higher than the flesh and therefore we are to be mindful of its proper worth, nobility, and its value in comparison to the flesh. Remember, it is not in flesh to think, nor is it in bones to reason. (20)

Direct = to take charge of; control. (21)

Discretion = the power or right to decide or act according to one's own judgment; the quality of being discreet, especially with reference to one's own actions or speech; prudent. (25)

Doth = do or does. (7)

Dust = fine, dry powder made up of tiny particles of earth; earth. (13)

Envy = a feeling of discontent or covetousness with regard to another's advantage.

→ Envy denotes a longing to possess something awarded to or achieved by another. In this instance the senses awarded to animals. (14)

Essence = the basic, real, nature of a thing or substances; the core of someone.

→ The essence of something is its true constitution, as opposed to what is accidental, phenomenal, illusory etc. Something that exists, especially a Spiritual or immaterial entity. (3)

Exalted = raised in rank, honor, power, character, quality, etc.; elevated.

→ *"exalted by virtues,"* means that it wouldn't have been Just to give us a Soul already possessing complete and unfolded virtues, or high in moral excellence or goodness because had this been so it would have robbed us of the experience needed for unfoldment. (11)

Examination = inspection; inquiry; investigation. (12)

External part = the physical body. (1)

Faculties = the power of the mind, as memory, reason, or speech; inherent capacities of the body.

→ *"Search it by its faculties,"* when studying the Soul, focus on its abilities to think, understand, reason, and will. These are the actions of the Soul. By beginning there we can travel backwards until we arrive at the Cause of the effects. (5)

Fallacious = deceptive; misleading. (26)

Flieth = to run towards or away from. (13)

Generality = the greater part or majority.

→ *"for the generality of men are ignorant,"* informs us that the majority of the populace lack in the true knowledge of Divine Truth, of the Soul, and of ALLAH. A good example of the generality of men being ignorant can be deduced from the article "Religious Controversy" in the Moorish Literature in which we are informed that "although the ignorant has finished college, he is a fool right on, being *trained* to jump through a hoop. The longer he stays in the schools, the better he can jump, and the more vivid will he defend his jumping." (Emphasis mine). (27)

Grateful = thankful. (2)

Hadst = have. (15)

Hast = have. (2)

Hath = have or has. (16)

Health = freedom from disease or ailment. (1)

Herb = a flowering plant whose stem above ground does not become woody. (13)

Hound = one of the several breeds of dogs trained to pursue game by scent, especially one with a long face and large drooping ears. (15)

Ignorant = lacking education, knowledge, or awareness about something in particular; unaware. (27)

Immortal = not subject to death; never to be forgotten; everlasting. (9)

Inquiry = question, examination, investigation.

→ In instruction 12, she is being questioned or examined; in instruction 23, she is doing the examining. (12, 23)

Inscrutable = incapable of being investigated, analyzed, or scrutinized; not easily understood. (2)

Irregular = unpredictable; fluctuating. (24)

Justice = fairness; righteousness.

→ Both JUSTICE and MERCY are of the Higher-self in man. But ALLAH has given man free will and in order for man to unfold, he must deal with the foes that come with this physical manifest. Man must develop his virtues just as he must develop and overcome his vices so that he may dethrone the demon self to ensure the exalting to the throne of savior LOVE. So, it was ALLAH displaying HIS justice upon man that HE did not give the Soul to us already exalted with virtues and in HIS compassion and kindness HE didn't give us a Soul deformed by vices. The other side of the coin is the fact that both virtues and vices are our own and it is on us to make or mar the Soul. They are ours and therefore we must be held accountable to them. (11)

Knowledge = the state or fact of knowing; facts, information, and skills acquired by a person through experience or study; the sum of what has been perceived, discovered, or learned; clear and certain mental apprehension. (28)

Lieth = lie (is in). (14)

Meek = showing patience and humility; gentle. (2)

Mercy = compassion; kindness. (11)

Mule = the offspring of a donkey and a horse (strictly, a male donkey and a female horse), typically sterile; usually considered not very smart. (4)

Nature = untouched and uninfluenced.

→ In this instance, it is referring to the moon remaining in its natural state even after darkness spreads before her. Remember that the moon serves a purpose and will fulfill its objective. So even though darkness spreads over the face of the moon, it is not of the moon. Even when darkness overshadows the moon, behind that darkness the moon remains unchanged. The Soul was given to us to serve a specific purpose and even though the fool may not know what the purpose is, the Soul will still do what it has to do because that is the way that Creative Fate meant it to be, and the Soul will follow that course. (8)

Perpetual = continuing or enduring forever; everlasting.

→ "*Her motion is perpetual,*" informs us that the Soul of man is always active and alert. (23)

Proportion = symmetry, harmony, or balance. (1)

Raise = to elevate; exalt.

→ "*Raise it not too high,*" don't make the Soul the pinnacle of your being. The Soul is not the greatest aspect of you, you are Spirit-man, not Soul-man! (4)

Rash = acting or tending to act too hastily or without due consideration. (24)

Reason = logical thinking. (26)

Reasoning = the process of forming conclusions, judgments, or inferences from facts or premises. (3)

Regions = the vast or indefinite entirety of a space or area or something compared to one. In this instance "the regions [vast space] of the stars." (23)

Resign = give up. (15)

Restrain = keep in check or under control; to keep or hold in a particular place, condition, or position. (24)

Senses = any of the faculties, as sight, hearing, smell, taste, or touch, by which humans and animals perceive stimuli originating from outside or inside the body. (14)

Shield = protect; cover. (12)

Stag = an adult male deer. (15)

Supple = pliant; moving and bending with agility; limber; pliable. (24)

Suppressed = subdued; stopped; inhibited, restrained, or hindered. (23)

Thee = you.

Therefore = for that reason; consequently. (16)

Thine = your. (11)

Thinking = to decide by reasoning, reflection, or pondering; rational. (3)

Thirsteth = to be thirsty; a strong and eager desire; craving. The Soul *craves* after knowledge. (23)

Thou = you.

Thy = your.

Tortoise = a turtle. (15)

Traverseth = to travel or pass across, over, or through. (23)

Treasures = valuable, wealth, or precious knowledge. (17)

Uncertain = unsure or undecided; wavering; inconsistent. (26)

Unchangeable = not capable of being altered; immutable. **Immutable** = not subject or susceptible to change; unchangeable; changeless.

→ The Soul will do as it was meant to do no matter how we may feel about it. It has a job and once we've embraced this fact, we can guide or direct the Soul in that which is right. (9)

Understanding = the ability to understand; comprehension; to grasp mentally; perceive; personal interpretation. (3)

Universal = present everywhere; applicable or common to all purpose, condition, or situations. (23)

Unto = to.

Uttered = sent forth with the voice; pronounced or spoken. (18)

Uttermost = most remote or outermost; furthermost; the outer or furthest part of the earth. (23)

Vices = evils, degrading or immoral practices or habits; serious moral failings; wicked or evil conduct or habits; shortcomings. (11)

Vigour = vigor: healthy physical or mental energy or power; vitality. (1)

Virtue = righteousness.

→ *"Beware that thou direct its course to virtue,"* means that we are to guide the Soul towards righteousness and truth. To do this we must first accept the Truth that we are Spirit-man, and not Soul-man or Physical-man. Once we have accepted this fact, we can develop and unfold so that the Soul is always directed to that which is beneficial to its learning process and not to that which hinders its growth. (21)

Virtues = moral excellence and righteousness; goodness; conformity of one's life and conduct to moral and ethical principles; a good and desirable personal quality. (5, 11)

Willeth = will; to influence by exerting will power.

→ *"even so it is one soul willeth contraries,"* means that the Soul brings about a duality It is not until the Soul is disciplined accordingly that the contraries begin to cease. As the Soul willeth, so it is. (7)

Willing = power of choosing one's own actions; the faculty of conscious and especially of deliberate action. (5)

Worship = the ceremonies, prayers, or other religious forms by which Love is expressed to ALLAH; the practices of showing deep respect for and offering sincere praise and prayers to ALLAH. (28)

Yielding = pliable; flexible. (24)

NOTES:

PINNACLE OF WISDOM = The highest point obtained in wisdom.

→ The theme that is reoccurring in this chapter is "LIFE." The word is used more than 11 times throughout and the word "LIVE" is found more than 3 times. The pinnacle of wisdom is the proper application of life. Amongst the various points made, the proper application of life reigns supreme. But what is the proper application? Without wisdom, life is fleeting. We are merely an animate existence going through the same process as animals: procreating, feeding, sleeping, etc. The proper application of life comes from the realization that there is greater in us. That we have a direct link with ALLAH and that because of men's ability to think, understand, reason, and will, he has a greater responsibility and a bigger role to play in Creation. Men is set apart for a purpose (Ch. 35:19; 36:9) and it is therefore sinful (willful disobedience to the laws of ALLAH) to live and lead a life that is contrary to the life ALLAH has deemed for men. "But ye love the fleeting life and leave alone the Hereafter." (Holy Qur'an, 75:20-21). "Man loves haste and things of haste. For that reason, he pins his faith on transitory things that come and go, and he neglects the things of lasting moment, which comes slowly, and whose true import will only be fully seen in the Hereafter." (Yusuf Ali, "The Meaning of The Holy Qur'an," footnote #5821, pg. 1567). Life gains its values by the means we apply to serving humanity. (Heading)

Abundance = a great or plentiful amount. (24)

Abuse = to use wrongly or improperly; misuse.

→ *"Are these [the crow and fawn] to be compared with thee in the abuse of life?"* The comparison between fawn, crow, and man is being made because in truth we abuse the life that we have. The fawn and the crow operate according to what they have to do. But man, on the other hand, abuses life and does as *he* feel. Unless man becomes conscious of his true essence, he will continue to abuse the gift of life. (20)

Accommodate = to become adjusted to; adapt. (9)

Alas! = used as an exclamation to express sorrow, pity concern, or apprehension of evil. (18)

Allotted = divided or distributed by share or portion; assigned as a portion. (8)

Art = are. (3)

Bloom = freshness; the time or period of greatest beauty, artistry, etc. (32)

Canst = can. (11)

Carcass = the dead body of an animal. (1)

Cares = concerns, inclinations, responsibilities, and worries. (12)

Clay = the human body, as distinguished from the Spirit-man and Soul; the flesh. (7)

Cloyeth = to cause distaste or disgust by supplying with too much of something originally pleasant, especially something rich and sweet; surfeit. (2)

Condemn = to declare to be bad, unfit; worthless. (4)

Content = to be satisfied with what one is or has. (8)

Corrupt = decayed, putrid; infected' (2)

Covet = to wish for longingly. (27)

Creator = ALLAH. (5)

Crow = any of several large flossy black birds of the genus corvus, having a characteristic raucous call especially C. Brachychynchos of North America. (20)

Cruel = willfully or knowingly causing pain or distress to others. (21)

Dazzleth = to overpower or dim the vision of by intense light.

→ *"Though bright, it dazzleth not;"* even though the rising sun produces a strong light, it does not overpower or blind the lark. (2)

Delusion = a false belief that is resistant to reason or confrontation with actual fact; a false belief or opinion. (28)

Desire = to wish or long for; want. (27)

Despiseth = to be unpleasant; cause displeasure. (33)

Dread = to fear greatly; to be afraid of. (30)

Duty = something that one is expected or required to do by moral obligation. (11)

Economy = careful, thrifty management of resources, materials, labor, etc.

→ In this instance, it is referring to the proper use (management) of one's life while on earth. (24)

Employ = to make use for a specific purpose or specific task. (5)

Employ = put to work. (22)

Employest = utilize or apply.

→ *"Badly thou employest the little thou hast;"* is referring to the fact that we ask, or desire

for longer life even though we misuse this span that we've been given. Make the best use of the current cycle that is given and there will be nothing to worry about. (18)

Enslave = to make a slave of; reduce to slavery bondage or dependency. (23)

Esteem = to regard highly or favorably; to consider as of a certain value or of a certain type.

→ *"Learn to esteem as thou ought,"* is to learn to regard favorably and take into consideration life's true value. By doing so we learn how to manage our time in this manifest more properly. (3)

Evil = morally wrong or bad; immoral; wickedness. (29)

Expectations = prospects, especially of success or gain; the degree or probability that something will occur. (29)

Fawn = a young deer, especially an unweened one. (20)

Fools = people who lack judgment, sense, or understanding; ones who act unwisely on a given occasion.

→ *"Fools, to dread as mortals,"* shows the complexity and contradiction of finite man. In one instance he is overcome by intense fear befitting a mortal, and the next he desires immortality. If he were immortal, he would only prolong his dreadfulness and then dread the circumstances even though he longed for immortality. (30)

Forbiddeth = to exclude or bar; to prohibit. (2)

Frequent = happening or occurring quite often or at close intervals; constant, habitual, or regular.

HOLY INSTRUCTIONS FROM THE PROPHET
* PINNACLE OF WISDOM *

→ *"Too frequent repetition, is it not tiresome?"* The phrase is used in the negative form. It is making reference as to what is it that man should want in life after having lived in this manifest. It is pointing out the individual who basically lives by fulfilling the desires of the flesh, e.g., breathing, eating, etc., and living a purposeless life. Life was shortened (limited by years) as a blessing. (17)

Generations = one's contemporaries; offspring. (20)

Hadst = have. (24)

Hast = have. (18)

Hateth = dislike; to dislike intensely or passionately; detest. (33)

Hath = has. (24)

Hence = for this reason; therefore. (7)

Hereafter = in the life or world to come; reincarnation. (19)

Ignorance = lack of knowledge or information; uneducated. (28)

Immortal = not subject to physical death; never to be forgotten; everlasting. (30)

Impossibilities = things or goals that are not capable of being accomplished; something impossible. (29)

Infancy = the state or period of being an infant; very early in childhood, usually the period before being able to walk; babyhood. (14)

Infancy = *"second infancy"* the period in life where one is dependent upon another for aid and assistance, as in old age. The period in life where an elder must be looked after because of the inability of caring for self due to old age. (14)

Infirmities = moral weaknesses; physical weaknesses or ailments; frailties; feebleness; lack of strength; diseased. (31)

Innocence of manners = pure and moral manners, without harmful or sinful intent; simple mannerisms. (21)

Just: actual, real, or genuine. (6)

Justice = reason; correctness. (33)

Knowledge = the state or fact of knowing; facts, information, and skills acquired by a person through experience or study; the sum of what has been perceived, discovered, or learned; clear and certain mental apprehension. (19)

Labor = work. (26)

Lark = any of various chiefly Old-World birds of the family alaudidae, especially the skylark, having a sustained melodious song. (1)

Licentiousness = lacking moral discipline; sexually unrestrained; unrestrained by law, or general morality; having no regard for accepted rules or standards. (31)

Lo = acknowledge; look! see! Used to attract attention or show surprise. (6)

Manners = a way of doing something or the way in which a thing is done or happens. (21)

Merciful = full of mercy; compassionate, kind and forgiving. (7)

Misadventures = instances of misfortune; mishaps. (28)

Neglecteth = to pay no attention to or too little attention to; disregard. (26)

Obscure = lacking in light or illumination; dark. (2)

Offspring = descendants collectively; children. (20)

Ought = this word is used to express duty or moral obligation. (3)

Oughtest = ought; must. (4, 11)

Outrage = wanton, cruelty, violence or indignity. **Wanton** = without regard for what is right, just, humane, etc.; careless; reckless. (31)

Owl = any of numerous, chiefly Old World oscine birds of prey, of the order Strigiformes, having a broad head with large, forward-directed eyes that are usually surrounded by disks of modified feathers. The owl is a night bird of prey and therefore embraces the shade of the evening as it prepares for the night. (1)

Perish = to pass away; cease to exist. (19)

Pinnacle = the highest or culminating point, as of success, power, fame, WISDOM, etc. (3)

Pleasure = the state or feeling of being pleased or gratified; enjoyment or happiness. (33)

Present moment = the here and now; this cycle of life. (26)

Preserve = to keep alive or in existence; make lasting. (11)

Pretended = false appearance intended to deceive.

→ *"pretended wise"* are those who claim to know and have wisdom but yet are insincere or falsely professed; a deceiver. (4)

Prodigal = wastefully or recklessly extravagant. (24)

Regardest = to take into account or consider; respect. (24)

Repetition = the act of repeating; repeated action, performance, or presentation. (17)

Repine = to be discontented or low in spirits; fret or complain. (19)

Repinest = complain. (24)

Revered = respected. (32)

Riotous = given to or marked by unrestrained revelry; loose; wanton; uproarious; boisterous. (21)

Scene = an area or sphere of activity.

→ "scene of delusion," means that life (on this manifest/plane/sphere) is but a plane of illusions; a view of false beliefs and erroneous perceptions. (28)

Series = a group of events of misfortune occurring one after another. (28)

Shalt = shall.

Sleepest = rest.

→ *"sleepest in security"* means that one's have nothing to worry about for they have created no conditions to warrant worry; to sleep in comfort. (10)

Sorrow = a feeling of deep distress caused by loss, disappointment, or misfortune, suffered by oneself or others; mental suffering; grief. (17, 28)

Span = a limited space of time, as the term or period of living. (16)

State = the condition or situation with regard to a set of circumstances; position or conditions in life. (8)

Straw = a single stalk or stem, especially of certain species of grain, chiefly wheat, rye, oats, and barley; a mass of such stalks, especially after drying and threshing, used as fodder (food for livestock). (10)

Strive = to exert oneself vigorously; try hard. (11)

Succeeding = being that which follows. (5)

Suffice = to be enough or adequate, as for needs, purposes, etc.; be sufficient. (22)

Superfluous = being more than is sufficient or required; excessive. (17)

Teareth = to pull apart in pieces by force or violence. (8)

Temerity = foolhardy disregard of danger; reckless boldness; rashness. (31)

Thee = you.

Therefore = for that reason; consequently. (11, 18)

Therein = in that place or thing. (7)

Thine = your.

Thou = you.

Thoughtless = not thinking enough; careless or heedless; characterized by or showing lack of thought; shallow.

→ *"thoughtless hours,"* those periods in our lives where ones produced negative, useless, or unproductive thoughts. (14)

Thy = your.

Thyself = yourself.

Tiresome = causing or liable to cause a person to tire. (17)

Toils = a net or trap. (7)

True = real; genuine.

→ *"its true value,"* the real worth, which is based on the good that your life may be of to others. (2)

Tyranny = arbitrary or unrestrained exercise of power. (23)

Ungrateful = unappreciative. (21)

Vainly = in a vain, senseless, or foolish way; without effect or avail. (8)

Valuable = of great importance; nothing is more valuable or worth more than life, especially when used righteously. (4)

Value = merit; importance; worth. (2)

Vices = immoral or evil habits or practices; faults; defects, or shortcomings. (16)

Virtue = moral excellence and righteousness; goodness. (18, 32)

Virtuous = having or showing virtue, especially moral excellence; upright; pure. (34)

Vulture = any of various large birds of prey, characteristically having dark plumage and a featherless head and neck and generally feeding on carrion (dead animals). (1)

Want = to be lacking or absent, as a part or thing necessary for completeness; lack.

→ *"the want of good is evil."* We are taught that ALLAH has given us no good without its admixture of evil, but that He has also given us the means of throwing off the evil from it. Just as well, if we were to throw off the good that is within us, evil would be the remainder. Hence, "the want [*lack*] of good is evil." (6)

Wilt = will. (26)

Wisdom = the quality of having experience, knowledge, and good judgment; the ability to recognize or judge what is true, right, or lasting; insight.

→ *"wouldst thou improve thy wisdom and thy virtue?"* would you enhance/increase in wisdom and virtue if you were given more years to live? Would you become a more virtuous person? If you were to state yes, why haven't you been able to do so yet? It is in the proper application of what has been given to us, life, in which we are lacking in. (18)

Wouldst = will you?; would you? (18)

Wrinkles = small furrows or creases in the skin, especially of the face, as from aging or frowning. (32)

NOTES:

····· **CHAPTER XL (40)** ·····
HOLY INSTRUCTIONS FROM THE PROPHET
* THE INSTABILITY OF MAN *

INSTABILITY = the quality or state of being unstable; the tendency to behave in an unpredictable or erratic manner; changeable; unsteadiness; unfixed; undependable.

→ In this chapter, the Prophet tackles one of our greatest foes, Vanity! Vanity creates instability in the life of man because his main objective is not based on sincerity of heart. He seeks to feed himself on the winds of illusion while reality is lost in his works. A stern warning is issued to us by the Prophet in that we should do that which is right without expectation or thought of praise. To do what is right because it is right in the sight of ALLAH, not because it is right in the sight of man, and not because we have a thirst to hear about our good deeds in order to feed the desires (vanity) of the flesh. (Heading)

Admiration = the act of looking in or contemplating with pleasure; a feeling of wonder, pleasure, or approval. (16)

Ashamed = feeling shame; distressed or embarrassed by feeling of guilt, foolishness, or disgrace. (5)

Behave = to act or react in a particular way (usually properly). (4)

Behold = look at; see; acknowledge. (1, 16)

Bespeaketh = to ask for in advance; make arrangements for. (9)

Bestoweth = to present as a gift or an honor; confer. (14)

Biddeth = command; order; direct. (12)

Bread = livelihood; food or sustenance. (4)

Bubbles = something insubstantial, groundless, or ephemeral, especially a fantastic or impracticable idea or belief; an illusion; a speculative scheme that comes to nothing. (17)

Butterfly = any of various insects of the order Lepidoptera, characteristically having slender bodies, knobbed antennae, and four broad, usually colorful wings. (12)

Calamities = events that bring terrible losses, lasting distress, or severe affliction; a great misfortune or disaster. (2)

Cares = state of mind in which one is troubled, worried, or concerned; grief, suffering. (8)

Casteth = to throw off (12)

Conspicuous = easily seen or noticed; attracting special attention, as by outstanding qualities. (7)

Content = satisfied with what one is or has; not wanting more or anything else. (11)

Dainties = things (food) delicious to the taste; a delicacy. (13)

Deceiveth = to mislead by a false appearance or statement; delude. (9)

Delighteth = takes pleasure in; enjoys. (15)

Deserveth = to merit, be qualified for, or have claim to (reward, assistance, punishment, etc.) because of actions, qualities, or situation. (13)

Deserving = worthy of reward, aid, etc. (See *"Deserveth"* above). (11)

Despair = to lose all hope or confidence; give up or be without hope. (1)

Endanger = subject oneself to danger or destruction; to put oneself at risk. (3)

Engageth = to bind, as by pledge, promise, contract, or oath; to assume an obligation or agreement. (10)

HOLY INSTRUCTIONS FROM THE PROPHET
* THE INSTABILITY OF MAN *

Engrosseth = to occupy completely, as the mind or attention; absorb. (1)

Exalted = elevated; lofty. (5)

Extendeth = to stretch out. (9)

Fear = to be afraid or frightened of something; a feeling of agitation and anxiety caused by present or imminent danger; a feeling of disquiet or apprehension. (1)

Fixeth = to set.

→ He who *sets* his heart (mind) on show (illusions) loseth reality. (17)

Flattery = excessive, insincere praise.

→ To flatter is to try to please by complimentary remarks or attention. (14)

Follies = foolish acts, practices, ideas, wickedness, etc. (2)

Gaudy = brilliantly or excessively showy. (7)

Gay = happy. (12)

Gaze = a steady or intent (fixed) look. (13)

Hath = have or has.

Hero = a man of distinguished courage or ability, admired for his brave deeds and noble qualities; a person who, in the opinion of others has heroic qualities or has performed a heroic act and is regarded as a model or ideal. (3)

Human state = position in life; the condition of a person, as with respect to circumstances or attributes; station; present cycle of life. (2)

Inconstancy = changing without reason; an act of being inconstant; fickle; variable; changeable; faithless; unreliable; instability. (1)

Instruction = direction; imparted knowledge. (14)

Intemperance = lack of moderation or due restraint, as in action, speech, etc.; unrestrained. (1)

Jasmine = any of numerous shrubs or vines belonging to the genus Jasminum, of the olive family, having fragrant flowers and used in perfumery. (12)

Joy = a cause of great pleasure and happiness. (16)

Lo = look! see! (6)

Mark = to make note of; a noting or concern of oneself. (16)

Merit = claim to respect and praise; something that deserves or justifies a reward or commendation. (7)

Neglecteth = to disregard.

→ *"The man who neglecteth his present concerns,"* the man who disregards the responsibilities he has during this cycle of life. (4)

Posterity = succeeding for future generations collectively; all of a person's descendants. (11)

Proclaim = to announce officially and publicly; to declare openly. (16)

Raiment = clothing; apparel; attire. (13)

Regardest = to take into consideration. (14)

Rejoice = to feel or show great joy or delight. (11)

Renowned = celebrated; famous. (3)

Revolve = to repeatedly go over in the mind; to think about; to ponder or reflect on. (4)

Shadow = illusion.

→ *"shadow of a dream,"* reflection of a dream; an illusion; a wild or vain fancy. (2)

HOLY INSTRUCTIONS FROM THE PROPHET
* THE INSTABILITY OF MAN *

Shalt = shall.

Shroud = a cloth or sheet in which a corpse is wrapped for burial. (10)

Solicitude = a cause of anxiety or concern; worry. (9)

Speak = to communicate vocally.

→ "*Speak in sincerity,*" speak genuinely, honestly, with truth and without deceit. (14)

Station = position or status in life.

→ "*thy present station,*" your current position, or status in life. The present cycle of life. (5)

Swayeth = to cause (the mind, emotions, etc., or a person) to incline or turn in a specific way; to move to and fro, up and down. (1)

Thee = you.

Therefore = for that reason; consequently. (2)

Therein = in that place, time, thing, or circumstance. (1)

Thou = you.

Thy = your.

Treads = to set down the foot or feet in walking; to walk. (17)

Tulip = any of various plants belonging to the genus Tulipa, of the lily family, having lance-shaped leaves and large, showy, cup-shaped, or bell-shaped flowers in a variety of colors. (7)

Ungrateful = unappreciative. (3)

Unmeaning = not meaning anything; meaningless. (14)

Unrivaled = having no rival or competitor; having no equal; incomparable; supreme; in total control. (1)

Unstable = not stable; not firm or firmly fixed; unsteady. (3)

Unto = to.

Vain = excessively proud of or concerned about one's own appearance, qualities, achievements, etc. (8, 15)

Vanity = excessively proud in one's appearance, qualities, abilities, achievements, etc.; conceited. (1, 2, 6)

Vesture = clothing; garments. (13)

Weep = to express grief, sorrow, or any overpowering emotion by shedding tears; mourn with tears or other expressions of sorrow. (2)

Whilst = while. (11)

Whither = whatever place; wherever. (1)

Widowhood = the state or period of being a widow.

Widow = a woman who has lost her husband by death and has not remarried. (10)

Wilt = will.

Wind = illusion; something fleeting. (4)

NOTES:

→ **INCONSTANCY** is defined as changing without reason; an act of being inconstant; fickle; variable; changeable; faithless; unreliable; instability. Fickle is defined as changeable with regard to one's loyalty to someone or some cause. Inconstancy is one of the biggest foes we face in a world of many dealings. This chapter affords us the ability to point out and deal with inconstancy accordingly. A point worth mentioning is that Chapter 41 begins by covering the nature of the physical manifestation but finishes by displaying a higher, more meaningful nature, the spiritual. (Heading)

Abide = to dwell or remain with. (22)

Accident = any event that happens unexpectedly, without a deliberate plan or cause; an unforeseen incident. (5)

Afar = from a great distance; a long distance. (31)

Anxiety = distress or uneasiness of mind caused by fear of danger or misfortune. (10)

Armed = to equip with what is needed for effective action.

→ "armed thee with resolution," is to be equipped with personal resolve and the ability to find a solution to a problem and decide firmly on a proper course of action. (3)

Arrogant = having or displaying a sense of overbearing self-worth or self-importance; overbearing pride; conceited. (17)

Art = are. (2)

Beyond = overpassing certain or set boundaries. (31)

Boasteth = an instance of bragging. (See "*Boasteth*" in Ch. 26). (4)

Body = flesh; human vehicle made of "earth." (3)

Boldly = fearlessly and daringly; courageously; with full confidence and courage. (32)

Brow = the forehead; the ridge over the eye; the eyebrow. (25)

Camelion = chameleon: any of the numerous Old-World lizards of the family Chamaeleontidae, characterized by the ability to change the color of their skin, very slow locomotion, and projective tongue. (19)

Concerneth = to engage or involve; those with which ones associate with or come in contact with. (14)

Constancy = the quality of being unchanging or unwavering, as in purpose, love, or loyalty; firmness of mind; steadfastness; faithful and dependable. **Steadfastness** = fixed or unchanging; steady, (10)

Contrarieties = being contrary; opposed, as in character or purpose to what is expected; adverse; conflicting. (7)

Countenance = appearance, especially the expression of the face.

→ "*the lightning serveth but to show the glories of his countenance.*" As to lightning, Yusuf Ali states, "To cowards lightning and thunder appear as terrible forces of nature: lightning seems to kill and destroy where its irresistible progress is not assisted by proper lightning-conductors." To the resolute man, lightning serves only as a source of light which shines forth and exposes his aura. Storms, thunders, and lightnings can herald disaster and chaos but are unable to impede the path of the resolute. (30)

Deigneth = to think fit or in accordance with one's dignity; to condescend to give or grant. (26)

Detested = intensely disliked; abhorred. Abhorred = to feel strong hatred for. (16)

Doeth = do or does. (4)

Ease = the condition of being comfortable or relieved; freedom from pain, worry, or distress; freedom from difficulty of effort. (14, 22)

Embattled = an army prepared and fortified for battle; a large military unit trained for combat. (29)

Employ = put to work; put to use: make use of. (3)

Enemy = one who feels hatred toward, intends injury to, or opposes another; a foe; adversary. (12)

Ensure = to make sure or certain; insure. (10)

Escapeth = gets away; breaks loose from. (8)

Establish = to set up on a firm or permanent basis.

→ *"Establish unto thyself principles of action,"* is to set up a system, set of rules, or moral standards on a permanent basis for yourself to adhere to and be sure you remain constant to those virtues. **Adhere** = stick firmly to; follow or observe. (9)

Establish thy heart = set your heart (mind) to do that which is right according to the dictates of ALLAH and His Prophet Noble Drew Ali. (33)

Event = something that occurs in a certain place during a particular interval of time; an occurrence; something that happens.

→ *"event of an impulse,"* an occurrence that happens from a sudden urge, without thought or consideration. (5)

Evil = morally wrong or bad; immoral; wicked. (11)

Exalted = elevated above or standing higher than the common.

→ *"Exalted form,"* one that stands out above others, fixed in the ways of righteousness. (24)

Execution = the act or process of carrying out a plan, wish, etc.; put into effect. (6)

Failings = defects or shortcomings; weaknesses. (6)

Faults = misdeeds or transgressions; defects or imperfection; character weaknesses, mistakes, errors, or offenses; failings. (12)

Firm = constant; steadfast; stable; fixed; not subject to change; solid. **Steadfast** = resistant to externally applied pressure; solid; immutable. (7)

Firmness = not susceptible to change; fixed and resolved.

→ *"firmness of mind,"* a mind that has established will power and carries out that which he/she sets out to do no matter what may appear in his/her way. A firm mind with no room for deviation. (7)

Fixed = to become stable, firm, or founded; to set definitely. (22)

Foundation = the basis on which a thing stands, is founded, or is supported. (23)

Furnished = supplied with; gave; equipped with something, in this instance weakness, which is of the flesh. (3)

Glories = great beauty or splendor. (30)

Grudgeth = to put into the mouth as an attempt to avoid anyone asking for some; unwilling to give or to give with reluctance. (18)

Hath = have or has. (13)

Hitherward = hither: to or towards this place. (24)

Humble = meek or modest; courteously respectful. (17)

Immutable = not susceptible to change; unchangeable; constant.

→ *"the greatest of human is to be immutable,"* is to say the greatest aspect, or quality of a human is to be unchanging, firm, and constant in that which is right. That is the unfoldment of the Higher-self which is the Mother of virtues and the harmonies of life and breeds Justice, Mercy, Love, and Right. (33)

Impulse = a sudden wish or urge that prompts an unpremeditated act; and abrupt inclination. (5)

Incapable = not capable; not open to, or susceptible to. Susceptible = easily influenced by. (8)

Inconstant = one who is fickle, always changing or varying. **Fickle** = changeable with regard to focus, sincerity etc.; instability. (20)

Inheriteth = to receive (a characteristic) from one's parents by genetic or cultural transmission. (2)

Instability = the quality or condition of being unstable; erratic, or unpredictable.

→ Instability is a condition of the human state. It is of the human nature derived from our physical father. (2)

→ *"beware of instability in the execution,"* is a caution extended to us to guard ourselves against erratic behavior in carrying out our actions. (6)

Intent = aim or purpose; intention. (6)

Irregular = unpredictable; fluctuating.

→ *"his motions are irregular,"* the inconstant in life is impulsive and his inclinations are uneven (he has no balance). He does not conform to moral law and is fickle minded. (15)

Irresolution = unsure of how to act; undecided; lack of decision or purpose.

→ "Beware of irresolution in the intent of thy actions," be on guard against irresolution, indecisiveness, unfirm, wavering with your intention; be firm in the decided actions you take. (6)

Joyful = a feeling or causing great pleasure and happiness. (20)

Just = right. (13)

Legions = any large group of armed men; a military or semi-military unit. (29)

Loins = the part of the human body between the hips and lower ribs, especially regarded as the seat of physical and generative power; the genital area. (2)

Majesty = supreme greatness. (25)

Mendeth = to set right; to remove or correct defects or errors in.

→ *"Mendeth not,"* not able to set right or correct due to the inability to control one's actions. (12)

Misfortune = adverse fortune; an unfortunate event. (10)

HOLY INSTRUCTIONS FROM THE PROPHET
* INCONSTANCY *

Moderation = the act of being moderate; being within reasonable limits; not excessive or extreme. (18)

Motions = movements; impulses, or inclinations of the mind, will, or desires. (15)

→ *"Nature urgeth thee to inconstancy,"* man's carnal nature/physical manifestation impels, or pushes him to state of being variable or fickle. It leads to an unstable lifestyle where ones fluctuate in their purpose. (1)

Obstacles = things that oppose, stand in the way of, or impedes progress. (26)

Oppose = to impede the process of.

→ "Oppose his passage," any attempt to deter, stop, slow down, or stand in the way of one's journey. (26)

Overspreadeth = to spread or extend over the surface of; diffuse over. **Diffuse** = spread over a wide area. (19)

Passions = powerful emotions, such as love, joy, hatred, or anger; emotions and desires, (10)

Perceiveth = to become aware of, know, or identify by means of the senses; to recognize, discern, envision, or understand.

→ *"perceiveth not,"* means that the individual lacks the proper understanding as to how he escapes from himself. (8)

Phantom = an appearance of illusion without material substance, as in a dream, image, mirage, or optical illusion; something seen in the imagination; not real (bearing no substance). (21)

Port = a place where a ship or person stops on a journey.

→ This is a metaphor for steadiness of mind. (25)

Possesseth = to have as belonging to one; to have as a faculty, quality, or the like. (10)

Principles = a person or specific basis of conduct or management; guiding sense of the requirements and obligations of right conduct.

→ *"principles of action,"* are a set of rules or standards used to develop good behavior, moral standards, and just standards. The "principles of action of the Moorish Science Temple of America are its laws, the five grand principles of Love, Truth, Peace, Freedom, and Justice, and the teachings of the Prophet Noble Drew Ali which are intended to make us better beings and aid in our spiritual unfoldment. (9)

Proceedeth = to arise, originate, or result; continues to go or move forward.

→ *"proceedeth not,"* does not derive from or is not produced from reason. (13)

Profuse = spending or giving freely in a large amount; extravagant. **Extravagant** = spending or using more than is necessary or more than you can afford. (18)

Rack = a cause or state of intense suffering of body or mind; under great strain or distress. (21)

Rarely = not often; seldom; infrequently. (4)

Reason = sound judgment or soundness of mind. (7)

Reason = logical or rational thinking; good judgment; good sense; intelligence. (13)

Reason = cause or explanation. (22)

Rely = trust or have faith in; be dependent on or have confidence in. (8)

Reproacheth = disgrace, discredit or blame incurred; to disappoint. (7)

Resolution = the mental state or quality of being resolute; firm or determined; unwavering; a firm decision; the act of resolving or determining upon an action or course of action, method, procedure, etc. (3, 31)

Riseth = to get up from bed, especially to begin the day after a night's sleep; to wake up. (21)

Servant = one who labors for or serves another; a person employed by another, especially to perform domestic duties. (17)

Servile = slavishly submissive; excessively willing to serve or please other people. (17)

Shalt = shall. (6)

Sighing = sight: to lament (mourn) with sighing; to sigh is to exhale audibly in a long deep breath, as from sorrow, weariness, exhaustion, sadness, etc. (20)

Sorrow = a feeling of deep distress caused by loss, disappointment, or misfortune suffered by oneself or others; mental suffering; grief. (22)

Soul = an independent principle of life.

→ A garb provided to Spirit-man in order to function independently on the plane of soul. The essence of the soul is the Spirit. The soul possesses actions. These actions are: Thinking, Understanding, Reasoning, and Willing. The soul is influenced by our thoughts and therefore we must forever be careful of what and how we think, because the soul is shaped by our thoughts, and as we expand our thought environment, we give the soul greater expression. The virtues or vices we feed the soul will be our reward. (14)

Steadiness = firmly placed or fixed; unwavering, as in purpose; steadfast. **Steadfast** = not changing in your attitude or aims; fixed; steady.

→ "*steadiness is in his port*," is to say that the mind of the resolute is firm, sure, steadfast, and unwavering. (25)

Subjection = being under the power or authority of another or others; to submit to the authority of someone or something. (17)

Suppress = to put an end to forcibly; subdue or prohibit the activities of. (7)

Tendencies = predispositions to think, act, behave, or proceed in a particular way. (7)

Terrors = fears; horrors.

→ "*terrors of death*," implies fears of dying, meaning that no matter what the circumstances are, even at the cost of death, he moves forward to the determined goal. (29)

Thee = you.

Therefore = for that reason. (1)

Thou = you.

Thy = your.

Tranquility = calmness; peacefulness; serenity.

→ "*and in his heart reigneth tranquility*," means that his soul is at peace because he has control over all that he faces in life. He knows how to deal with the cares of the world accordingly. (25)

Tread = to walk.

→ "The mountains sink beneath his tread," is metaphorically stating that though the man with a resolute will may face difficult problems, he does not allow them to hinder his progress toward his set objective. (27)

Triumph = to be victorious over. (6)

Tyrant = a ruler who exercises power in a harsh cruel manner; an oppressive person. (17)

Uncertainty = uncertain; unpredictable; doubt; not known, questionable, or unsure.

→ "*born of uncertainty*," coming about, or originating unpredictably from an unknown region, or area. (5)

Unequal = not the same in any measurable aspect; irregular.

→ "*His life is unequal*," meaning that because of his lack of resolution, his life is always fluctuating, never balanced, therefore he has no control over events that may unfold. (15)

Uninterrupted = moving freely, continually, and in a steady fashion. (24)

Unregarded = unaffectedly.

→ The point being made here is that the man with a resolute will is not affected by signs of danger. He shows no regards to them, but he acknowledges that danger does exist. (28)

Unto = to.

Urgeth = to drive forth by the impulses of the body; to push or drive into action by a strong desire or impulse. (1)

Utmost = the most distant limit or point; farthest degree. (31)

Vain = without real significance, value, or importance; fruitless. **Fruitless** = failing to achieve the desired results; unproductive; without success. (28)

Various = presenting or having many different qualities or aspects; marked by, exhibiting, or possessing diversity; inconsistent or unstable. (2)

Verdure = green vegetation, especially grass or herbage. (19)

Wavering = becoming unsteady; to show inconsistency; to feel or show doubt, indecision, etc.; inconstancy. (2)

Weepeth = to express emotion, such as grief or sadness, by shedding tears; cry; to be in a state of sadness or grief. (21)

Wherefore = for what purpose or reason?; why? (16)

Will = of one's own accord or power. (4)

Willeth = the act or process of using or asserting one's choice.

→ "*Willeth*" (will), denotes fixed and persistent intent or purpose. One day the inconstant in life is willing to do something, the next, because of his inconstancy, he changes his mind and is no longer willing. The only consistency he displays is in the changing of his mind. (21)

Wise = the ability to discern (recognize) or judge what is true, right, or lasting; judicious or prudent. (3)

Womb = the uterus of the human female which hold the developing fetus (the belly); a place where something is generated or helped to germinate. (2)

Wonder = to cause to think or speculate curiously.

→ The question being asked is rhetorical in nature. If ones are lacking a sure foundation on which happiness is built upon, why be surprised or amazed when it no longer remains with us? If it's built upon a sure foundation, no matter the circumstances, it will remain with it. (23)

NOTES:

HOLY INSTRUCTIONS FROM THE PROPHET
* WEAKNESS *

WEAKNESS = the condition or quality of being weak; lack of strength, firmness, vigor, or the like; likely to fail under pressure, stress, or strain; lacking firmness of character or strength of will. (Heading)

Absolute = complete; not mixed; pure. (13)

Admiration = the act of looking on or contemplating with pleasure; a feeling of wonder, pleasure, or approval. (13)

Admixture = a mixture; the act of mixing; the state of being mixed. (14)

Agonies = the suffering of intense physical or mental pain; the struggle that precedes death. (22)

Alas = used as an exclamation to express sorrow, pity, concern, or apprehension of evil. (6)

Allotted = divided or distributed by share or portion; assigned as a portion. (19)

Alloy = mixture; blend. (15)

Arrest = to withhold or restrict the movement of; to have under one's control.

→ *"arrest not."* Weakness is the one thing that physical man does not have control over and will continue to be subservient to if he does not elevate beyond the body of desires. (8)

Art = are. (2, 3, 4)

Behold = to observe; look at; see. (22)

Blended = combined or to combine. (18)

Bosom = intimate or confidential.

→ Your wife as being the one you have bestowed trust and given affection to prior to your passing form and her entering into widowhood. (20)

Burnedeth = burn; to feel strong emotion, passion, or longing for. (12)

Canst = can.

→ *"Rejoice that thou canst not [cannot] excel in evil"* is to be glad of the fact that everything has a limit within the flesh. However, I think it important to point out that evil is evil no matter what. It is the degree of evil that must be addressed. The greater the evil we indulge in, the harder the task of redemption. Good and evil from a finite perspective are limited to the realm of things that are made manifest. When viewed through infinite wisdom we are viewing it from the true essence of men: SPIRIT-MAN, in which there is no evil. (18)

Cease = to come to an end; discontinue. (10)

Circumstances = conditions or facts that determine or must be considered in the determining of a course of action. (8)

Content = the substantive or meaningful part. (13)

Content = satisfied; satisfy; desiring no more than what one already has. (4, 18)

Contenteth = to satisfy.

→ *"it contenteth thee not,"* even when one's have obtained what they most longed for they are still left with an emptiness within. This is the outcome of the desires of the flesh, the carnal nature of man. No matter what we may desire, if what we wish for is of the physical manifest and not directed by reason, it will never suffice. (3)

Contentment = happiness or satisfaction. (20)

Couldst = can. (5)

Creator = ALLAH. (5)

Danger = a source or an instance of risk or peril; a cause of harm. (1)

Declareth = to reveal or make manifest; show. (6)

Dejection = sadness, depression, or lowness of spirits (thoughts). (12)

Delighteth = to offer great pleasure or joy. (6)

Delights = things that give great pleasure. (10, 12)

Desires = objects of longing; things longed or wished for. (3)

Desiring = longing, craving, or wishing for. (9)

Despised = disliked intensely. (20)

Despiseth = to dislike intensely; to feel hatred or disgust for. (7)

Destruction = ruin; the condition or being destroyed. (17)

Dictates = to command or order. (23)

Divisions = a splitting into factions; disunion. (21)

Doubts = feelings of uncertainty about the truth, reality, or nature of something. (23)

Duty = moral obligation. (21)

Ecstasy = a state of emotion so intense that one is carried beyond rational thought and self-control; an intense feeling of joy or delight. (13)

Enjoyment = something that gives pleasure. (10)

Entirely = wholly; completely. (18)

Escape = to avoid; to break free or get free from someone or something. (1)

Esteem = to hold in favorable regard; respect. (13)

Evil = morally wrong or bad; immoral; wicked. (18)

Excel = to surpass. (18)

Extremity = the greatest or utmost degree; any extreme degree. (16)

Forbiddeth = to command against doing something; refuse to allow. (16)

Founded = based on; to establish or set up upon. (11)

Frail = morally weak. (3)

Frailty = a fault resulting from moral weakness. (1)

Glorieth = the height of achievement, enjoyment, or prosperity; to rejoice. (2)

Grief = strong mental suffering or painful state; miserable mental pain; torment. (15)

Grieve = to cause to be sorrowful; distress; to feel or express grief. (19)

Hast = have. (3)

Hath = have or has. (14)

Hast not = have not or has not. (18)

Imperfection = the quality or state of being imperfect; having flaws; having defects or weaknesses. (1)

Inconstancy = changing without reason; an act of being inconstant; fickle; variable; changeable; faithless; unreliable; instability. (1)

Inconstant = always changing; unpredictable; unreliable; fickle. (1)

Infirmity = a moral weakness; physical weakness or ailment; frailty; feebleness; lack

HOLY INSTRUCTIONS FROM THE PROPHET
* WEAKNESS *

of strength; a feeling or defect in a person's character. (1, 6)

Join = combine. (13)

Joy = a cause of great pleasure and happiness. (15)

Justice = fairness; the quality of being just; sincere at heart. (21)

Knowledge = an awareness or understanding. (23)

Languishment = to assume an expression of tender, sentimental melancholy. **Melancholy** = deep and long-lasting sadness. (12)

Liberality = the quality of being liberal in giving; generous. (20)

Means = an agency, instrument, or method used to attain an end. (14)

Melancholy = sadness or depression of the soul; deep and long-lasting sadness. (16)

Mercy = compassion; relief, clemency. (22)

Mingled = mixed together. (16)

Mischiefs = harm or trouble, especially as a result of an agent or cause; damage, destruction, or injury caused by a specific person or thing. (1)

Moderate = being within reasonable limits; not excessive or extreme. (11)

Nature = the particular combination of qualities belonging to a person by birth, origin, or constitution; the instincts or inherent tendencies directing conduct. (18)

Nauseates = to cause to feel extreme disgust; repulse. (12)

Objects = material things; things sought after with passion; desires. (12)

Obtained = acquired; having gained possession of. (3)

Pain = mental suffering; distress. (10)

Period = ending. (22)

Permanent = lasting or remaining without essential change; forever. (6)

Pleasure = the state or feeling of being pleased or gratified; enjoyment or happiness. (6, 15)

Portion = a part or share; an amount. (15)

Possess = have in one's control. (19)

Possessing = having. (2, 9)

Possession = ownership; control. (11)

Pre-eminence = superior to or notable above all others; superiority; importance; outstanding. (23)

Preferring = choosing; favor; to like better; to place above other persons or things. (8)

Quarreleth = fight. (8)

Raising = to have as a source.

→ Our doubts emanate from our own ignorance. (23)

Raptures = intense pleasure or joy. (13)

Reason = logical thinking; good judgment; intelligence.

→ Our reason is to be founded not on common thinking or intelligence, but upon the teachings of Prophet Noble Drew Ali. (11)

Rejoice = to feel or show great joy or delight. (18)

Relish = a pleasing or enjoyable quality; great enjoyment. (4)

Repenteth = to feel sorry for; regret. (7)

Satiety = satisfied, as one's appetite or desire to the point of boredom; surfeit. **Surfeit** = to indulge to excess in anything. (12)

Shalt = shall. (1)

Sighs = to sigh is to exhale audibly in a long deep breath, as from sorrow, weariness, relief, or exhaustion. (12)

Sink = to drop or fall slowly, as from weakness or fatigue, both mentally and/or physically. (21)

Sorrow = a feeling of deep distress caused by loss, disappointment, or misfortune suffered by oneself or others; mental suffering; grief. (11)

Soughteth = to seek; to search for. (3)

Sources = supplies. (10)

Stations = positions. (19)

Succeedeth = to follow; to come after. (8)

Surpasseth = to be greater; to go beyond the limit, power, or capacity. (13)

Terminate = end. (12)

Thee = you.

Thou = you.

Throwing off = rejecting; the means or method of pushing something not wanted away. (14)

Thy = your.

Thyself = yourself.

Tranquility = calmness; peacefulness. (13)

Unite = to come or bring together as one; to form a whole. (13)

United = combined or joined. (15)

Ushered = attended or brought at the coming or at the beginning; precede or herald. (12)

Vain = (Archaic) senseless or foolish. (1)

Vanity = excessive pride in one's appearance, qualities, abilities, achievements, etc.; conceited. (1)

Variety = a number or collection of varied things, especially of a particular group; an assortment; many things; a multitude of different things. (6)

Various = of different kinds; different. (19)

Virtues = moral excellence and righteousness; goodness; conformity of one's life and conduct to moral and ethical principles; a good desirable personal quality. (23)

Wearied = to become physically or mentally exhausted; fatigued; tired; impatient or dissatisfied. (4)

Weary = tired. (12)

Wherefore = for what purpose or reason?; why? (4)

Wherein = in what way or respect; in what or in which? (2)

Wise = having or showing experience, knowledge, and good judgment; the ability to discern (recognize) or judge what is true, right, or lasting; judicious or prudent. (17)

Wouldst = would you?; will? (3, 20)

NOTES:

INSUFFICIENCY = the quality or state of being insufficient, especially moral, or mental incompetence; deficiency (lacking) in amount; inadequate; not enough. (Heading)

KNOWLEDGE = the state or fact of knowing; facts, information, and skill acquired by a person through experience or study, the sum of what has been perceived, discovered, or learned; clear and certain mental apprehension. (Heading, l, 15)

Affright = to arouse fear in; terrify; to frighten. (27)

Amiable = friendly and agreeable in disposition; good-natured and likable; lovely or lovable. **Disposition** = the natural qualities of a person's character. (20)

Anguish = agonizing physical or mental pain; torment. (10)

Apprehend = to grasp mentally; understand. (19)

Art = are. (8, 27)

Ascend = to go or move upward; rise; advance. (13)

Ashes = mortal remains, especially the physical body as liable to decay. (22)

Attaineth = to gain, reach or accomplish by mental effort; achieve. (1)

Authorized = to have given permission to do. (4)

Bareth = bear: to support, withstand.

→ "*bareth not*" is not to support or withstand. (20)

Bid = to summon; to command; order. (12)

Behold = look at; see; acknowledge. (22)

Boldness = without fear. (25)

Breedeth = to bring about; produce. (18)

Cause = good or sufficient reason. (11)

Claimeth = to assert and demand the recognition of (a right, title, possession, etc.). (2)

Command = to have control or authority over; rule; order. (4)

Commandest = to order, rule, dictate, or the like.

→ "*commandest to the torture,*" to give an order or command by someone in authority, *i.e.*, a ruler, to torture someone in order to get them to reveal something, whether it is the truth or not. In this there is sin, because the pain would cause one to admit to things they may actually be innocent of. (9)

Commandeth = orders. (28)

Condemn = to give grounds or reason for convicting or censuring.

→ "*Surely thine own words condemn thee,*" is the use of one's own words as grounds or reason for convicting or censuring. (7)

Conduct = to direct in action or course.

→ "*attention is the pilot that must conduct thee into her port.*" To be able to arrive at the knowledge of truth, one must be attentive to what goes into the soul. By avoiding corrupt thinking, we produce creative and righteous thoughts that lead to unfoldment. (17)

Confess = to acknowledge or avow (a fault, crime, misdeed, etc.); to make confession.

→ "*confess his guilt,*" is to mislead the criminal into admitting a crime, sin, or misdeed with the intent of never carrying out an agreement. (8)

Connivance = tacit (unspoken) encouragement or assent (without participation) to wrongdoing by another; to cooperate secretly or conspire. (3)

Council = a group of people meeting regularly to advise on, consult, discuss, deliberate, or organize something. (3)

Countenance = appearance, especially the expression of the face. (14)

Criminal = a person guilty or convicted of a crime. (8)

Dazzle = to dim the vision of by intense light; to blind someone temporarily; (14)

Deceive = to deliberately cause someone to believe something that is not true; mislead. (23)

Decree = an authoritative order having the force of law. (3)

Demanding = insisting upon; urgently asking for. (6)

Denial = an assertion that something said, believed, alleged, etc., is false.

→ "He that giveth a denial with reason," is dealing with one who may have been accused of some wrongdoing but in exercising reason is able to explain the wrong of such an allegation. (26)

Desirable = worth having, wanting, or seeking; worth achieving. (1)

Desire = to wish or long for something; crave; want. (6)

Devotions = earnest attachment to a cause, person, etc.; religious observances or worship. (21)

Dissimulation = hypocrisy; to conceal one's true motives, thoughts, feelings, etc., by some pretense; to speak or act hypocritically; deception. (18)

Dost = do; does. (11)

Doth = does. (22)

Emerald = a bright green precious stone consisting of a variety of beryl, used as a gem stone. (16)

Enemies = a group who feel hatred toward, intense injury to, or opposes another; foes; adversaries. (18)

Enforce = make; to obtain by force or compulsion. (10)

Entreaty = an earnest request or petition; a plea. (28)

Executed = put into effect; carried out. (7)

Flattereth = to portray favorably; excessively compliment in order to get something in return. (8)

Flattery = to praise or compliment insincerely or excessively. (18)

Footstep = a step on which to go up or down. (13)

Footstool = a low stool upon which to rest one's feet when seated. (15)

Forgetteth = fail to remember. (6)

Frailty = the quality or state of being weak and delicate; moral weakness; a fault resulting from moral weakness. (22)

Guiltless = free from guilt; innocent. (8)

Hath = have or has. (2)

He = ALLAH. (6)

Honest = truthful and sincere. (23)

Ignorance = lack of knowledge, information, or awareness in general; uneducated.

→ *"thine own ignorance."* It has often been said that the more one knows, the less he actually knows. In this instance, we must humble ourselves and accept our own ignorance if we are to gain true knowledge. (15)

Infirmities = weaknesses. (21)

Inform thyself = to make oneself aware by careful study and analyzation. (15)

Instituted = established; put into operation. (21)

Insufficience = the quality or state of being insuffrcient, especially moral or mental incompetence; deficiency (lacking) in amount; inadequate; not enough.

→ "insufficience of the wisdom of the wise" means the lack of TRUE wisdom which is possessed by wise men. (12)

Insufficient = not sufficient (enough); lacking in what is necessary or required; inadequate. (13)

Just = honorable and fair in one's dealings and actions; consistent with what is morally right; righteous. (23)

Just = fair; impartial. (28)

Justice = the principle of moral righteousness; fairness.

→ *"Sayeth thou, that justice cannot be executed without wrong?"* If you believe, or say, that one's cannot carry out justice without someone first doing wrong, these words bear witness against you. Justice is not only punishing a wrong. It is also rewarding what is right. The Higher-self is the Mother of virtues and the harmonies of life and breeds Justice, Mercy, Love, and Right. (7)

Labor = physical or mental exertion, especially when difficult or exhausting; work. (17)

Maintenance = the act of keeping in existence or continuance; the act of maintaining; upkeep.

→ *"maintenance of justice,"* upkeep, perseverance, or maintaining justice and a continuance of righteousness. (13)

Manfully = with boldness, courage, or strength. (16)

Moderation = temperance (self-control). (26)

Mount = to climb; to go up; get up on. (15)

Numerous = consisting of many. (5)

Oath = a solemn appeal to some revered person to witness one's determination to speak the truth or keep a promise. (23)

Objects = material things.

→ "objects of thy desire," things you long for or wish to possess. (6)

Obstinate = stubborn; hard or difficult to deal with. (28)

Obtained = acquired. (18)

Passions = powerful or compelling emotions or feelings, as love and hate.

→ *"thou must hear without thy passions,"* to be fair in your dealings with men, you must put aside all your personal feelings and go with the law. The law is neutral, and it is up to the individual whether they bring reward or punishment upon themselves. (28)

Patience = the ability to accept or tolerate delay, trouble, difficulty, provocation, annoyance, or suffering without becoming angry or upset; understanding. (25)

Pearls = small, hard, shiny white balls formed within the shell of an oyster and having great value as a gem when lustrous and finely colored. (16)

Permitted = allowed. (3)

Pilot = to steer or control the course of; a guide or leader. (17)

Possesseth = to have, gain, or acquire; to cause to own, hold, or be proficient in something, such as property or knowledge. (2)

Proclaimeth = to announce officially and publicly; to declare openly. (2)

Purpose = a result or an effect that is intended or desired; an intention. (10)

Pursue = to strive to gain or accomplish. (16)

Rack = ruin or destroy; torture.

→ "*rack the innocent*," to ruin or destroy an innocent person. (9)

Radiance = shining brightness; radiant brightness or light. (14)

Raiseth = breeds; to bring about. (18)

Rendered = caused to be or become; made. (28)

Repentance = the act or process of repenting; remorse or contrition for past conduct or sin. Contrition = sincere remorse for wrongdoing. (22, 23)

Reprove = to voice or convey disapproval of; criticize or reprimand (correct) someone. (25)

Repulse = a refusal or rejection; a denial. (26)

Requisite = required; necessary.

→ Evil is not essential or required of man. The essence of man is spiritual, not demonic. What is required of man is the good that is within him. (3)

Ruby = a deep red translucent variety of the mineral corundum, valued as a precious stone; a gem. (16)

Ruler = a person who rules or governs. (2, 4)

Sapphire = a clear hard variety of corundum used as a gemstone that is usually blue but may be any color except red. (16)

Seek = to go in search or quest of. **Quest** = to search or seek for; pursue. (16)

Shalt = shall.

Splendor = magnificent or gorgeous appearance; great brightness. (20)

Statesman = a person who is experienced in the art of government or versed in the administration of government affairs. (2)

Subject = a person under the rule of another. (2)

Supplications = to make humble or earnest requests. (28)

Suspected of ill = one who is thought to have done a wrong, usually with no evidence of actually having done so. (9)

Swearest = to promise or pledge with a solemn oath; vow. (23)

Tender = gently and kind; easily moved to sympathy or compassion; considerate. (28)

Thee = you.

Therefore = for that reason; consequently. (16)

Thine = yours; that which belongs to you.

Thou = you.

Thy = your.

Toil = to labor continuously; work. (17)

Tolerated = allowed without prohibiting or opposing; permitted; put up with; endured. (3)

Unto = to.

Vice = an evil, degrading, or immoral practice or habit; a serious moral failing; bad conduct or bad habits; a personal shortcoming. (3)

View at thy devotions! = examine what you pledge your allegiance to; examine your religious observances or worship, that you may be made more aware of its purpose. (21)

Weary = to get physically or mentally exhausted; fatigued; tired; impatient or dissatisfied. (17)

Wilt = will. (23)

Wisdom = the quality of having experience, knowledge, and good judgment; the ability to recognize or judge what is true, right, or lasting; spiritual insight. (21)

Wise = having or showing experience, knowledge, and good judgment; the ability to discern and execute what is true, right, or lasting; a judicious or prudent person. (4, 12)

Worthy = of commendable excellence or merit; having adequate or great merit, character, or value. (1)

Wouldst = would you; will. (15)

NOTES:

MISERY = great mental or emotional distress; extreme unhappiness; a cause or source of suffering. (Heading)

About thee = connected, associated, in, or somewhere near a person (you). (12)

Account = a statement of reason, causes, etc., explaining some event; reason, basis.

→ "account of thine action;" a reason given for a particular course of action taken by you. Your deeds are personal, and you must bear the weight of them, be they good deeds or bad. (23)

Admitted = allowed or permitted; to have the capacity for. (14)

Adorn = to decorate; enhance. (4)

Affliction = a cause of mental or bodily pain; a condition of suffering or distress. (20)

Allotted = distributed; given; issued. (19)

Alloy = a mixture. (16)

Anguish = agonizing physical or mental pain; torment. (18)

Anticipateth = to look forward to; expect; to think, speak, etc., or feel an emotional response in advance. (22)

Apprehension = anticipation of adversity or misfortune; suspicion or fear of future trouble or evil. (22)

Art = are.

Beaver = a large amphibious rodent of the genus Castor, having sharp incisors, webbed hind feet, and a flattened tail, noted for its ability to dam streams with trees, branches, etc. (22)

Begetteth = to father, sire, produce (a male child). (5)

Behold = to observe; look at; see; to acknowledge. (2)

Being = life. (2, 8)

Bitterness = distress; causing pain. (16)

Blaze = flame; fire. (15)

Blessings = something which you are very grateful for.

→ A child is a gift from ALLAH thereby bringing you happiness. ALLAH alone gives life, and we must learn to appreciate the ability to reproduce because it affords us a chance to perpetuate the race as not just as Asiatics, but also as a clean and pure nation reproclaimed by ALLAH through His divine prophet Drew Ali. (9)

Cast = to put or place behind you; to throw off. (12)

Character = the combination of qualities or features that distinguishes one person, group, or thing from another. (2)

Curseth = to wish or invoke evil, calamity misfortune, injury, or destruction upon; damn. (10)

Custom = the practice followed by a people of a particular group or origin.

→ *"Custom cannot alter the nature of truth."* Custom is a common practice or tradition of a people handed down generation after generation, yet this practice or tradition does not change what is Truth. *"[n]either can the opinion of man destroy justice,"* no matter what any man's opinion or point of view is, it will not destroy true, divine justice. *"The glory and the shame are misplaced,"* the *"glory"* of killing and the *"shame"* of begetting should be switched. Glory should be given to life while shame extended to the taking of life. (6)

Delight = great pleasure; joy.

→ *"delight must be purchased,"* delight must be obtained, gained. (13, 16)

Destroyed = put an end to; kill; completely ruined; demolished; done away with. (7)

Destruction = the act of destroying or the state of being destroyed; to put an end to; extinguish; kill; slay. (4)

Doth = does. (10)

Error = wrong. (6)

Exert = to make a physical or mental effort; to put, oneself, through strenuous effort. (3)

Feeble = lacking physical, mental, or moral strength; physically weak.

→ *"Feeble and insufficient as thou art, O man, in good,"* as inadequate and weak as we are in producing good deeds. (1)

Fly = to flee (run) or escape. (18)

Forseeth = to see or know beforehand. (20)

Frail = mentally weak; weak. (1)

Frequent = occurring or appearing often. (16)

Garments = clothing. (4)

Glorious = having or deserving glory esteem, etc. (4)

Glory = great honor, praise, or distinction.

→ *"the glory and the shame are misplaced,"* the glory should go to the producing of another being, and the shame should go to the taking of another's life. But people tend to glorify murder and are ashamed of bringing life into the world. (6)

Grief = strong mental suffering or painful state; misery; mental pain; torment.

→ *"Grief is natural to thee,"* due to the fact that man encounters grief so often in this life, it is simply a part of our physical make up which is connected to the base desires of the flesh. (12)

Hath = have or has. (9)

Honored = to be honored is to be revered, or highly respected. (5)

Hound = one of any several breeds of dogs trained to pursue game either by sight or by scent, especially one with a long face and large drooping ears. (22)

Human ills = mental (psychological) illness, *i.e.*, inconstancy, weakness, misery etc., that is within human nature. (11)

Inconstant = always changing; unpredictable; unreliable; fickle. (1)

Instruments = tools; an implement, especially one held in the hand, as a hammer, saw, or file, for performing or facilitating mechanical operations. In this instance, tool (instruments) used to cause death. (4)

Insufficient = not sufficient or enough; lacking in what is necessary or required; inadequate. (1)

Joy = great pleasure and happiness. (12, 17)

Justice = the principle of moral righteousness. (6)

Kindled = set fire to; ignite; start. (15)

Lo! = look!; see!; Used to attract attention or show surprise. (4)

Malady = a disease, disorder, or ailment; an illness or sickness. (17)

Misplaced = to place or bestow improperly, unsuitably, or unwisely. (6)

Nature = inborn or inherent qualities; innately. **Innately** = Innate: existing in one from birth; natural to the flesh or lower instincts. (2)

Nature = reality, as distinguished from any effect of art; the constitution (make up) of something. (6)

Notwithstanding = in spite of; regardless of; nevertheless. (6)

Passions = powerful emotions, such as love, joy, hatred, or anger; emotions and desires. (2)

Perceived = recognized, discerned, envisioned, or understood. (17)

Perverseness = willfully determined to go counter (against) what is expected or desired; persistent or obstinate in what is wrong. (11)

Pleasure = the state or feeling of being pleased or gratified; enjoyment or happiness. (1, 12, 14, 18)

Praise or honor = used to place one within admiration and high public esteem. (8)

Premeditated = planned in advance. (23)

Prerogative = an exclusive right, privilege, etc.; limited to a specific person or to persons of a particular category.

→ *"prerogative of thy nature,"* it (misery) is a natural, undeniable exclusive right of the carnal nature of man. (2)

Produced = procreated. (7)

Prudent = wise in handling practical matters; exercising good judgment; acting with or showing care and thought for the future. (12)

Purchase = to acquire by effort, sacrifice, flattery, or money, etc. (18)

Rare = uncommon; not frequently occurring. (16)

Reason = logical thinking; good judgment; intelligence. (3, 12)

Reflection = a fixing of the thoughts on mental concentration; careful consideration; meditation.

→ "Reflection is the business of man," careful consideration is man's rightful or proper concern and duty; his true endeavor. "A sense of his state is his first duty," a perception, or understanding, of his condition (mental, emotional, spiritual, physical, etc.) is his obligation. (19)

Resideth = to be inherently present. (2)

Seize = take or grab. (22)

Shalt = shall.

Shameful = causing shame; disgraceful; indecent. (4)

Simply = in a simple or easy manner. (14)

Sorrow = a feeling of deep destress caused by loss, disappointment, or misfortune suffered by oneself or others; mental suffering; grief. (12, 13, 16, 17, 19)

Sorrow is frequent = mental suffering occurs or appears quite often. (16)

Soundest = free from defect, damage, disease, or injury; in good condition. (17)

Source = point of origin. (2)

Spear = a weapon consisting of a long shaft with a sharply pointed end. (22)

Stag = an adult deer. (22)

Subdue = conquer, defeat, control, etc. (3)

Thee = you.

Thine = pertaining or belonging to you; yours. (23)

Thou = you.

Thy = your.

Thy frame = the human body. (13)

Trample = to beat down with the feet so as to crush or destroy; to conquer or gain mastery over. (3)

Triumph and empire = exultation (joy) resulting from victory and an extensive enterprise or territory. (8)

Unmixed = not mixed; pure. (16)

Unshaken = stable; solidified; solid. (1)

Unto = to. (19)

Wanteth not = lacks not; does not lack its alloy or mixture. (16)

Weepeth = to express emotion, such as grief or sadness, by shedding tears; cry. (21)

Weeping = crying. (21)

NOTES:

* THE DIVINE ORIGIN OF THE ASIATIC NATIONS *

DIVINE ORIGIN = the spiritual aspect of humans; the group of attributes and qualities of humankind regarded as Godly or God-like.

→ We are dealing with the true essence of man. The original stage of the Asiatic Nations as the true civilizers of the world. Gaze upon the glory of ALLAH as He created this world and placed the Asiatic Nations here to bring about civility and civilization. Trace back the beginning stages of the fellowman (European) and you will see who his civilizer was and is. (Heading)

Asiatic Nations = consists of Puerto Ricans, Cubans, Columbians, Dominicans, Mexicans, Brazilians, Chinese, Japanese, Korean, Arabians, etc. and all the Asiatic people or nations within the human race possessing the melanin that distinguishes those from Africa, Asia, North America, etc., from the pale skin nations of Europe.

→ According to Brother Jose V. Pimienta-Bey, "The etymology of the root word: 'Asia,' is traceable to Akkadian, which was an ancient 'Semitic' language and culture of Mesopotamia, a region occupied by the peoples of western Asia and east Africa. The term comes from **asu** which means 'to go out from' or 'to rise.' Consequently, we see that the M.S.T. is using a term whose ancient origins compel those who use it, to identify with Asia and Africa in a unified fashion." (Othello's Children in the "New World.") (5)

Ancient = very old, aged. The civilized peoples, nations, or culture of antiquity. **Antiquity** = ancient times, especially the times preceding the Middle Ages. (2)

Arabians = of or pertaining to Arabia or its inhabitants.

→ Today Arabia includes Saudi Arabia, Yemen, Oman, the United Arab Emirates, Qatar, and Kuwait: divided in ancient times into Arabia Deserta (an ancient division of Arabia, in the North part between Syria and Mesopotamia), Arabia Petraea (an ancient division of Arabia in the Northwestern part), and Arabia Felix (an ancient division of Arabia, in the Southern part: sometimes restricted to Yemen). The original Arabians are the descendants of Ishmael. Ishmael is sometimes referred to as The Father of the Arabs. His mother was Hagar, and his father was Abraham. (3)

Canaanites = descendants of Canaan, or inhabitants from the land of Canaan. **Canaan** was the grandson of Noah and the son of Ham. (4)

Central America = Central America is a land bridge (isthmus) connecting South America to North America. The land bridge consists of Beliz, Guatemala, Honduras, El Salvador, Nicaragua, Costa Rica, and Panama. (5)

Chinese = a native or inhabitant of China. China is a country in East Asia.

→ According to the book "Blacked Out Through Whitewash" by: Suzar, the fust Chinese Emperor, Fu-Hsi (2953-2838 B.C.) was a wooly haired "black" man. (3)

Civilization = an advanced state of human society, in which a high level of culture, science, industry, and government has been reached. (2)

Command = order or authority. (7)

Descendants = a person or people whose (Bloodline) can be traced back to a particular individual or group of people; offspring; children. (4)

Egyptians = descendants or inhabitants of Egypt. Egypt is located on the N.E. Corner of Africa. It is the home of the Nile Valley which

* THE DIVINE ORIGIN OF THE ASIATIC NATIONS *

stretches some 550 miles. Egypt's ancient civilization can be dated as far back as 4000 B.C. or better. (3)

Etc. = (et. cetera); and others; and so forth; and so on. (1)

Fallen = to debase or bring down from an original state or stage. **Debase** = to lower in character, quality, or value; degrade. (1)

Founder = one who establishes a particular thing; an author or originator. (7)

Hagar = Hagar was an Egyptian and the second wife of Abraham. She was the mother of Ishmael. (7)

Hamitites = descendants of Ham. Ham was the son of Noah and the youngest of three. Shem and Japheth were the other two brothers with Japheth as the eldest. (3)

Higher-Self = The Higher-Self is the true essence of man.

→ The Higher-Self is human spirit, clothed with soul, made in the form of ALLAH, the Higher-Self is ALLAH in Man. The Higher-Self is everlasting. By describing the Higher-Self as the mother of virtues and the harmonies of life, our Prophet teaches us that the Higher-Self gives birth to and is the source of all virtues and harmonies - virtues such as sincerity, faith, hope, charity, gratitude, compassion, modesty, diligence, temperance, justice, mercy, love, etc. And wherever harmony exists, the Higher-Self is present, for the Higher-Self promotes, fosters, and gives rise to all the harmonies of life. Thus, all of the harmony, justice, love and positive activity we see around us are different expressions of the Higher-Self (ALLAH in Man). The Higher-Self is the embodiment of Truth. (In part by Brother Nathaniel Chambers-El.)

Brother Jose V. Pimienta-Bey, Ph.D. says: "Moorish Science Moslems call the spiritual (or most Godly) essence of Man, the 'Higher-Self.' The 'Higher-Self' is essentially that which always follows the *will* of ALLAH (Love, Truth, Peace, Freedom and Justice) at all times - over and above the 'Lower-Self.' The 'Lower-Self' represents the will of the flesh, the individual self or *Ego*." (1)

Hindoos = also spelled Hindu: persons, especially of Northern India, who adheres to Hinduism. (4)

Hittites = descendants of Heth. Heth was a son of Canaan. (4)

Holy City of Mecca = the birthplace of Prophet Mohammed in 570 A.D. It is currently located in W. Saudi Arabia. (2)

India = a republic in S. Asia: a union comprising 25 states and 7 union territories. Buddha is said to have been born in India circa 566 B.C. (4)

Instructing = the act of imparting instructions to another, especially to achieve a specific objective; to provide with knowledge, esp. in a methodical way; transmit. **Transmit** = to pass along (information); communicate. (1)

Islam: see *"Islam"* in Ch. 48. (7)

Japanese = a native or inhabitant of Japan. Japan is made up of 4 main islands: Honshu ("mainland"), Hokkaido, Kyushu, and Shikoku. Japan is located off the East coast of Asia. It is recorded that Japan was founded in 660 B.C. (3)

Key = the key being spoken of is none other than a deep abiding spirituality. This key was the cause giving rise to our Science, Technology, Medicine, etc., our Civilization. (2)

Land of Canaan = some of what is considered to be the land of Canaan consisted of Palestine, Israel, Syria, and Phoenicia. (4)

Lower-Self = the body of illusions. Among these illusions stand the lower passions and desires of man which cause him to sin. The lower-self is anything that stands in the way of man reaching deific life, the *oneness* of man and ALLAH. The lower-self breeds hatred and everything that harms, it is the carnal self, the body of desires, it is an illusion and will pass away. (1)

Mexicans = natives or inhabitants of Mexico.

→ A majority of those born in Mexico can trace their lineage back to the Aztec and/or Mayan civilization. The Aztec Empire reached the height of its power during the early 1500's, covering much of what is now South-Central Mexico. It 1521, Spaniards (from Europe) led by the explorer Hernando Cortes conquered the Aztec and destroyed their civilization. The Mexicans gained independence from Spain in 1821. A social revolution began in 1910, when the people of Mexico started a long struggle for social justice and economic progress. During this struggle, the government took over huge, privately owned farmlands and divided them among millions of landless farmers. The government established a national school system to promote education, and it has built many hospitals and housing projects. More than a third of the people still live in poverty, and the government keeps expanding its programs to help them. (5)

Mizraim = Mizraim was the son of Ham and brother of Cush, Phut, and Canaan. (3)

Moabites = of or pertaining to the ancient kingdom of Moab, its people, or their language. Descendants of Moab. Moab was the son of Lot and the father of the Moabites. The land of Moab was located between the Dead Sea and the Arabian Desert. (See "*Moabites*" in Ch. 47.) (2)

Mohammed = also spelled *Muhammed* or *Mahomet* = "There is a well-known misconception that Mohammed spread Islam with the sword. There should be a distinction made between the two Mohammeds. Prophet Mohammed of 570-632 A.D. was of Arabian descent and recited the Holy Qur'an to the people; upon hearing him read the Qur'an the people would weep and also convert to Islam due to the Beauty, Eloquence, and Truth of what they heard. Mohammed used his sword to protect himself against unbelievers who wanted to kill him, because he professed what seemed as new. Islam is the fastest growing religion in the world." (7)

Mohammed II 1430-1481 A.D. this is the Mohammed of 1453 Byzantine who was of Turkish descent and spread Islam by the sword. This is the Mohammed being spoken of in our Koran Questions for Moorish Americans (Questionnaire) in Key # 83 &. 84. Constantine XI Palaeologus's head was cut off in the battle of April 6, 1453. "Also, the cross on the dome of St. Sophia was replaced by the crescent of the Moslems." (Quote from Sister Rashida-El/D.M.).

Moorish = Here we break away from the norm. Instead of repeating what key #14 of our Koran Questions for Moorish Americans (Questionnaire) says, we will attempt, in brief; to excavate a bit deeper.

First, let us break this word "*Moorish*" down. First, we have "MOOR." According to Wayne B. Chandler, in his chapter "The Moor: Light of Europe's Dark Age," from the book "African Presence in Early Europe," he states that "the term Moor has been put to diverse use. Its roots are still traceable circa 46 B.C., the Roman army entered West Africa where they encountered black Africans which they called 'Maures,' from the Greek adjective maures, meaning dark or black." Now, we fully know that man cannot be "black," for black signifies death. But we know that the Moors are the first inhabitants of this earth and therefore we equate Moors with the original man.

Our next move is to address the suffix "-ish." According to the Webster's Encyclopedic Unabridged Dictionary of the English Language (1996 Ed.), "-ish is a suffix used to form adjectives from nouns, with the sense of 'belonging to,' 'after the manner of,' 'having the characteristics of,' etc."

So, *"Moorish"* would mean "pertaining, belonging, or in the manner of the Moors." (l)

MOORISH AMERICANS = Why is the so-called black person a Moorish-American? Because we are descendants of Moroccans and born in America. We are not saying that all so-called black people come from Morocco. The Moabites were driven out of the land of Canaan and received permission from the Pharaohs of Egypt to settle and inhabit North-West Africa. In later years, they formed themselves kingdoms, one of these kingdoms was Morocco. Therefore, the so-called black man was a Moor even before the founding of Morocco, thus saying Moroccan is just a modern term for Moabite. A Moor can trace his line genealogy all the way back to the Garden of Eden, because the Moabites (the ancestors of the so-called black race) were the founders of the Holy City of Mecca, and the modern name for the Garden of Eden is Mecca. Morocco was a Moorish rock; a foundation for which later became an empire. The dominion and inhabitation of the Moroccan empire extended from North-East and South-West

Africa, across the great Atlantis even unto the present North, South, and Central America and also Mexico and the Atlantis Islands; before the great earthquake which caused the great Atlantic Ocean. Thus, saying the so-called black people of America are Moors who were stripped of their nationality and birthrights. The Holy Koran of the M.S.T. of A. teaches that, "What your ancient forefathers were, you are today without doubt or contradiction." Thus, showing we are descendants of Moroccans and born over here in America, making us *Moorish Americans.* (l)

Moslems = Moslem is one who submits his swill to the will of ALLAH. A Moslem is a follower of Islam[ism]. Our Prophet Noble Drew Ali says that "a follower of Islam in the true sense of the word is one whose hands, tongue and thoughts do not hurt others." (6)

Nation = a large group of people who share common customs, origins, culture, language, or history and inhabiting a particular area; tribe; a nationality. (1)

North America = the Northern continent of the Western Hemisphere, extending from Canada to Mexico. The continent of North America consists of Canada, United States of America, and Mexico. America is also referred to by Prophet Noble Drew Ali as "Babylon." And we must bare in mind that the fall of Babylon was a tragic one. (1)

Origin = the first stage of existence; beginning; ancestry. **Divine Origin** = a Divine Source from which man obtains his spiritual existence; coming into being. (Heading)

Seed = offspring; descendants. (3)

South America = South America is the continent located below the United States. It consists of Columbia, Venezuela, Guyana, Suriname, French Guiana, Brazil, Peru, Chile, Ecuador, Argentina, Uruguay, Paraguay, and Bolivia. (5)

Teaching = the act of imparting knowledge or skill to another. Impart: to pass on; transmit. **Transmit** = to pass along (information); communicate. (1)

Turks = natives or inhabitants of Turkey, located today in Asia Minor. The Turks, or Ottoman Turks, ruled the Byzantine Empire for over 400 years, starting from 1453 A.D.; the Turks (who were the Ottomans) waged war against the Christians (Roman Empire) in order to defend and protect the Islamic Creed. The Romans wanted to kill everyone who didn't convert to Christianity. So, the war of 1453 occurred. Key #83, they protected Islam with that war. (7)

Uniting = the process of bringing together into a whole unit; to join and act together in a common purpose or endeavor. (1)

NOTES:

CHRISTIANITY = the doctrine based on the life and works of Jesus, the Christ.

→ Christianity as a "religion" has been high jacked by those hungry for power. The faith established by Jesus has taken different turns throughout history. It has been used to enslave the people instead of granting them true *liberation*. To get a true understanding of the works of Jesus, we must travel back in history. This must be done in order to seek out the *TRUE* meaning of Jesus's teachings since throughout the centuries the teachings have been distorted by the power-hungry heads of states and other religious leaders. (1)

Africa = a continent located below Europe and between the Atlantic and Indian oceans and consisting of over 50 countries; about 11,700,000 square miles. Africa is the second largest continent in the world. (2)

Ancient = very old; aged. The civilized peoples, nations, or culture of antiquity. **Antiquity** = ancient times, especially the times preceding the Middle Ages. (2)

Canaanites = descendants of Canaan, or inhabitants from the land of Canaan.

→ **Canaan** was the grandson of Noah and the son of Ham. In the Amarna Letters, the Phoenician coast is described as the land of Canaan. (2)

Church = a building or structure designed for public worship, usually by Christians. (1)

Common People = those set aside from the rulers, i.e., the poor, oppressed, etc. (5)

Crucified = Crucify: to put to death by nailing or binding to a cross. A form of execution exercised by the Romans. (1)

Destiny = Fate. The fate to which a particular person is destined; Man's final abode. **Fate** = the supposed force, principle, or power that predetermines events. (8)

Europe = a continent in the western part of the landmass laying between the Atlantic and Pacific oceans, separated from Asia by the Ural Mountains on the East and the Caucasus Mountains and the Black and Caspian seas on the Southeast. (3)

Forefathers = our ancestors; a person from whom one is descended; ancestral descent or lineage. A forefather also means "a founder or originator." (8)

Foundation = beginning; the act of founding, setting up, establishing, etc. (1)

Founded = to set up or establish on a firm basis or for enduring existence. (1)

Fulfilled = to bring into actuality; to bring to an end; to complete. (4)

Inhabitants = ones who inhabit a place, especially as permanent residents. **Inhabit** = to live or reside in. (2)

Jesus = Jesus was a Prophet of ALLAH, the Son of Joseph and Mary.

→ Prophet Jesus was a righteous and holy man, but a man, nonetheless. In spite of how righteous or holy Jesus was, he was merely a *man* and a servant of ALLAH and therefore not worthy of worship or praise. Prophet Jesus said, "I am your brother man, just come to show the way to ALLAH; you shall not worship man; praise ALLAH the Holy One." (MHK 8:24) Prophet Jesus was a Moslem who submitted his will to ALLAH, and he never told anyone to worship or praise him as ALLAH. We as Moorish

Americans *Honor* man, and give *Praise* to ALLAH, and to Him alone belongs worship, adoration, thanksgiving, and praise. Jesus's life stands as the best (known) example of how Man can locate and master the God-force within himself. (1, 5)

Lamb = symbolic to one who is gentle, meek, or innocent, etc. (5, 8)

Law = any rule or injunction that must be obeyed. (1, 3)

Lion = symbolic to one of great importance, strength, or influence. (5, 8)

Moabites = of or pertaining to the ancient kingdom of Moab, its people, or their language. Descendants of Moab. Moab was the son of Lot and the father of the Moabites. The land of Moab was located between the Dead Sea and the Arabian Desert. Also see the definition of *Moabites* in Chapter 47. (2)

Modern Days = is in reference to this era of time; present times. (9)

Mohammed The First = See the "Mohammed" in Chapter 45. (4)

Nation = a large group of people who share common customs, origins, culture, language, or history and inhabiting a particular area; tribe; a nationality. (1)

Nazareth = a town in Northern Israel: the childhood home of Jesus. (4)

Obtained = acquired; to gain possession of. (9)

Oppress = to burden with cruel or unjust imposition or restraints. (See "*Oppress*" in Chapter 31.) (5)

Pale Skin = "Pale Skin" is used when speaking of Europeans. Europeans (pale skin) do not produce the same amount of melanin as Asiatics, thus giving them a pale appearance. (3)

Poor = having little or no money, goods, or other means of support. (7, 8)

Principles = an accepted or professed rule of action or conduct; rules or beliefs governing the way you behave; the Principles of our forefathers are Love, Truth, Peace, Freedom, and Justice. The Holy and Divine Laws are the dictates, the Instructions of our Moorish Holy Koran. (8)

Redeem = to free, liberate, rescue, or save. **Liberate** = to set free, as from imprisonment or bondage and to bring back to an original state. (1, 3)

Rich = having wealth or great possessions; material items. (6, 7)

Roman Yoke = the oppressive laws and rules applied by the Romans. (1)

Rome = an ancient empire founded by Romulus circa 753 B.C. It extended at one point in time to include Carthage, Sicily, parts of Spain, Greece, Britain, Gaul, Asia Minor, and Egypt, though not in that exact chronological order. (1)

Ruler = a person who rules or governs. (5, 6, 7, 8)

Scene = the place where some action or event occurs. this event, the arrival of Prophet Mohammed upon world to fulfill the works of Jesus. (4)

Seek = to go in search or quest of. **Quest** = to search or seek for; pursue. (8)

Seeking = to try; to attempt. (3)

Seeking Peace = means searching for a way to live without being hindered or subjugated by the laws, principles, or politics of others. (9)

Teachings = acts or practices. (6)

Ten Commandments = the set of laws spoken by ALLAH to Moses on Mount Sinai. Just as many religious bodies have done, these Ten Commandments were twisted by the oppressive rulers to fit their selfish purposes. (6, 7)

Universally = of, relating to, extending to, or affecting the entire world or all within the world; worldwide. (9)

Universally = *"Being taught Universally,"* is spreading the principles of Love, Truth, Peace, Freedom, and Justice to all intelligent beings, in all lands: all over the world. (9)

Unjust = lacking in justice or fairness; unfair or dishonest. (5)

Vine and Fig Tree = the Vine and Fig Tree here is *Islam[ism].*

→ Vine and fig tree was a tree in which people would sit and enjoy fellowship while being shaded from the heat of the day. Islam will shade us from the great wrath of ALLAH which is sure to come upon the earth.

Also, the vine is like the vein of which the blood line of the Asiatics course through. The fig tree begins at the roots of all Asiatics and branches out to the various Asiatic Nations in Asia, Africa, Aboriginals of Australia, South, Central, North America and Mexico. This is our Asiatic Tree. (8)

Worship = the ceremonies, prayers, or other religious forms by which this love is expressed; ardent devotion; adoration; homage; the practice of showing deep respect for and offering praise and prayers to ALLAH. (8)

NOTES:

* EGYPT, THE CAPITAL EMPIRE OF THE DOMINION OF AFRICA *

→ Prior to the arrival of foreigners, the country known today as Egypt was known as Kemet by its original inhabitants. It was considered the empire of the ancient African kingdoms and was the largest and richest and maintained one of the strongest militaries on the continent. They offered to the world one of the most advanced spiritual perspectives and was the center of initiation for many civilizations that came afterwards. (See *"Egypt"* below).

Africa = modern name for the continent located below Europe and between the Atlantic and Indian oceans. It consists of over 50 countries and it's about 11,700,000 square miles. It is the second largest continent in the world second only to Asia. (Heading, etc.)

Amorite = a member of one of the principal tribes, or nations, of Canaan before its conquest by the Israelites; a member of one of several ancient Semitic peoples primarily inhabiting Canaan and Babylonia (Mesopotamia).

→ The term "Amorite" is often used to refer to the Canaanite tribe and/or its descendants. The Amorites were descendants from the line of Ham, Noah's son, therefore making them Hamitic. (6)

Ancient = very old; aged; the civilized peoples, nations, or culture of antiquity. **Antiquity** = ancient times, especially the times preceding the Middle Ages. (1, 8, 9, 10)

Asia = the continent bounded by Europe and the Arctic, Pacific, and Indian oceans.

→ When Moorish-American Moslems speak of Asia, we are referring to the times of old before the continents received their current shapes and names. (5)

Asiatics = non-Europeans (pale skin).

→ Those classified as Asiatics amongst the followers of Prophet Noble Drew Ali are the descendants of the original inhabitants of the islands of the Caribbean, *e.g.*, Cubans, Jamaicans, Haitians, Puerto Ricans, Dominicans, as well as the inhabitants of South America, including the Venezuelans, Brazilians, Chileans, Colombians, etc. Mexicans, Japanese, Chinese, Koreans, certain Arabians, etc., are all classified as Asiatics by members of the Moorish Science Temple of America. In a general sense Noble Drew Ali gives us two races of people, Asiatics and Europeans (Pale skin), unlike western scientists who at one time classified the people of the world according to the continent of which they inhabited, e.g., European, African, Asiatic, and American. Later, they designated the terms Mongoloid, Negroid, and Caucasoid. (14)

Atlantic Ocean = a body of water bounded by North America in the western hemisphere and by Europe and Africa in the eastern hemisphere. It is about 41,000,000 square miles. (7)

Atlantis = a legendary island-continent, mentioned by Plato and said to have existed in the Atlantic Ocean west of Gibraltar and to have sunk beneath the sea.

→ That Atlantis existed there is no doubt. The Prophet makes reference in Oral Statement #138, where Brother J. Blakely-Bey told the Moors that the Holy Prophet said, "Atlantis is going to arise again." In the writings of the ancient "Egyptians" there's been reference found dealing with Atlantis as well. It was on his way home from Egypt that Plato fust heard of the legendary island of Atlantis. (7)

Black = a name used to degrade the Asiatics of America, in particular the so-called Negro. The re-naming (labeling) was initiated by the European (pale skin) nations as part of the process of making a slave.

→ It is a sad occurrence today when we try to make this degrading mark a term of beauty. ALLAH never created a "black person." Black was created by the Europeans (Pale skin) as a beast of burden for themselves. Brother Jose V. Pimienta-Bey, author of "Othello's Children in the 'New World'" covers this perspective well. He states, "a person calling themselves black trying to make it positive is like pushing an elephant uphill on roller- skates." Sheik/ Divine Minister, Brother Azeem Hopkins-Bey, referenced this point in his work "What Your History Books Failed to Tell You." He mentions that "If you do not know yourself then you leave the authority to someone else to identify you, and through time you will be accustomed to that label. Black is an adjective; which is a descriptive word, and not a noun. A noun is a person, place, or thing; therefore, a person cannot be black." (pg. l3). Brother N. Chambers-El states in his "Moorish Questionnaire Commentaries" that "the marks Negro, Colored and Black have no cultural integrity and fails to connect our people, alienating and separating us from our glorious history culture, and accomplishments. As applied to human beings, Black is a term of disrespect and abuse whose roots go no further than the institution of slavery. It is a term of degradation used to vilify and denigrate us in the minds and imaginations of others. What your [our] ancient forefathers were you [we] are today, without doubt or contradiction. There is no one who is able to change man from the descendant nature of his forefathers, unless his power extends beyond the great universal Creator ALLAH himself. In light of the above, man cannot be what he's not, but can only be what he is. And the custom of labeling our people Negro, Black, Colored, and Ethiopia alter the nature of truth." Black according to science means death. (9)

Brethren = brothers. (5)

Canaan = son of Ham and grandson of Noah. (2)

Capital = chief, especially as being the official seat of government; most important. (Heading)

Colored = anything that has been painted, stained, varnished, or dyed.

→ Colored indicates that something has been altered and therefore made weak and is no longer in its original state. The suffix -ed as applied to the word color-ed forms the past tense of a weak verb. Two things must be kept in mind when dealing with such marks: 1) anything that has been colored is not original; 2) only *things* can be colored. A simple reading of the definition in a dictionary will suffice to make the point. Under the word "colored" we find the following: 1) having color. 2) Often Offensive, belonging wholly or in part to a race other than white, especially the black race [emphasis mine]. 3) Often Offensive, pertaining to the black race. 4) influenced or biased. 5) specious, deceptive. 6) of some hue other than green. 7) Often Offensive, (a) a black person (b) black person as a group. Colored was a mark (label) used to degrade the Asiatic nations of North America by the European (Pale skin) and it was predominately used during the institution of slavery. (9, 17)

Confess = to make known; to acknowledge as one's belief or faith; own or admit as true.

→ "*Confess his own,*" is to make known one's faith.

→ "*Every tongue must confess his own,*" states the Moorish Holy Koran. As individuals and followers of Prophet Noble Drew Ali we are to make known our religion of Islam(ism) as brought by the Prophet. The Prophet brought us back our national and divine creed and we must make it known at all times and live accordingly whether in the public's eye, or in the privacy of our household. (15)

Conjunction = in union with another body of doctrine or idea; combination.

→ Laws and customs made by any subordinate Temple of the Grand Major Temple must not be at variance with the laws of the Prophet and the Grand Major Temple. This indicates that one's seeking to create laws and customs must first be familiar with the laws of the aforementioned individuals. (14)

Contradiction = a statement or proposition that contradicts or denies another or itself and is logically incongruous.

→ The statement ". . . *without doubt or contradiction*" implies a degree of certitude made by the Prophet. The Prophet is making it abundantly clear that only One has the power to change one's descendant nature and that is ALLAH, none other. (10)

Covenant = an agreement between ALLAH and His Prophet(s); a formal agreement between two or more persons to do or not to do something specified; a binding agreement. (14)

Create = to make or bring into existence. (14)

Creed = any system, doctrine, or formula of religious belief; a faith. **Doctrine** = a set of beliefs or principles held and taught by a religious group.

→ For members of the Moorish Science Temple of America, our religious creed is Islam(ism). (16)

Creed and Principles = The Creed and Principles of our forefathers are Islam(ism) and Love, Truth, Peace, Freedom and Justice. (16)

Cush = son of Ham and brother of Mizraim, Phut, and Canaan. He was also the grandson of Noah. (2)

Customs = a group pattern of habitual activity usually transmitted from one generation to another.

→ Custom, applied to a community or to an individual, implies a more or less permanent continuance of a social usage. In the Temple, customs can also be additional rules created by Head Officials to better help in the development of its membership. These "rules" are to be made in conjunction with the Prophet's laws and not at variance. (14)

Demarcation = the determining and marking off of the boundaries of something.

→ Demarcation line was a dividing line between the land of the father, Ham, and the son, Cush. Ethiopia is the line that separated their lands. Cush's dominion was the North-East and South-East regions of Amexem (Africa) and Ham's dominion encompassed the North-West and South-West regions of Amexem. (3)

Descendants = people whose bloodline can be traced back to a particular individual or group of people; one's offspring; children. (9)

Descent = derivation from an ancestor; a person's origin or ancestry; lineage.

→ Nationality is also indicative of a person's descent, or lineage. (17)

Disobedience = disregard or transgressions; lack of obedience or refusal to comply. (16)

Dominion = a territory usually of considerable size, in which a single rulership holds sway; territory. (7)

* EGYPT, THE CAPITAL EMPIRE OF THE DOMINION OF AFRICA *

Dredged = unearthed or brought about by the removal of sand, silt, mud, etc., from the bottom of. (8)

Egypt = a republic in NE Africa with a civilization dating back over 6,000 years.

→ It is imperative to point out that the Egypt of today is NOT the Egypt of the past. Egypt was known as Kemet in the past. Historian's mark Kemetian history from the time of the uniting of the upper and lower kingdoms by King Menes around 3200 B.C. Today we study the history of Kemet by way of its dynasties. The first dynasty is attributed to King Menes. There was a total of 30 dynasties, ending with the invasion of the Macedonians under the leadership of Alexander "the Great" in 332 B.C. From that moment onward the rulership of Egypt came under the Ptolemies. Here began what has been considered the Greek Period which lasted until the death of Cleopatra VII in 30 B.C. It is also worth noting that these periods of rulership should be distinguished along with the names given to Egypt. It is best stated that the periods prior the Greek invasion and during the rulership of native-born "Egyptians," this land was commonly called Kemet. In today's history books "ancient Egypt" would be Kemet and the word "Egypt" is used to describe the period of European rule. Since we are dealing with the labels given to the land mass known as Egypt today, it is also worth stating that the Hebrew Scriptures, *i.e.*, the 39 books in the Bible from Genesis to Malachi, refer to Egypt as Mizraim. Mizraim is listed as the second son of Ham. (See *"Egyptians"* in Ch. 45). (6, 8)

Empire = a number of territories or nations of people ruled over by a single supreme authority, such as an emperor, empress, king, or other powerful sovereign or government. (Heading, 6)

Ethiopia = a republic in East Africa, formerly known as Abyssinia.

→ As in the case of Egypt, the country known today as Ethiopia is not the same as in the days of old. The land of Cush, as it is known in the Hebrew Scriptures, is believed by many historians to pre-date the civilization of Kemet. Ethiopia (Cush) at one time encompassed the Sudan and had as its seat of power Napata and Meroe. (3)

Europe = a continent in the western part of the landmass laying between the Atlantic and Pacific Oceans, separated from Asia by the Ural Mountains on the east and the Caucasus Mountains and the Black and Caspian seas on the Southeast.

→ Europe is said to be the place of origin of the pale skin (European) nations. (17)

Forefathers = ancestors; persons from whom one is descended; ancestral descent or lineage. (16)

Founder = one who establishes a particular thing; an author or originator. (12)

Grand Major Temple = The Grand Major Temple is the first and primary Temple which all other temples answer(ed) to or derive(d) from. (14)

Ham = son of Noah and father of Cush, Mizraim, Put, and Canaan. Among Ham's descendants are the Hamitites. (3)

Hittite = descendants of Heth, second son of Canaan. (6)

Inhabit = to exist or be situated within; populate. (6)

Inhabitants = people that inhabit a place, especially as permanent residents. (2)

Inhabitation = place of residence. (7)

Kingdoms = territories or domains (areas) controlled by a king. (8)

Members = people that belong to a group or an organization. (13)

Mexico = the northernmost country of Latin America. It lies south of the United States. The Rio Grande forms about two-thirds of the boundary between Mexico and the United States.

→ Among all the countries in the Western Hemisphere, only the U.S. and Brazil have more people than Mexico. Mexico City is the capital and largest city in Mexico. It is also one of the world's largest metropolitan areas in population. To understand Mexico, it is necessary to view the nation's long history. Hundreds of years ago, the Indians of Mexico built large cities, developed a calendar, invented a counting system, and used a form of writing. The last Indian empire in Mexico - that of the Aztec - fell to Spanish invaders in 1521. For the next 300 years, Mexico was a Spanish colony. The Europeans (Spaniards) plundered Mexico stripping it from much of its riches and placed the native population in a subservient status thus forcing them to remain poor and uncultivated (uneducated). Many changes were also introduced into Mexican culture in the areas of farming, government, industry, and religion. Mexico has 31 states and 1 federal district. Each state has an elected governor and legislature. The federal district is governed by the elected mayor of Mexico City. The Mexicans gained their independence from Spain in 1821. (See *"Mexicans"* in Ch. 45). (7)

Moabites = descendants of Moab the eldest son of Lot.

→ An interesting and plausible definition is extended by Sheik/Divine Minister Brother Azeem Hopkins-Bey. He mentions that "Moabite breaks down to Mo-ab-ite; which translated to "mo" a Semitic term meaning from; "ab" a Semitic term which means father similar to "abu" in Arabic which means father (Abraham - father of many nations), and -ite is a suffix which means tribe. The Moabites are the tribe or nation that comes from the father, and ALLAH is the father of the universe, (The human seed that came forth from the heart of ALLAH... [Holy Koran of the M.S.T. of A.]). Moor is short for Moorish." ("What Your History Books Failed to Tell You," pg. 27). (See *"Moabites"* in Ch. 46). (6)

Nation = a large group of people who share common customs, origins, culture, language, or history and inhabiting a particular area; tribe.

→ John F. Kennedy once said, "A nation reveals itself not only by the men it produces but also by the men it honors, the men it remembers." (15)

Nationality = the status of legally belonging to a particular nation by origin, birth, or naturalization; the descendant birth attachment through a special nation or tribe; (See *"Nationality"* in Ch. 48). (17)

Nature = a particular combination of characteristics and qualities belonging to a person by birth, origin, or constitution. (11)

Negro = a disparaging mark placed upon the Moors by the European (pale skin) nations, meant to hold ones in perpetual bondage.

→ Negro was used during slavery to degrade the Asiatics enslaved by the Europeans, in particular in America and the Caribbean. Brother N. Chambers-El states, "...today our people are now attempting to redefine and rationalize

·····CHAPTER XLVII (47)·····
* EGYPT, THE CAPITAL EMPIRE OF THE DOMINION OF AFRICA *

that despicable, God-awful term "Nigger" or "Nigga," which like the term Black, originated in the institution of slavery. For centuries now we've been marked and stigmatized by this term, which drags along with-it centuries of shame, pain, oppression, and terror. This term has been so thoroughly ingrained in the mind of our people that one can say its connotations have become part of our "collective unconsciousness." Feeling powerless to distance ourselves from this wretched term or eliminate it from the mind and speech of others, many of our people are now attempting to redefine it, rationalizing it as a "term of endearment" disconnected from its awful history...." ("Moorish Questionnaire Commentaries," note #111, pg. 245). (9)

Niger River = a river in West Africa, rising in S. Guinea, flowing NE through Mali, and then SE through Nigeria into the Gulf of Guinea. It is about 2600 miles long. (8)

Nile River = the longest river in the world extending over 4,000 miles and located in E. Africa.

→ The Nile River was of great importance to the inhabitants of the Nile Valley. By being able to determine the flooding seasons of the Nile the inhabitants were able to establish their farming and when to move inland to avoid destruction. The Nile was known as "Hapi" to the inhabitants of the Nile Valley and is responsible for one of the greatest civilizations recorded. (8)

Pharaoh = a title of an ancient Egyptian king.

→ "Pharaoh" has been used since ancient times for Egypt's kings. The word itself means "Great House" and had been a term used since at least as far back as the 18th Dynasty under Amenhotep IV (Akhenaton). (6)

Preserved = kept up or maintained. (13)

Repent = to make a change for the better as a result of remorse for one's sins; to feel or express sincere regret or remorse for past conduct.

→ To "repent from their sinful ways" is expressed as a warning from Prophet Noble Drew Ali. The verb "repentance" demonstrates action on behalf of the person requesting forgiveness. It takes courage for ones to admit their wrongs and vow to make a change for the better. The Prophet is issuing a warning to those with ears to hear that they turn from their sinful ways and return to ALLAH in Islam(ism). We Moors have better heed. (14)

Seeking = trying to find; in search of. (6)

Sin = willful disobedience to the mandates of ALLAH; an act that breaks a religious or moral law; something regarded as shamefully deplorable, or utterly wrong.

→ The Prophet informs man that the sin lies in the wish, in the desire, not in the act. All sins begin as a thought. Thoughts are things unmanifest. It is important that as Moslems we. become conscious and cautious of our thoughts. Constant thoughts create our habits and if these thoughts are based on naught our habits will soon reflect the same. (16)

Slavery = the complete control of a human being by another as master; a person who is the property of and wholly subject to another; a person entirely under the domination of some influence or person; bondage. (16)

Sojourned = journeyed; stayed for a time in a place. (6)

Strayed = deviated, as from a moral, religious, or philosophical course; to have deviated from the direct course, left the proper place, or gone beyond the proper limits, especially without a fixed course of purpose; to have gone astray. (17)

Strictly = in a strict manner; in a precise or exact manner; no deviation.

→ "Strictly preserved" means that the laws given are to be enforced and obeyed by all members and they must keep these laws in perfect or unaltered conditions. We are to maintain them without alteration, and they are to be kept in a pure state. (13)

Subordinate = subject to or under the authority of a superior; placed in or belonging to a lower order or rank.

→ A "subordinate temple" is subject to the authority of the primary temple. Sister Rashida-El states in her Moorish Dictionary and Study Guide that a Subordinate Temple is any legal Temple, Branch temples included. (14)

Temple = a divine habitation, sacred place, or sanctuary, either physical or spiritual, that is employed for worship; a building dedicated to religious public and private worship. (14)

Tongue = the language of a particular people, region, or nation.

→ Our own vine and fig tree is Islamism and as followers of the Prophet we are to confess, admit our own, individually and as a nation of people in whatever language we may speak. (15)

Trade = the act or process of buying, selling, or exchanging commodities within a country or between countries or kingdoms. (8)

Transportation = the act of transporting; to convey. **Convey** = to carry, bring, or take from one place to another. (8)

True Possessors = actual owners; original owners. (6)

Vine and Fig Tree = Islamism. (See *Vine and Fig Tree* in Ch. 46 & 48). (15)

Warn = to give notice, advice, or intimation to (a person, group, etc.) of danger, impending evil, or possible harm.

→ When prophets are given warnings, they are speaking plainly and strongly as directed by ALLAH. (14)

Worship = the ceremonies, prayers, or other religious forms by which love, and devotion is expressed to ALLAH: ardent devotion; homage; the practice of showing deep respect for and offering praise and prayers to ALLAH. (15)

1774 = September 5, 1774, the year the first Continental Congress (meeting) was held in Philadelphia, Pennsylvania (the first capital of the United States of America). This is where they decided to strip the Moors of their nationality and birthrights and the slave names (marks) of Negroes, Black, Colored, and Ethiopia were given to the Asiatics of America, whom were of Moorish descent. This was the consensus (agreement) of the 13 colonies represented in the 1774 Continental Congress (meeting). (17)

→ "What your ancient forefathers were, you are today without doubt or contradiction." (Ch. 47:10). In studying this statement, we can clearly see that there is no error in what is being stated. There is no two ways about the point being made. Things are plain and simple for the infinite mind. There is no room for doubt or contradiction when you are absolutely **SURE** of something, and the Prophet is the voice through which ALLAH has spoken to the sheep. The debasement of the Asiatics during the Trans-Atlantic slave trade served to change man from his true line to ALLAH.

Brother N. Chambers-El made the point plain in the following example: "If you take an apple seed from an apple in Africa and later plant that seed in American soil, an apple tree will come forth from it, not an orange tree. Similarly, if we were Moors in Africa prior to the African slave trade and our arrival here in America, how could we be anything but Moors? In the Moorish Holy Koran Prophet Noble Drew Ali says: "What your ancient forefathers were, you are today without doubt or contradiction." ("Moorish Questionnaire Commentaries").

NOTES:

·····CHAPTER XLVIII (48)·····
* THE END OF TIME AND THE FULFILLING OF THE PROPHESIES *

→ "Time is a continuum marked by periods we call events. These events are what we use to measure time, *i.e.*, sunrise, seasonal changes, earth rotation, etc. These measures are like "demi-times" (time v. time), and we refer to these "demi-times" as minutes, hours, days, months, years, centuries, millenniums, eras, etc. The "End of Time" is in reference to the end of an era. Noble Drew Ali is the last Prophet in these days and times - in this era of time. The "Fulfilling of the Prophesies" is in reference to all the ancient predictions coming to pass, as well as to what Noble Drew Ali said would happen with and during the third and fourth generations of Moors on these shores of America." (Brother James "Jimmy" Collins-El).

Amalgamate = to mix or merge so as to make a completion; blend; unite.

→ When we speak of amalgamating, we as Moorish American Moslems and Asiatics, as true followers of Prophet Noble Drew Ali, are referring to a new era in time when we were declared as a clean and pure nation by the Prophet. This means that we do not desire or wish to marry or have children with members of the European/Pale nations. Nor do we wish to embrace their philosophical perspectives since it was created by their forefathers for *their* earthly salvation. The Prophet forgave us for all that we had done before his coming and now we are held responsible for our decisions. Ignorance is no longer an excuse. (6)

Ancient = the civilized people, nations, or cultures of antiquity; very old; aged; antiquated. Antiquity: ancient times, especially the times preceding the Middle Ages. (10)

Birthrights = any rights or privileges to which a person is entitled to by birth.

→ Our Birthright is being the Lord of all the plane of manifest, of protoplast, of mineral, of plant, of beast. This is our Birthright from ALLAH. But man gave up his rights just to gratify his lower self. But not a thought is lost for man will regain the title to his vast estate as has been dictated by the WILL of ALLAH through His Prophet. Among other aspects of birthrights, we have FREEDOM. Religious freedom grants us the means of discovering truth that we may be able to march forward toward a nobler life. Freedom as a birthright also grants you the ability and power to act, speak, or think freely as well as the capacity to exercise choice, to be that which you aspire to be. It is a birthright to be granted the freedom to follow your ancestral customs and traditions and be given all rights afforded to all men equally. In the case of Moorish American Moslems, we are to live in accordance with the teachings established by Prophet Noble Drew Ali. Our laws and customs are to be in conjunction to those brought by Drew Ali. By living thusly, the umbrella of the covenant made by ALLAH through the Prophet will cover us all. (10)

Charter = the organic law of an organization; loosely, the highest law of any entity.

→ In the case of the M.S.T. of A., a document by our national representative outlining the principles, functions, and the conditions under which our organization must operate, define its rights, privileges, and purpose. A charter is also an authorization from a central or parent organization to establish a new branch, chapter, etc. In the time of the Prophet the charters were issued by him. (See MHK, Ch. 48:4). (4)

Chartered = documented and defined as a formal organization. (4)

Christianity = the doctrines that are supposed to be based on the life and works of Jesus of Nazareth. (See "*Christianity*" in Ch. 46.) (7)

* THE END OF TIME AND THE FULFILLING OF THE PROPHESIES *

Church = a building designed for public worship usually by Catholics/Christians; the doctrines of the Catholic/Christian Church. (7)

Clean and Pure Nation = This refers to Moors not being influenced by the corrupt, wicked nature and mentality of others who have no mercy in them, whether in their politics, cultures, creeds, etc. We as Moorish American Moslems do not promote or advocate racism. Our Prophet was not a racist. He spoke the Truth regardless of the consequences. His love and interest were always geared toward the promotion and wellbeing of the human race. We are not to contribute to anything that will cause the public to disagree with our Holy and Divine Movement. Our Prophet Noble Drew Ali says that you (WE) must learn to love instead of hate! This is an everlasting movement founded by the Prophet through the WILL of ALLAH to redeem his people from their sinful ways. We are working on getting back to the state of mind of our forefathers based on the principles of Love, Truth, Peace, Freedom, and Justice, hence a Clean and Pure Nation. As stated previously, the Prophet forgave us for all that we did before he came (before we became conscious of these divine teachings), now we are held accountable for our actions. (6)

Covenant = a binding agreement, compact or promise from ALLAH to man and from man to ALLAH. **Binding** = adherence to a commitment, obligation, or duty.

→ Our Prophet has established several Covenants that we must adhere to. In the Moorish Holy Koran, we find three specific covenants. They are as follows: l.) Chapter 25, A Holy Covenant of the Asiatic Nation; 2.) Chapter 47:14, the Covenant of Love, Truth, Peace, Freedom, and Justice; 3.) Chapter 48:9, the Covenant of the great God-ALLAH: "Honor thy father and thy mother that thy days may be longer upon the earth land, which the Lord thy God, ALLAH hath given thee!" We must follow the teachings of the Prophet so that we can fall under the protection of the covenants made by ALLAH to Him (Noble Drew Ali), who came to lead us back to the path of the Universal Creator. (9)

Creed = any system, doctrine, or formula of religious belief; a faith. **Doctrine** = a set of beliefs or principles held and taught by a religious group. In our case, Islam(ism). (6)

Descendants = one's whose bloodline can be traced back to a particular individual or group of people; offsprings, children. (5)

Descended = to come from an ancestor or ancestry; offspring. (6)

Desire = to wish or want; long for. (6)

Divine Creed = spiritual path to ALLAH; spiritual belief; religion. (3, 10)

Divine Salvation = intended for Spiritual deliverance from the bondage of the physical plane.

→ Being free from hatred, slander, lewdness, murder, theft, and everything that harms. When man has truly unfolded into the harmonious intentions of the Universal Creator ALLAH. This is also when Perfected Man has passed through all the ways of life and has attained unto the Blessedness of Perfectness and at ONE with his Father, God-ALLAH. (8)

Due Time = "In due time" means at the proper or appropriate time as appointed by ALLAH. (1)

Earth = the 3rd planet from the sun of which we inhabit. (See *Earth* in Ch. 1). (1)

Earthly Salvation = dealing with the physical world.

* THE END OF TIME AND THE FULFILLING OF THE PROPHESIES *

→ Our teachings, if followed accordingly, will save us from ignorance, oppression, poverty, danger, or other crippling circumstances which prevent us from unfolding to become as intended, that is God-Like. It is living out ALLAH'S laws on earth. It is making the appropriate decisions in life that follow the laws of the Prophet that we may be able to save ourselves. It is stretching out our hand to the assistance of others such as family, friends, the community and in general serving humanity It is knowing thyself and thy Father, God-ALLAH. It is being able to think in that which is right by making good choices, displaying good moral excellence, and honoring the principles and Creed of our forefathers. Jesus described salvation as a ladder reaching from the heart of man to the heart of ALLAH. It has three steps, Belief, Faith, and Fruition. (See MHK 7:27). (8)

Everlasting = lasting forever; eternal; beyond the concept of time from a finite perspective. (3)

Everlasting Gospel = Everlasting means "lasting forever," and Gospel means "good news."

→ Everlasting Gospel is the saving power sent from ALLAH and delivered to us through His Holy and Divine Prophet Noble Drew Ali. It is through this everlasting gospel that the true relationship between ALLAH and man is restored. It is the means through which the salvation and spiritual transformation of humanity is achieved. "It saves us from ignorance, laziness, drug addiction, alcoholism, self-hatred, conceit, greed, selfishness, envy, vanity, fear, indifference, hypocrisy, hopelessness, misery failure, ruin, disbelief, etc." (Brother N. Chambers-El, "Moorish Questionnaire Commentaries"). In a profound sense, it sets us free from everything that harms and brings us peace and happiness. Our Prophet came with a message of Love, Truth, Peace, Freedom and Justice, which has the power to save humanity from sin and its consequences. Through his teachings and exemplary role, Prophet Drew Ali shows humanity the way to peace and reconciliation with ALLAH.

This Everlasting Gospel also saves by teaching us who we are: a Spirit and a part of ALLAH and who our Creator is. Indeed, in the knowledge of who we are and who our Creator is lies an invincible power against which nothing can prevail, a power which gives us the ability to overcome all obstacles/problems that stand in the way of our spiritual unfoldment and ultimate success. This power also saves us by teaching us that as a Spirit and a part of ALLAH, we all have unlimited capacities for progress and that everyone has within him the seed of perfect development and it rests solely with us to make our fortune; to master our fate, and to create our own destiny. (See Moorish Literature, *"What is Islam,"* pg. 10.)

Islam has a saving power. Of that there is no doubt. The Moorish Holy Koran, the Koran Questionnaire for Moorish Americans (Questionnaire), the Moorish Literature, the Humanity Pamphlet, The Divine Constitution and By-Laws, and everything that was brought and taught (Islamism) by the Prophet of ALI to us are part of the Everlasting Gospel. Within all the aforementioned literature there is a saving power. However, it is up to each individual possessing the will to choose, and as Moorish American Moslems, to apply these lessons to uplift ourselves. Within this application is a power strong enough to uplift a nation. Prophet Noble Drew Ali told the Moors, "I brought you everything it takes to save a nation, now take it and *save yourself.*" It is reported that when the Prophet made this declaration, he was holding up the Holy Koran and Questionnaire. (3)

Forefathers = one's ancestors; a person or persons, from whom one is descended; ancestral descent or lineage.

→ A forefather can also mean "a founder or originator." (8, 10)

Forerunner = a person who goes or is sent in advance to announce the coming of someone; harbinger. (2, 3)

Founded = set up or established on a firm basis or for enduring existence; to provide a basis or ground for. (8)

Founders = ones who establish a particular thing; authors or originators. **Establish** = to set up, found. (6)

Fulfilling = carried out, or brought to a realization, as a prophecy or promise. (Heading)

Gospel = something regarded as true and implicitly believed; a doctrine regarded as of prime importance.

→ The word "gospel" translates to "good news" in the Greek Language. (3)

Great Wrath = Divine retribution for sin; punishment by ALLAH; a manifestation of anger from ALLAH. (See *Retribution* in Ch. 35). (l)

Hath = has. (9)

Honor thy Father and thy Mother = "What is the Covenant of the Great GOD-ALLAH? Honor thy Father and thy Mother, that thy days may be long upon the Earthland which the Lord thy GOD-ALLAH hath given thee." (Questionnaire question #42).

→ Brother N. Chambers-El states, "A Covenant is a solemn, binding agreement between two or more parties. The solemnity of this Covenant is evidenced by the fact that it is the Covenant of the Great GOD-ALLAH," as opposed to the covenant of man. In other words, this Covenant did not originate with mankind; it originated with ALLAH and was sent down to mankind as a mandate and divine instruction to be followed.

"When our great ancestor, Moses, led the Israelites out of bondage to freedom, he gave them a divine code of law that had been observed among our people for thousands of years, but had been lost to the Israelites due to their 400 years of enslavement. Among these laws issued by Moses were those which are traditionally called the 'Ten Commandments,' one of which says: "Honor thy Father and thy Mother that thy days may be long upon the earth which the Lord thy God hath given thee." (See Holy Bible, Exodus 20:12). It is truly prophetic that after 400 years of enslavement, Prophet Noble Drew Ali would reintroduce this ancient Covenant among us.

"To honor one's father and mother means to keep alive their hopes, dreams, aspiration, values, creed and principles. But more than that, it means to preserve their name, identity, history, and heritage. In doing so we remain culturally nourished by the Spirit of our ancestry." (See Brother N. Chambers-El, "Moorish Questionnaire Commentaries.") (9)

Incorporated = to become united or combined into an organized body; formed as a legal corporation or organization. (4)

Incorporated Organization = an organization that is legally united with the corporate U.S. government and is therefore protected by its laws. (4)

Inhabitants = ones that inhabit a place, especially as a permanent resident. **Inhabit** = to live or reside in. (6)

* THE END OF TIME AND THE FULFILLING OF THE PROPHESIES *

Islam = The religious faith of the Moorish American Moslem is Islam; their religion is Islamism. Islam is an Arabic word which translates to mean "submission." Thus, Islam as faith means complete submission to the Will of ALLAH, the Father of the Universe. Islam derives from the root Salaam, which means "peace." Islam in the profoundest aspect means PEACE. Islam is preeminently the religion of PEACE. The Prophet Noble Drew Ali states that "Islam is a very simple faith. It requires man to recognize the supreme duty of living at peace with one's fellow creatures. It teaches the supreme duty of living at peace with one's surroundings." (Moorish Literature, "What is Islam?" pg. 10). Islam did not originate with Prophet Mohammed. As stated in the Holy Qur'an of Mecca, "Islam was before Mohammed."

As Moorish American Moslems we are returning to Islam as it was prepared by our forefathers for our earthly *and* divine salvation. Islam as taught by Prophet Noble Drew Ali emphasizes the importance of living by the divine principles of Love, Truth, Peace, Freedom, and Justice.

Prophet Noble Drew Ali said, "A follower of Islam in the true sense of the word is one whose hands, tongue and thoughts do not hurt others." "The goal of man's life according to Islam is peace with everything, peace with ALLAH, and peace with man." The whole point of our existence is to be perfected in the way of ALLAH; to make our way back to HIM (this is what it means to be in Islam).

Our religion as stated by our Holy and Divine Prophet Noble Drew Ali is ISLAMISM. Islamism is the doctrine (set of beliefs or principles) and practice of Islam; it is our faith in total application. The application of Islamism is to be demonstrated in our every act, whether they be scholastically, philosophically, whether we are at the job, in a family gathering, at a funeral or in a recreation center. No matter what it is that we are indulging in, Islamism is to be demonstrated as we endeavor to give others the best that is in us. The suffix -ism means the process, action, or the practice of something, in this instance Islam as revealed by ALLAH to the Prophet. We as followers of Noble Drew Ali, as Moorish American Moslems, are to display daily the principles of Love, Truth, Peace, Freedom, and Justice through our words, actions, and deeds. The Prophet rejuvenated and ignited the Divine Light of Islam on these shores of the Western hemisphere and brought it as dictated by ALLAH for our conditions at this time.

Brother R. Jones-Bey, who took over the mantle as the National Grand Sheik of The Moorish Science Temple of America, Inc. from Brother R. Love-El, states in the 2004 revised edition of the Branch Temple Information that there has been misunderstanding in the past concerning the manner in which Moorish Americans practice Islam as opposed to more traditional forms of the religion. Many have concluded that because we don't adhere to certain rituals, we are not actually practicing Islam. However, nothing could be further from the truth. Our lessons support this in that we are taught that rites and forms are but symbolic and are not the essence of religion but a means to help men comprehend. Custom does not alter the nature of truth. Our Prophet has brought us a higher form of Islam and has told the Moors: 'You are going to have to take these lessons and go straighten out your brothers in the East.'

"One area that needs to be addressed is the erroneous assertion that *Prophet Mohammed* was the *last prophet* that ALLAH would ever send to this earth. Many base this belief on the fact that the Holy Qur'an of Mecca states that *Prophet*

* THE END OF TIME AND THE FULFILLING OF THE PROPHESIES *

Mohammed was the "seal" of the prophets. The word *"seal"* has been interpreted by some to mean the *end* or *conclusion*, as one might seal an envelope so that no more material could be put in it. However, this interpretation has *always* been in dispute by *many* Islamic scholars.

"A *seal* is also a sign of authority, something that confirms or authenticates. *Prophet Mohammed* was the *"seal"* of the prophets in that he came with the authority from ALLAH to confirm the religion of *Islam*. Our lessons teach us that a Prophet is a thought of ALLAH manifested in the *flesh*. The thoughts of ALLAH are infinite and cannot be circumscribed. As *Moorish Americans* we should be able to stand on the fact that *Noble Drew Ali* is a Prophet that was sent by ALLAH in due time to redeem man from his sinful and fallen stage of humanity back to the highest plane of life with his *Father God ALLAH;*" (emphasis on original). (*Branch Temple Information*, 2004 ed., pg. 6). (3, 8)

John the Baptist = forerunner of Jesus, son of Elizabeth and Zacharias.

→ John is also recorded as being the cousin of Jesus. Elizabeth and Mary (mother of Jesus) were cousins. John the Baptist was purity made flesh and came to prepare the way for the welcoming of Jesus, who was Love made manifest. (2)

Lawfully = recognized and permitted by law to operate; legitimate. (4)

Lawfully Chartered = having the legal right to operate as an organization recognized and protected by law. (4)

Link = join, connect, unite, bond, or tie. (11)

Marcus Garvey = forerunner of Prophet Drew Ali.

→ Born August 17, 1887, in St. Ann's Bay, Jamaica. His parents were Sarah and Marcus Garvey. He founded the Universal Negro Improvement Association (U.N.I.A.) in 1914 while living in Jamaica. The organization failed to attract a large following. In 1916 Garvey arrived in New York. Not long after his arrival he established the U.N.I.A. on American soil. The organization was a success and gained a following of over 4 million globally. His success at organizing the so-called Negroes did not come without a price. Marcus Garvey became the target of the F.B.I. He was arrested and eventually charged with mail fraud. After serving over 18 months in a federal prison in Atlanta he was expelled from the United States and deported back to Jamaica. His mail fraud charges later proved to have been fabricated by the government and its lackeys. Marcus Garvey passed form on July 10, 1940, while living in London, England. (3)

Marry = to take as a husband or wife; to take as an intimate life partner by formal exchange of promises in the manner of traditional marriage ceremony.

→ Prophet Noble Drew Ali says in our Moorish Literature "We Moors cannot marry no one, but we obligate you, according to our divine laws and covenant and the laws of the land. This must be proclaimed and made known to every temple so that there will be no misunderstanding about I, the prophet, and my teachings because ALLAH alone can bind two hearts together as a unit." (6)

Modern Days = the present cycle or era of time; this age. (3)

Moorish = pertaining or belonging to the Moors and their culture. (See *"Moorish"* and *"Moorish American"* in Ch. 45). (4)

* THE END OF TIME AND THE FULFILLING OF THE PROPHESIES *

Nation = a large group of people who share common customs, origins, culture, language, or history and inhabiting a particular area; tribe. (2)

Nationality = the status of legally belonging to a particular nation by origin, birth, or naturalization; the descendant right attachment through a special nation or tribe; free national name, lineage, or identity **Origin** = a person's ancestry. **Ancestry** = a person's ancestors or the people that they are descended from. **Naturalization** = to grant full citizenship to (one of a foreign birth).

"Nationality is acquired at birth according to either of two principles. The first of these is *jus sanguinis*, or right of blood, which gives the child the nationality of one of his parents, usually the father. The second, called *jus soli*, or right of soil, makes a person a national of the country in which he is born. Most countries use both principles." (Sister Rashida-El, D.M., *"Dictionary and Study Guide"*).

Prophet Noble Drew Ali teaches us that "Nationality is the foundation of mankind, and whosoever fails to proclaim his nationality, is a slave in whatsoever land he finds himself." Our nationality is Moorish American. Our Prophet came to free us from the condition of mental slavery therefore it is of the utmost importance that we stop clinging to names and principles that delude to slavery and go back to the state of mind of our forefathers. Proclaiming our nationality and acknowledging ourselves as Moorish Americans is a very important part of our salvation as a nation of people, for it helps us consciously to re-connect to our history culture, and the religion of our antecedents. (See Moorish Literature, "A Divine Warning by The Prophet for The Nations," pg. 5).

When a person proclaims his nationality, he/she makes use of their tribal name from that point onward. By using your tribal name, you are saying to the world that you are *conscious* of who you are, and your forefathers were. The names El, Bey, and Ali are tribal names, so says the Prophet. They are not titles. Prophet Noble Drew Ali told the Moors not to use the name Ali and further instructed us not to name our children Ali. (10)

Prophet = a thought of ALLAH manifested in the flesh; *messenger*. In a profound sense one who is sent by ALLAH. **Noble** = *illustrious*; having admirable qualities or high moral principles; magnificent upstanding. **Drew** = *strong*. **Ali** = *mighty* or *The Exalted One* - The Great. **El** = Creator. This attribute describes the Creative nature of those who possess it. **Bey** = *Governor*. This attribute describes the *Governing* nature of those who possess it.

Old Time Religion = Islam(ism).

→ Islam(ism) is the oldest religion. Although not recognized, or called "Islam," man has practiced peaceful coexistence with his surroundings from the beginning of human history. It wasn't until man submitted to his carnal nature that he debased himself from the oneness with ALLAH. Because of this debasement we must labor, toil, and face unnumbered foes so that we can become the strength of ALLAH made manifest and attain back to the ONENESS which is ALL(AH). (3)

Organization = an organized group of people with a particular purpose. (4)

Pale Skin = Europeans.

→ "*Pale Skin*" is used when speaking of Europeans. Europeans (pale skins) do not produce the same amount of melanin as Asiatics, thus giving them a pale appearance. When speaking of Europeans, we must always

* THE END OF TIME AND THE FULFILLING OF THE PROPHESIES *

point out specifically who it is that we are addressing because many Asiatics lived, and live, in Europe. (6)

Prepare = to make ready beforehand for a specific purpose, as for an event or occasion; get ready. (3)

Prepared = made ready beforehand for a specific purpose. (3)

Prepared Divinely = Divinely Prepared = made ready by ALLAH (Divinely Inspired). (1, 3)

Prophesies = that which is made known by Divine Inspiration; the "predictions" of future events as dictated by ALLAH to His prophets and/or messengers; to reveal the Will or Message(s) of ALLAH. (Heading)

Prophet = a thought of ALLAH manifested in the flesh.

→ Prophet Noble Drew Ali, born Timothy Drew (January 8, 1886 - July 20, 1929, A.D.) in the state of North Carolina, is the Prophet sent to redeem the Asiatics of America. A prophet is a person chosen to speak for ALLAH and guide the people to their destiny. The Hebrew meaning for "prophet" is "one who is inspired by God," one who speaks for ALLAH by way of Divine Inspiration. Prophets come as warners to a set of people or to humanity as a whole. A prophet's warning is intended to give the warned people a chance at redemption before ALLAH releases His divine chastisement upon them. A prophet speaks what ALLAH instructs him/her to speak and carries messages to men from ALLAH. ALLAH speaks to man through man. The Holy Qur'an of Mecca informs us that "a Messenger is appointed for all people," (10:47). For the Asiatics of North America, our prophet is Noble Drew Ali, who was prepared and sent in due time to return us to the path of our ancient forefathers. It is of great importance to note that prophets do not speak before ALLAH! ALLAH alone makes prophets, not men. (1)

Redeem = to save from a state of sinfulness and its consequences; to bring back to an original state or possession.

→ It is worth noting that the word "redeem," or "redemption," emphasizes the releasing accomplished as a result of something else. In other words, redemption comes from letting go of the mundane and living in the spiritual (Higher Self). It is the exchange of the low, for the High. The trial and tribulations that we experience on the physical as well as the soul plane are the consequences of our fall. It is the price that we must pay, *i.e.*, the ransom, for our debasement from ALLAH. Giving up the fetters of the flesh will enable our unfoldment into the God-Man of today. (1)

Redemption = the act of redeeming or the state of being redeemed; deliverance from sin; salvation; rescue. (5)

Salvation = deliverance from the power or penalty of sin and its consequences, and the coming to peace and reconciliation with GOD-ALLAH; redemption. **Reconciliation** = to reestablish a close relationship between you and the Supreme Creator, ALLAH. (8)

Sinful Ways = deliberate disobedience to the known Will of ALLAH; the willful violation of religious or moral laws. (1)

Stir = to rouse from inactivity; excite. **Rouse** = to bring out of a state of sleep, unconsciousness, inactivity, depression, etc. (2)

Subordinate = subject to or under the authority of a superior. (See "*Subordinate*" in Ch. 47). (4)

Thee = you.

Thy = your.

Uplift = to raise to Spiritual heights; to improve socially, culturally, intellectually, and/or morally; to lift up; exalt. (11)

Uplift Fallen Humanity = raising the fallen sons and daughters of the Asiatic race from a dead state of mind and bringing them out of mental slavery away from the destructive mentality that they now have and guiding them into the light of consciousness, sovereignty, and true knowledge of self. Prophet Noble Drew Ali's mission was to establish a movement and an organization with the expressed purpose and goal of uplifting fallen humanity. He came to warn all Asiatics of America to repent from their sinful ways, before the great and lawful day which is sure to come, and returning the nationality, divine creed, culture, etc., back to the Moors of America for their earthly and divine salvation.

"Fallen humanity are those whose humanity has been debased - those whose thoughts, words, and deeds are uncharacteristic of what it really means to be human - those whose consciousness is disconnected from the realization of the Divine Presence of (ALLAH)." "Prophet Noble Drew Ali uplifts us by teaching us: that we have embedded within us the potencies and attributes of ALLAH; that we have within us unlimited capacities for progress; that our ancient forefathers were the founders of the first civilization of the Old World; that we were the authors of science, technology, literature, mathematics, medicine, chemistry, astrology, theology, architecture, philosophy, and all other branches of learning. For sure, in this knowledge of self is a saving power, a redemptive power, which lets all Moorish Americans know that true success, happiness, and fulfillment in life can only come from the knowledge of self and God." (Brother N. Chambers-El, "Moorish Questionnaire Commentaries," pg. 45)

The Prophet established the Moorish Science Temple of America as a vehicle from which we can start the process of uplifting fallen humanity. By getting right with ourselves and applying the teachings established by the Prophet we will be in a better position to better serve humanity and do our part in this great mission. (11)

United States = a part of the North American continent made up of 50 states and sharing a border with Canada and Mexico.

→ Even though the United States is made up of 50 states, only 49 of those are located within the North American continent. The 50th state is Hawaii, and it is located in the Pacific Ocean. (4)

Vine and Fig Tree = Islam(ism).

→ Brother G. Williams-Bey, member of the Moorish Science Temple of America, Inc., in an unpublished essay quoted by Brothers R. Thomas-Bey and M. Jeffreys-Bey state, "The 'Vine' is symbolic to an individual and its own culture. The 'Fig Tree' is symbolic of the Divine Laws and Instructions that each nation is granted through the Love and Mercy (the Prophet) of ALLAH." (See *Catechism on The Holy Koran of The M.S.T. Of A.*), (See *Vine and Fig Tree* in Ch. 46). (3)

Worship = the ceremonies, prayers, or other religious forms by which devotion and love is expressed to ALLAH; ardent devotion; adoration; homage; the practice of showing deep respect for and offering praise and prayers to ALLAH.

→ There is no better form of worship than doing the Will of ALLAH. It is this type of devotion that is at the root of true worship. It is the Spiritual nature of man to worship ALLAH, but because of our carnal thoughts, words, and deeds we debased ourselves from ALLAH. It now takes stages of growth for the God-Man to unfold within. As ceremonies and forms served a deeper spiritual purpose, our worship of ALLAH in our every way also serves a spiritual purpose. It is because of this that we must be sure to adhere strictly to the teachings found in the Moorish Holy Koran. (3)

Wrath = Divine Retribution for sin(s); punishment from ALLAH.

→ The wrath of ALLAH is not released upon a nation until ALLAH has sent to them a warner. ALLAH'S wrath is always justified. Simply put, it is brought upon a person or nation because of their deeds. This Divine Wrath is distributed upon everyone according to their deeds as it is stated in the Moorish Holy Koran, "The high and the low, the rich and the poor, the wise and the ignorant, when the soul hath shaken off the cumbrous shackles of this mortal life, shall equally receive, from the sentence of just and everlasting retribution, according to their works." (MHK Ch. 35:27). (See "*Retribution*" in Ch. 35). (1)

→ The Moorish Science Temple of America embraces five main/grand principles. These principles when applied righteously will aid and assist in achieving the unfoldment of the God-Man, or higher nature within each one of us. These five principles are LOVE, TRUTH, PEACE, FREEDOM, and JUSTICE. These principles are Spirit-Based. As one of the laws of physics state, two things cannot occupy the same space at the same time, so too the Prophet teaches that the heart of man cannot attend at once to too many things. (MHK Ch. 40:17).

LOVE = Our first principle of LOVE is not based on carnal desires. We must always bear in mind that ALLAH is LOVE, and this LOVE is what lead to the creation of all things. ALLAH did not create the universe and everything within it out of hate; He created it in LOVE and perfect balance. When we as students and followers of Prophet Drew Ali look at LOVE, we are reviewing it from a divine perspective. This deep-seated affection is directed to all of humanity; to see it lifted from the unwholesome depths of poverty, misery and suffering and placed on the solid rock of salvation. This LOVE is divinely inspired, and Jesus came as a demonstrator of LOVE DIVINE as did Prophet Noble Drew Ali. ALLAH'S prophets all speak in the same spirit. LOVE is the bond that holds all principles together. (5)

TRUTH = TRUTH is the spiritual fact that we are a part of the Supreme Creative Force which created all that ever was, is, and evermore to be. TRUTH is not based on the flesh, for the wise man knows the TRUTH that man himself is not the body nor the soul, but a Spirit and a part of ALLAH. In addition, TRUTH is the establishment/fruition of the teachings themselves. The truth of the flesh (lower-self) is directed by the body of desires and is therefore an illusion. It is truth reversed and therefore it is falsehood. The TRUTH of ALLAH is everlasting and therefore will never pass away. In a profound sense, it is directed by the HOLY BREATH. TRUTH is to speak as directed by the HOLY BREAIH. The Prophet spoke as directed by ALLAH and we are to imitate the Prophet in words, actions, and deeds. Our teachings are the words of TRUTH. Just as Jesus taught for 18 years TRUTH, the same breath speaks through the Prophet. (5)

PEACE = "Peace is a state of inner calm. An inner calm so complete that nothing can disturb it. The Peace which comes only from the knowledge that it is ALL. Fathomless Peace is meant by the Peace of the Spirit. This is the

* THE END OF TIME AND THE FULFILLING OF THE PROPHESIES *

peace to which Jesus referred to when he said, 'Peace I leave with you, my peace I give unto you.' The Infinite is always at peace because there is nothing to disturb it. A realization of our Oneness with Omnipotence brings peace. The peace which is accompanied by a consciousness of power." (Ernest Holmes, *"The Science of Mind,"* pg. 617). The Prophet gives us a more spiritual definition of PEACE when we look in our Moorish Literature. He informs us that "The goal of man's life according to Islam, is peace with everything. Peace with ALLAH and peace with man." (Moorish Literature, pg. 10, paragraph 1). Also, in paragraph 2 we are informed that "the FINAL abode of man is the House of Peace." (See also Holy Qur'an of Mecca, 10:25). This clearly reveals to us that we are not dealing with a simple physical, or mundane, definition. In order for PEACE to be found, we must first battle and overthrow the Goliath of the dark, i.e., the body of desires. We must be mindful that mundane peace is based upon earthly circumstances whereas our Spiritual PEACE is based upon Spiritual unfoldment. (5)

FREEDOM = In this instance, we are referring to the FREEDOM received from ALLAH from the judgment handed down at the end of times; the great wrath which is sure to come upon the earth. (MHK 48:l). The man who depends upon finite man for his freedom can just as well lose it at any given time. ALLAH being the Supreme Creator of ALL(AH) dictates the occurrences of men through His prophets and messengers. We are to govern our lives according to the teachings of the Prophet Noble Drew Ali. Our laws are the Moorish Holy Koran, and we are to govern our lives accordingly. Our final judgment will come from ALLAH, and so our ultimate FREEDOM will also come from Him. In our acceptance of ALLAH, we will lack nothing for ALLAH will

make the ways of the road simple for us to travel. In order for FREEDOM to manifest itself, we must make it happen. A man's ideal is his God and so, as man unfolds, his God unfolds. It is the will of man that makes possible the action of the Holy Breath and so we must place our will in tune with the WILL of ALLAH. This holds true to our perception of what FREEDOM is (as well as to the other principles). In order for FREEDOM to be a fact, the mind must be liberated. This liberation (FREEDOM) comes from breaking the chains that binds our minds to the flesh, the mental slavery which we still suffer from as a people. It is what the Prophet spoke to us about when he informed us that he "was sent to redeem this nation from mental slavery which you have now. . . (Moorish Literature, *"The Voice of The Prophet,"* pg. 8, paragraph 2). And therein lies the problem. The fact of the matter is that many of us don't truly believe that these chains can be broken. We do things that we know are counterproductive and no matter how hard we may try we cannot break away from these activities. The reason for this is that within the body of flesh we have this thing (the lower self)

which continues to pull us back. A lot of times the reason why we can't defeat this mentality is because we don't take the time to meditate, or as the Prophet informed us to do, "contemplate thine frame." We must exercise our will power and sit by the flowing spring of life and go into silent meditation as Jesus demonstrated. (5)

JUSTICE = Justice is to be demonstrated through divine inspiration. Without JUSTICE, we cannot fulfill the WILL of ALLAH, for ALLAH is a JUST God. In order for JUSTICE to be, we must have already been able to completely unfold into the thought of righteousness. Otherwise, we will still deal with justice from a physical perspective, that of the flesh. And as it is evident, the justice of the flesh is based on lewdness, murders, theft, and everything that harms. Righteous JUSTICE is based upon the Mother of virtues and the harmonies of life and breeds Justice, mercy, love, and right. To be just we must be able to hear without our passions. (MHK Ch. 48:28). (5)

NOTES:

REFERENCE AND SUGGESTED READING MATERIAL

Ali, Noble Drew. Moorish Literature

Ali, Noble Drew. The Holy Koran of The Moorish Science Temple of America, (1927)

Asad, Muhammed. The Message of The Holy Qur'an. Dar ai-Andalus Limited, Gibraltar.

Browder, Anthony. Nile Contributions to Civilization: Exploding the Myth: Vol. 1. The Institute of Karmic Guidance, Inc.

Chambers-El, Nathaniel. Moorish Holy Koran Commentaries. Moorish Vanguard Publications.

Chambers-El, Nathaniel. Moorish Questionnaire Commentaries. Moorish Vanguard Publications.

Holmes, Ernest. The Science of Mind. Martino Publications.

Hopkins-Bey, Azeem. What Your History Books Failed to Tell You. Author House.

James, George G.M. Stolen Legacy. U.B. & U.S. Communications System, Inc.

James, King. King James Study Bible.

Musashi, Miyamoto. The Book of Five Rings. Wisdom Editions.

Pleasant-Bey, Elihu. The Exhuming of A Nation (2nd ed.). Seven Seals Publications.

Pimienta-Bey, Jose V. Othello's Children in the "New World". 1st Books Library.

Rashida-El, Aisha. The Moorish Science Temple of America Dictionary and Study Guide.

Suzar, S.E. Blacked Out Through Whitewash.

Thomas-Bey, Ronald; Jeffreys-Bey, Michael. Catechism on The Holy Koran of The Moorish Science Temple of America. Moorish Vanguard Publications.

Three Initiates. The Kybalion. Teacher Cornerstone Editions.

<u>DISCLAIMER</u>

Islam:

The author respectfully requests that the readers of this material excuse any and all mistakes in the form of quotations, misspellings, and/or other grammatical errors. This is not to be reflective of any of the teachings and Spiritual material found within the literature of Prophet Noble Drew Ali and the Moorish Science Temple of America. Any and all errors found herein are reflective of the author's fallibility and bears no substance on the Prophethood of Drew Ali.

Material found following the " → " (NOTE:) sections in this work are based, for the most part, on the opinions of the author and is meant only to extend further clarity to the instruction in which the specified word is found. Any and all errors found therein are to be attributed to this author and no one else as I feel my imperfections and therefore humbled

Peace and Love

Printed in the United States
by Baker & Taylor Publisher Services